PENGUIN BOOKS

THE NEXT MOON

When the war in Europe ended André Hue was parachuted into Burma. Like many other members of SOE, he became an MI6 officer and, eventually, the British Military Attaché in Phnom Penh, where he met his wife Maureen. He retired as a Lieutenant Colonel in the Parachute Regiment with a DSO, Légion d'Honneur and Croix de Guerre – all earned within the three-month period covered by this book and when he was no older than twenty-one. Back in England he became a founder member of the Special Forces Club. He and his wife live in West Sussex.

Ewen Southby-Tailyour served for thirty-two years with the Royal Marines, before retiring as a Lieutenant Colonel in 1992. He is the author of three works of military history, as well as the definitive topographical guide to the shores of the Falkland Islands. In the writing of *The Next Moon* he has used as his primary source André Hue's own manuscript account of his activities in France written soon after the events.

D1638287

The Next Moon

*The remarkable true story of a British
agent behind the lines in wartime France*

ANDRÉ HUE AND
EWEN SOUTHBY-TAILYOUR

Foreword by Professor M. R. D. Foot

PENGUIN BOOKS

In association with Spellmount Publishers, Staplehurst

PENGUIN BOOKS

Published by the Penguin Group
Penguin Books Ltd, 80 Strand, London WC2R 0RL, England
Penguin Group (USA) Inc., 375 Hudson Street, New York, New York 10014, USA
Penguin Books Australia Ltd, 250 Camberwell Road, Camberwell, Victoria 3124, Australia
Penguin Books Canada Ltd, 10 Alcorn Avenue, Toronto, Ontario, Canada M4V 3B2
Penguin Books India (P) Ltd, 11 Community Centre, Panchsheel Park, New Delhi – 110 017, India
Penguin Group (NZ), cnr Airborne and Rosedale Roads, Albany, Auckland 1310, New Zealand
Penguin Books (South Africa) (Pty) Ltd, 24 Sturdee Avenue, Rosebank 2196, South Africa

Penguin Books Ltd, Registered Offices: 80 Strand, London WC2R 0RL, England

www.penguin.com

First published by Viking 2004
Published in Penguin Books 2005
2

Typeset by Rowland Phototypesetting Ltd, Bury St Edmunds, Suffolk
Printed in England by Clays Ltd, St Ives plc

Published in association with Spellmount Limited,
The Old Rectory, Staplehurst, Kent TN12 0AZ
Tel: 01580 893730
Fax: 01580 893731
E-mail: enquiries@spellmount.com
Website: www.spellmount.com

For Francesca Emily Bennett (André Hue's granddaughter),
in the hope that she and her generation will never
experience such events

Contents

List of Illustrations

Picture Acknowledgements

Grateful acknowledgement is made for permission to reproduce the following: André Hue: 1, 2, 3, 4, 5, 37, 38; Alan J. Bangay: 6; the Pondard family: 15, 18, 19; Ewen Southby-Tailyour: 16, 30, 31, 32, 35, 36; and Le Musée de la Résistance Bretonne, Saint-Marcel, Brittany: 11, 12, 13, 14, 17, 20, 21, 22, 23, 24, 25, 26, 27, 28, 29, 33, 34.

Every attempt has been made to contact copyright-holders. Any errors or omissions will be corrected in subsequent editions.

List of Maps

Foreword by Professor M. R. D. Foot

A few exceptionally vivid books explain what the life of an SOE agent was like on the ground: George Millar's incomparable *Maquis*, John Mulgan's *Report on Experience*, Ben Cowburn's *No Cloak, No Dagger* and Freddie Spencer Chapman's *The Jungle is Neutral*. This is the only book I have met fit to be mentioned in the same breath; it too expounds exactly what it felt like to organize subversion against an Axis enemy during the world war of 1939–1945.

Like Millar's and Cowburn's books, it deals with resistance to Nazi occupation in France. André Hue can add an extra edge: for, before he went into subversion, he was at work as a spy – his cover was that he was a teenage railway clerk. (Millar had a different extra edge. Before he went into subversion, he had succeeded in escaping from Germany back to England – see his *Horned Pigeon*, as astonishing a book as *Maquis*, though less well known.)

Hue's book comes out long after the event, but is largely based on notes made by its author soon after the liberation of France. He is now, alas, too ill to read it in proof; but has the advantage of having secured in Ewen Southby-Tailyour an editor fully qualified to understand the ins and outs of the secret life, from having worked over another heroic tale of resistance in France, Blondie Hasler's attack on and escape from Bordeaux in 1942 – an expert, moreover, on the secret side of the Falklands campaign of forty years later.

Between them, they have set down what happened to this young man, half Welsh and half French. I have read the story with the more interest because I was myself on the edge of part of it. I was forbidden to go to France in the early stages of the Normandy invasion, because I had read the plan for it months before while I was a staff officer at Combined Operations Headquarters, from which I had moved, in February 1944, to become intelligence officer of the Special Air Service Brigade. Getting as far forward as I could, I went to Fairford airfield in Gloucestershire on the evening of 5 June 1944, and saw the French SAS party emplane. Just before the aircraft door shut, I was led back away from it; a car turned up from nowhere; two figures draped in parachuting gear got out of it and went up into the aircraft's belly. One of them, I now know, was André Hue.

I sat in at the debriefing of his pilot, when the aircraft came back early next morning, and knew at least that all the parachutes had opened. I read all the SAS traffic from Brittany, as it came in, and played a small part through supplying maps and anything else on the intelligence front that was needed and that I could lay hands on. I chose the code name for, and helped to plan, Operation Cooney. This was a simultaneous attack on several Breton railway lines, a few days after the main landing, which broke them all at once, and so forced any Germans in Brittany who wanted to reinforce the Normandy front to walk there, or go by road transport under air attack.

I also organized the air support for the Battle of Saint-Marcel. The brigade major, the unflappable Esmond Baring, asked me to look after brigade headquarters while he walked across to the great house at Moor Park, Rickmansworth, for lunch. Jakie Astor, who ran our signals, looked in a few minutes later and told me that he thought a bomb line was coming through from 'Dingson', the SAS group in southern Brittany. A few minutes later still, it was in front of me on an army message form.

Now SAS had just formed a distant but warm friendship with the tactical air force that supported the invasion, by providing them with the target for the best petrol fire they remembered, at Châtellerault station. I thought for a moment: even if a German spy intercepted the call, there would be no time for him to pass the fact over to the Germans in Brittany before the aircraft struck. So I rang up my opposite number in the tactical air force, on an open line – he had no scrambler – and read the bomb line out to him in clear; he passed it to a Thunderbolt group; they put in the attack André recounts in his eighth chapter.

All over Brittany, word went round: these SAS are not only Frenchmen, they can get air support. We never in fact mounted another such operation, but it did do exactly what the one-armed

Colonel Bourgoin wanted it to do: relieved the pressure on him enough for him to make an orderly withdrawal. SAS thereafter dispersed, all over the peninsula, until the BBC broadcast the message '*Le chapeau de Napoléon, est-il toujours à Perros-Guirec?*', which to thirty thousand Bretons meant, 'Parade at 23.55 tonight in the village square, armed' – and almost every Breton village was in resistance hands by midnight, leaving the Americans to fight their way through to Brest down the main roads.

I can therefore recommend this book from personal knowledge secured at the time, as well as on general literary and historical grounds, as an admirable read. It brings out wonderfully well the degree of tension and suspicion under which a secret agent working against the Nazis had to live, trusting nobody at all but himself, and taking care not to trust himself too far.

M. R. D. Foot
Nuthampstead
January 2003

Prologue by André Hue

When the Germans entered Paris on 14 June 1940, Britain was forced to carry the burden of war against Germany for several months by herself. In the meantime, in France, citizens of courage and decision resolved that France had not yet lost the war and, following their leader, General Charles de Gaulle, men and women from all classes of French society began their own fight against the occupying power. This movement became known as the French Resistance, and was to prove a magnificent and powerful weapon in the hands of the Allies.

Over four years the men and women of the Resistance were tracked day and night by the German Gestapo, by the SS, by Russian troops, and even by their own home-grown traitors, the *Milice*.[1] Hundreds of French men, women and children were arrested, killed or sent to concentration camps, but, for every dead or missing person, ten were ready to take over his duty – to fight and die if necessary.

Between May and June 1940 the German armies had made their powerful drive westward, aiming for Paris and the heart of France. Dive-bombing attacks by the Luftwaffe preceded massive thrusts by the Panzer divisions: the SS poured in, while fear and discouragement replaced an earlier confidence among the French population. This was a new style of war for those who knew little of the methods to deal with the relentless bombing of towns and villages, roads and communications, whether legitimate military targets or not.

Life was grim: the Allied armies were in full retreat – the most difficult of all military operations, and one made even more arduous as the roads were crammed with near-panic-stricken refugees flocking towards the capital. But the German army was not to be deterred from its merciless drive: large numbers of innocent refugees, mixed with the retreating army, became the victims of its bestial attack. Nothing could stop this rout. Towns were burned, harbours were mined. Paris was declared an open city, and the French government removed itself to Bordeaux, while all the time the German army drove on and on, until one-quarter of France was conquered.

Then one day an old, broken voice came over the French radio, informing the French people that they had lost the war and that he, Marshal Philippe Pétain, was now head of the French state. He had asked for an armistice to save France from complete destruction, but the French did not know what to make of this. They could think no more, their army was beaten; the unthinkable, the impossible, had happened.

With everything appearing lost, the people of France, weak, crestfallen and dazed, were suddenly woken by a new, strong and confident voice from London – the voice of another, very different, Frenchman. General Charles de Gaulle was calling from across the Channel, denying that his country was defeated. He was in England and taking over the destiny of France, he said. This was a global war, many countries would be involved, and the Free French would be among them. His voice brought new hope to our hearts.

With the approval of the British military authorities, the General invited all Frenchmen to join him in the struggle, and, with the voice of Winston Churchill also challenging the German army, preparations were begun for the fight which was to decide the fate of the world: slavery or freedom. In their towns and villages French men and women listened to the voices of these two leaders, and they made their own decision. For many it was to fight on, come what may, until the German army was beaten – or they would die in the process. Many did.

France was cut in two. The north, including the Channel and Atlantic coasts, was occupied by the German army, while the south was run by a collaborationist French government under Marshal Pétain based at Vichy, the demarcation line being patrolled by German sentries aided by French gendarmes. There remained just two ways to reach England to join de Gaulle: across the Channel in small fishing boats, or through the Pyrenees, across Spain to Gibraltar, and thence by RAF aircraft or Royal Navy ship.

Before long, people were making the dangerous journey to the South of France and the difficult trek across the mountains, enduring nights of cold and ice with neither food nor shelter. On and on they plodded, with nothing but an indomitable, bloody-minded spirit to keep them going. First the Germans and the *Milice* had to be dealt with, then the customs authorities, and finally the Spanish – whose loyalties and beliefs could not be trusted. For those who failed, there were months of internment in the infamous Miranda de Ebro concentration camp while frantic efforts were made to acquire false papers acceptable to the British consulate officials, who would normally be granted permission to visit an internee. This was also the route by which many SOE agents and Allied escapers and evaders would make their way home.[2]

Others chose the shorter, but no less perilous, journey across the Channel in small fishing boats. All along the Brittany coast on dark nights tiny dinghies, crammed too tightly with people, would steal out to the waiting craft with their oars muffled. But not all who set out reached the far shore. Sentries on the lookout for just such attempts returned many, only to have them try again on release. Three or four attempts might be made before a 'home run' could be recorded – and that after days at sea and arrival in such an exhausted condition that passengers and crew could barely walk. Yet, in spite of these hardships, more and more took up the challenge and joined their comrades in England.

Once identity had been established beyond all doubt and with sufficient evidence to prove that these Frenchmen were loyal, they were interviewed by the staff of General de Gaulle's London headquarters, where they were heartened by the sight of the *tricolore* flying above the building: from that moment, any privations suffered began to count as naught.

It was during this period that the Germans tried to win over the nation they had conquered. They were instructed to be courteous, but the people could not be deceived, for the memory of the brutal treatment they had experienced was too vivid – it could not be wiped out overnight. Gradually the locals devised little ways of annoying the Germans, such as painting 'V' (for victory) signs on walls, wearing small red, white and blue emblems, and doing all manner of little things for which they could not be imprisoned but which irritated the Boche.

Others began to think a little more deeply. Local Maquis[3] units of armed maquisards were established across the country. Ammunition dumps were raided, communications were cut, and information was gathered which would be of use to friendly forces when they returned.

All this started in a small way, but soon it was clear that this could be developed and more formally organized. Liaison was established with the British, and plans were made to help these bands of French men and women who were apparently harmless citizens by day but strived to be a deadly striking force at night.

Providing such help was hazardous work, but there was no lack of volunteers as French and English trained side by side before returning across the Channel, determined to win. If we could not beat the Germans openly at first, we could fight in other ways: sabotage and demolition would be our weapons; we would force the enemy to mobilize all his troops to protect his trains, men and communications.

In the course of all this I lost many civilian friends, and I remember especially the bedridden Madame Le Blanc, an eighty-three-year-old lady murdered by the Germans during one of their many reprisals merely because her farm was in the Saint-Marcel area.

When, each year, we celebrate the Allied landings of 6 June 1944 I know where I should be (and until recently always was), and that is with my friends at the monument to the memory of our Maquis de Saint-Marcel in Brittany.

I wish to take this opportunity to thank one of our commanding officers, Colonel Maurice Buckmaster, for his understanding and comprehension of the problems and difficulties we faced, and to pay tribute to my friend Pierre Marienne, captain in the Free French forces, *Compagnon de la Libération*, executed by the Germans on 12 July 1944. Rightly, Marienne was known as '*Le Lion du Maquis de Saint-Marcel*'; without his professionalism and remarkable courage our task might never have been completed. I also remember the other friends whom I see no more since their fate was death in a concentration camp or against a wall early one morning.

This book is my simple account of the life I lived in those days of uncertainty and fear, and I am grateful to Ewen Southby-Tailyour for deciphering my hundreds of pages of notes, made on my return to England in August 1944 and which were then typed up the year after the war ended.

André Hue
West Sussex
Spring 2000

Introduction

On Trafalgar Day (21 October) 1940, Winston Churchill broadcast to the French people in their own language. Whether this was a co-incidence or whether the day was chosen with care is unclear. What is certain is that the Prime Minister was unequivocal with his promises:

Frenchmen! . . . Herr Hitler . . . and his little Italian accomplice . . . both wish to carve up France and her Empire as if it were a fowl: to one a leg, to another a wing or perhaps part of the breasts . . . You will excuse my speaking frankly, but this is not a time for mincing words. It is not defeat that France will now be made to suffer at German hands, but the doom of complete obliteration . . . Frenchmen – rearm your spirits before it is too late . . . Never will I believe that the soul of France is dead . . .

The soul of France was not dead, but it needed stirring and a little guidance.

While this is not a history of the Special Operations Executive, it might be helpful to take a glance at SOE and its overall achievements before we tell the story of one of its most remarkable operations. As M. R. D. Foot has written:

The crumbling of the land front in Europe precipitated a revolution in British strategic thinking. As early as 25th May, 1940, the Chiefs of Staff submitted to the War Cabinet that if France did collapse 'Germany might still be defeated by economic pressure, by combination of air attack on economic objectives and in Germany and on German morale and the creation of widespread revolt in her conquered territories.'[1]

To emphasize this view, the Right Honourable Hugh Dalton, Minister of Economic Warfare, wrote to the Earl of Halifax, then Secretary of State for Foreign Affairs:

We've got to organise movements in enemy occupied territory, comparable to the Sinn Fein movement in Ireland, to the Chinese guerrillas now operating against Japan, to the Spanish irregulars who played a notable part in Wellington's campaign or – one might as well admit it – to the organisations which the Nazis themselves have developed so remarkably in almost every country in the world. This 'democratic international' must use many different methods, including industrial and military sabotage, labour agitation and strikes, continuous propaganda, terrorist acts against traitors and German leaders, boycotts and riots.

It is quite clear to me that an organisation on this scale and of this character is not something which can be handled by the ordinary departmental machinery of either the British Civil Service or the British military machine. What is needed is a new organisation to co-ordinate, conspire, control and assist the nationals of the oppressed countries who must themselves be the direct participants. We need absolute secrecy, a certain fanatical enthusiasm, willingness to work with people of different nationalities, complete political reliability. Some of these qualities are certain to be found in some military officers and, if such men are available, they should undoubtedly be used. But the organisation should in my view, be entirely independent of the War Office machine.[2]

Lord Halifax put the case to Churchill, and on 16 July 1940 the Prime Minister invited Lord Dalton to 'take charge of subversion': thus the Special Operations Executive, a department of the Ministry of Economic Warfare and not the Foreign or War Office, was conceived to 'set Europe ablaze'.

When the war in Europe was over, General Dwight D. Eisenhower wrote:

Special mention must be made of the great assistance given us by the FFI (Forces Françaises de l'Intérieur) on the task of reducing Brittany. The covert resistance forces in this area had been built up since June around a core of SAS troops of the French 4th Parachute Battalion to a total strength of some 30,000 men. On the night of 4/5th August the État-Major was dispatched to take charge of their operations. As the Allied columns advanced, these French forces ambushed the retreating enemy, attacked isolated groups and strong points and protected bridges from destruction. When our armor had swept past them they were given the task of clearing up localities where pockets of Germans remained, and of keeping open the Allied lines of communication. They also provided our troops with invaluable assistance in supplying information of the enemy's dispositions and intentions. Not least in importance, they had, by their ceaseless harassing activities, surrounded the Germans with a terrible atmosphere of danger and hatred which ate into the confidence of the leaders and the courage of the soldiers.[3]

Eisenhower also wrote to SOE's director, General Sir Colin Gubbins, on 31 May 1945:

While no final assessment of the operational value of resistance action has yet been completed, I consider that the disruption of enemy rail communications, the harassing of German road moves and the continual and increasing strain placed on the German war economy and internal security services throughout occupied Europe by the organized forces of resistance, played a very considerable part in our complete and final victory . . .[4]

Within SOE it was assumed, originally, that all the Frenchmen not supporting the Germans would work in harmony, but this was not to be the case. For instance M. R. D. Foot in his book *SOE in France* explains that

Strong anti-nazi elements in Vichy France refused to have any dealings with General de Gaulle, who in turn rejected anything and anybody that savoured of co-operation with Pétain's regime. So, on Foreign Office insistence, F Section was called the 'independent French' section and was kept out of all contact with the Free French authorities in London . . . a separate country section had to work with the Free French . . . and pressure of necessity compelled SOE to make direct contact with the Gaullists, who provided men for the earliest work that was done. Reports from these men, when they returned, impressed SOE with the strength of support for de Gaulle in France; and the RF [SOE Gaullist section] was the result.

To quote further from *SOE in France*:

SOE's politics were simply anti-nazi; they did not favour or disfavour any other political creed at all. Notoriously, SOE supported monarchists against communists in Greece and communists against monarchists in Yugoslavia because that seemed the best way to defeat Hitler. On the French political front, SOE only took sides to the extent that it was always against Pétain and came, more and more as time went on, to support de Gaulle . . . SOE was ready to work with any man or institution . . . that would help it beat the nazis.

It was also supporting the Allied cause elsewhere in the world: indeed, after the period covered by this account, André Hue – still with SOE – was parachuted into Burma.

Half of all agents were expected to be killed and, although volunteers were accepted into its ranks, SOE was, as one member pointed out, a rather exclusive club which, by and large, could be joined only by invitation. Nor was it foolproof in its conduct: partly due to its secrecy, a number of 'double-bookings' took place. A notable example was the raid on Bordeaux by Lieutenant-Colonel 'Blondie' Hasler, Royal Marines, in December 1942.[5] Hasler's limpet mines (paradoxically, supplied by SOE) exploded on their merchant-ship targets at the precise moment that an SOE team was carrying out its own final recce for just such an attack.

Nor did SOE's desire to beat Hitler give it a carte-blanche call on the wherewithal to do so. Marshal of the Royal Air Force Lord Harris, always loath to supply aircraft to 'carry apparent ragamuffins to distant spots, in pursuit of objects no one seems anxious to explain',[6] concurred with Lord Portal, Chief of the Air Staff, who told one SOE officer, 'Your work is a gamble which may give us a valuable dividend or may produce nothing . . . My bombing offensive is not a gamble. Its dividend is certain; it is a gilt-edged investment. I cannot divert aircraft from a certainty to a gamble . . .'[7]

Thankfully aircraft were 'diverted', although it is perhaps interesting to compare this attitude with that of the admirals, who also had extreme calls on their coastal and submarine forces: they too were unwilling at the start to supply what was asked of them by SOE and other 'special forces', but later relented.

None of this is a reflection on the aircrews and the ships' companies, who tended to revel in such work and who for the most part exercised courage and ingenuity to see their individual operations through – attributes matched by the even more remarkable men they were supporting. It has to be said, though, that some pilots were concerned less with accurate navigation and more with a safe return and the avoidance of flak. On a number of documented occasions passengers were forced to produce pistols in order to make their point, and Max Hastings has recorded that many parachutists, on D-day in particular, 'were released with near-criminal carelessness'.[8] Sadly, this habit did not entirely end on 6 June 1944.

Remembering General Eisenhower's views on the effectiveness of SOE in France at the time of, and subsequent to, the D-Day landings, it is fair to suggest that Lords Harris and Portal were blinkered to the many other factors that make for a winning combination in modern warfare. Bombing certainly has its place, but, except in the unique case of the atomic bombs on Japan, it does not end wars on its own.

Here, then, is one man's story of his work for the Special Operations Executive, which in under three months and at the age of just twenty earned him the British Distinguished Service Order, the French *Croix de Guerre avec Palmes* and appointment as a *chevalier de la Légion d'honneur*.

It has been a great privilege to record the life of a man whose deeds make one marvel at the courage of a past generation. Our own generation faces difficult enough odds, it is true, but it is hard to imagine, in modern warfare, human beings – civilian and military; male and female; elderly, middle-aged, juvenile and infant – being put through similar tests to those endured in occupied Europe, and for such a length of time. It would be wonderful to know that a regime so terrible as that of the Nazis could never be allowed again, but history does repeat itself – and, as I write, is repeating itself in Iraq – and present-day religious extremism is a spur to the wicked equal in destructive power to the extreme nationalism of the 1930s.

If history does repeat itself, I hope that André Hue's story – and those of all the men and women who fought in his war – will be an encouragement to others that, in the end, good can prevail.

André Hue lived under a variety of names during the period covered in *The Next Moon*. By SOE and on some of his false papers he was known as 'Hubert'; to the Maquis and the French SAS he was 'Capitaine André', for he had known many of them before and at the beginning of the war; but to Marienne and to his personal friends in France he was simply 'Bob'. At times he was – among a number of other *noms de guerre* which have not survived – also 'Alfred Marie Havet', 'Hunter-Hue', 'Hendrik', and 'Fernand', and known too by the name of his first 'circuit': 'Hillbilly'. Except in direct speech, I refer to him throughout as 'André Hue'.

Ewen Southby-Tailyour
South Devon
Spring 2003

Acknowledgements

I am grateful to Leo Cooper for introducing me to Jamie Wilson of Spellmount Publishers – a meeting that led to Jamie's much appreciated interest in André's story. My agent, Robin Wade, and Tony Lacey of Penguin together (and with some tact) then managed to control my wayward enthusiasm, while Bob Davenport's part in helping to turn the narrative into a readable story was heroic.

Professor M. R. D. Foot, CBE, has given incomparable guidance on SOE matters in general,[1] but I am especially indebted to him for his continued support and for writing the generous foreword: evidence of how much I relied on his knowledge will be found in the footnotes and in the quotes that he has allowed me to use from his books. The late Sir Brooks Richards, KCMG, DSC, produced invaluable information on Coastal Forces affairs: his book *Secret Flotillas* was vital to my research. Duncan Stuart, CMG, gave unprecedented help with André's SOE records, while Commander Peter Williams, DSC, RNVR, aided by his daughter-in-law, Jenny Williams, supplied superb descriptions of motor-gunboat operations. Mark Seaman of the Imperial War Museum proffered general advice on associated SOE subjects.

Just before he died, Monsieur Patrick Andersen Bö of Le Musée de la Résistance Bretonne at Saint-Marcel allowed me total freedom to search his archives and tap into his large collection of contemporary illustrations without hindrance – or cost: a unique freedom of access so rarely offered to authors. Madame Gorel (Anna Pondard) escorted me for two humbling days around the Maquis de Saint-Marcel in what must have been a haunting journey down her own memory's lane. As courageous and as lively now as she was in her youth, her example is vibrant proof that the human spirit, when at its very best, is quite indomitable. On the second day she proudly – and with a touching hesitancy – showed me the silver medal around her neck (the King's Medal for Courage in the Cause of

Freedom) that had been presented to her by King George VI in recognition of her bravery in support of Allied forces. Her father and sister Geneviève had received the same medal: all, plus her mother, were also honoured with the French Resistance Medal, while her father was invested as a *chevalier de la Légion d'honneur*.

André's daughter, Nicola Bennett – with her knowledge of the area and the people, plus her bilingual French – has been a constant link with the past and present and a most entertaining guide through the hills and woods of the Landes de Lanvaux across which her father fought while he and his companions tied up German troops who should otherwise have been defending Normandy.

During my researches 'on location' my wife, Patricia, was hugely helpful with her map-reading, note-taking and sensible powers of deduction.

Most thanks are due to Maureen Hue for asking me to undertake the daunting task of piecing together this brief period of André's life, particularly while a debilitating disease began to rob her of his companionship.

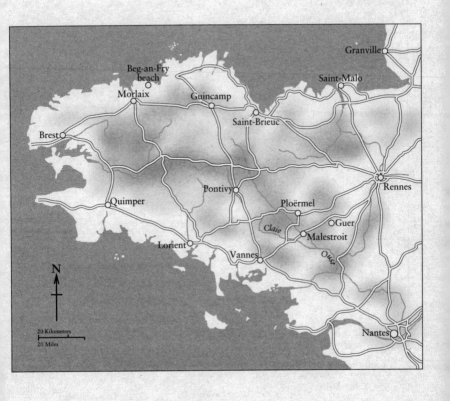

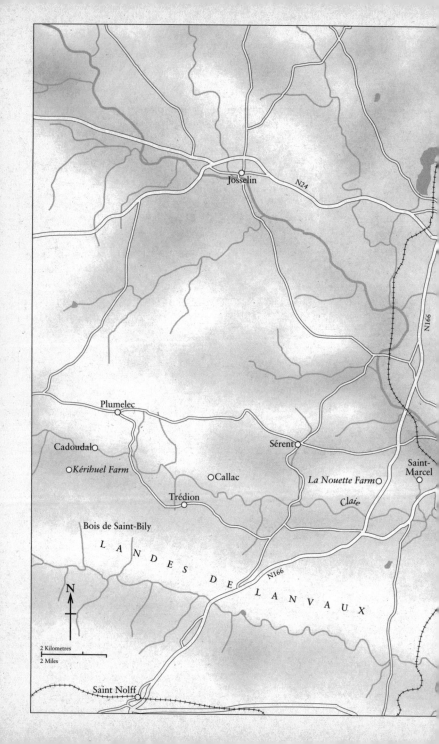

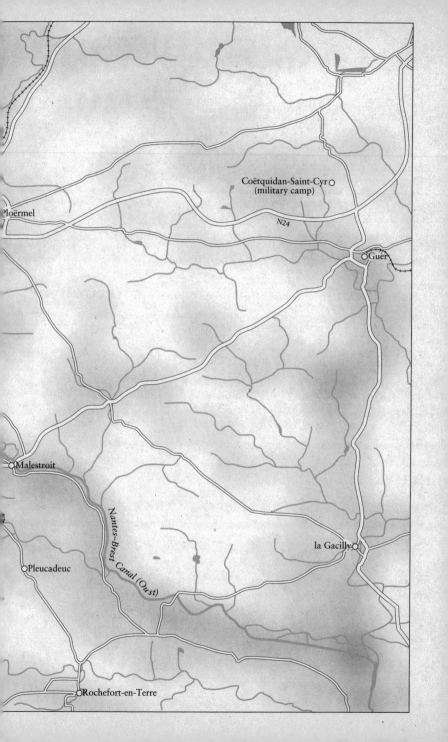

1. Shipwrecks and Marshalling Yards

'Abandon ship!'

'Abandon ship!'

I was under a hot shower, and froze. A few minutes earlier a deep rumble had vibrated through the liner, but I had thought little of it for I was still tired from the night before and not due to return to my duties for another hour or so.

But now that terrifying cry, echoing down the passageways, drove away all fatigue, ending my own phoney war and launching me upon adventures undreamed of in my tiny cabin. It was Monday 17 June 1940. I was sixteen, and stark naked.

Until that moment abruptly relieved me of my official duties as a junior trainee purser, I had thought only of becoming a senior officer in the French Mercantile Marine. On board La Compagnie Générale Transatlantique's 28,124-ton SS *Champlain* I paid little attention to the war, for that was all happening to others, on land and far to the east.

The previous day we had called in briefly at Saint-Nazaire, but we were now anchored in the fairway off La Pallice, La Rochelle's commercial port a hundred miles further south, down the Biscay coast of France. The 600-foot, eight-year-old liner, laden with war supplies and 381 passengers and crew, was bound for Casablanca from St Lawrence in Canada, and had called in to refuel and take on fresh food for the final leg of our journey. She had also been ordered to La Rochelle for the captain to be shown, in person, a route for the North African coast that was considered safe from German submarines.

Few passengers had wanted to travel east across the Atlantic and so with spare cabin capacity, as rather fewer than the available 1,053 bunks were occupied, we were now instructed to take on as many French families as we comfortably could from among those who wished to flee the advancing Nazis, including politicians anxious to continue the fight from abroad.

Puffing on an American cigarette after a long spell of duty the night before our arrival, I had been conscious of aircraft droning low overhead as I leaned against the guard rail and stared at the darkened sky. Unable to work out their purpose, or, indeed, their nationality, I had turned in thinking only of the run ashore in Casablanca. Later, I was to learn that aerial mines had been laid across the southern entrance to La Pallice's harbour, and that one of them must have drifted into the *Champlain*'s side as she swung to her anchor. The previous *Champlain* had died nobly twenty-two years earlier, after being torpedoed off Portugal on 21 August 1918. Now her namesake was about to join her on the seabed.

But I knew little of this as I stood covered in soap. I had had a long night, as often just before we reached a port, and was looking forward to a good breakfast and the arrival of new passengers.

Nine months earlier I had lied about my age – I was tall for a fifteen-year-old – and so was enlisted 'on probation' as a trainee purser to look after first-class passengers aboard the *Normandie*. Unable to prove when I was born, the shipping company had been hesitant, but I was determined to go to sea and argued my case forcibly.

War had been declared while the *Normandie* was in mid-Atlantic and in company with a number of other ships on passage between Le Havre and New York. The brief wireless announcement had meant little to me, although I was surprised by how unsurprised everyone else was. With other tasks on their minds for the great liner – the French national flagship – the owners paid me off on completion of that round journey, but, after a brief visit to Le Havre to reassure my mother, I was allowed to continue my transatlantic voyages in the *Belgrasse* before being sent to the *Champlain*.

Now the ship was settling quickly and with an increasing list. The lights flickered; the water dwindled to a trickle; I was still covered in soap.

'Abandon ship!' Another steward ran down the darkening passageway outside our crew's quarters.

Stunned, but struggling to keep my wits, I thought for a few seconds. My only possessions within reach were a towel and a bar of soap, which was already sliding downhill across the tiles. There was obviously no time to collect more useful items from my cabin, so, swinging the towel around my waist, I made my way towards the upper deck.

I pushed open a door to the boat deck to meet a warm, still Charente-Maritime morning, with the nearest land beckoning from less than half a mile away. I had survived the explosion and was dressed for swimming, but my elder half-brother, Jean, was also on board and, as a junior electrical officer, might well have been nearer the explosion.

There was little time to scan the frightened faces on the upper deck, and no time to search the ship, but thoughts of how I would break the news to my already widowed mother swept swiftly through my mind. Yet if I did return below decks I might put her at risk of being doubly bereaved.

'Maybe he's safe. Maybe he's thinking the same.' I stifled my thoughts and sought the best place from which to jump.

Lurching along the sloping deck, men and women stumbled uncertainly, not wanting to believe that their only hope lay with a thirty-foot dive. Their eyes were wide with horror as the reality sunk in that this was not a nightmare, this was real: this was war.

The *Champlain* shuddered violently, telling me there was no more time left. Looking down, I could see the oily-flat surface littered with shouting faces and waving arms anxiously encouraging friends and loved ones to follow. The deck shook, then sloped sharply beneath my bare feet.

I bellowed one last '*Jean!*' along the boat deck, but there was no reply. Taking a deep breath, I climbed the solid, wooden-topped guard rail and jumped. As I surfaced, my last possession slipped from my waist and so, unencumbered, I swam clear with ease as the *Champlain* slipped past towards the seabed, where, without heeling further, she was to settle almost upright with much of her superstructure and her two distinctive funnels visible until demolished in the 1950s.

Sturdy trawlers now mingled with the few ship's lifeboats that had managed to get away, bringing with them strong fishermen's arms to haul in their human catch. I struck out for the nearest boat, and was dragged roughly but firmly over a gunwale.

'*Merci, monsieur,*' I coughed. '*Merci.*'

Lying for a few moments on the scaly bottom-boards, catching my breath and recovering from the not unpleasant effects of a hot shower followed by a cold swim, I collected my thoughts. Thankful that I was fit and unharmed, I took my place among the rescuers bending to their task. It did not occur to me that I was naked.

From the twin forts that face each other across the entrance to La Rochelle's inner harbours, dozens of spectators watched the rescue vessels making their way along the narrow waterway into the heart of the town itself. More people thronged the wide streets around the outer fishing dock, many offering bundles of clothes, blankets and towels. This was their first chance to help, for up to that moment these men and women had been looking eastward across France's lush summer countryside daring to hope that, somehow, all would be solved. Now, and with a suddenness they could not have foreseen, the Nazis had blighted their peaceful stretch of coastline. It had taken nearly a year.

Red Cross volunteers hopped aboard from the western quay.

'*Mon dieu!*' a woman whispered in my ear, blushing. 'Put these on – immediately!'

I looked down. 'You're right,' I said, affecting an unembarrassed Gallic shrug before stepping into the ill-fitting underpants held in an outstretched arm.

She took a pace backwards and checked. '*Parfait,*' she muttered, then pointed to the quayside. 'Hot coffee, croissants, Gauloises.'

Better than those was a warm embrace from Jean, who had been watching the arriving fishing craft as anxiously as I had called out his name earlier. Unharmed but wet, he was at least fully clothed.

With the partition of France imminent, Marshal Pétain was on that same day establishing his French government ninety-five crow-miles to the south-east at Bordeaux and already laying the foundations for a one-sided armistice with Germany. It was, although I did not know this at the time either, the day that General de Gaulle, the French Under-Secretary of State for National Defence, had returned to his native land from a meeting with Winston Churchill in London the day before. It was also the day that de Gaulle, with some subterfuge engineered by the Br[i] government, then flew back to England to continue the strug[gle] on behalf of his fellow patriots. As Winston Churchill was to wr[ite] in June 1949, 'De Gaulle carried with him [back to England] in this small aeroplane the honour of France.'[1]

Meanwhile, the *Champlain*'s survivors – she had lost eleven of her crew – were encouraged to head for Bordeaux, from where there lay a greater chance of escaping the inevitable division of France. As a member of the ship's company I had no option but to obey company orders – although that was not what I wanted, for the fire of retribution, revenge even, had been lit, suddenly, in my young head. But I was still employed by La Compagnie Générale Transatlantique, and another of its liners was already earmarked and waiting to take up where the *Champlain* had been forced to leave off.

The minor roads between La Rochelle and Bordeaux, down the east banks of the Gironde and Dordogne rivers and thence across the Garonne, have altered little over the years, and it was past the timeless vineyards of Saint-Emilion and Pomerol that we were driven in commandeered buses and *camions*, making our way – unwillingly as far as I was concerned – to La Compagnie's SS *Savoie*, moored at one of Bordeaux's riverside quays.

The air was warm, the winds were light, the grapes were forming well: that year's harvest would be rich and colourful, the vintage long-lasting. As I gazed for the first time across those aristocratic, vine-covered slopes, I could only guess at the dreadful fate that awaited France: the country of my father's birth, but not of mine.

I was born on 7 December 1923, in Swansea, where my mother, Caroline Annie Hunter, had, a year or so earlier, met a French widower, André Hue, then an engineer officer in a merchant ship plying between Le Havre and South Wales. The courtship was conducted intermittently during my father's irregular visits, with the added disadvantage that neither party spoke one word of the other's native tongue. Yet love has its own patois, and will thrive if the omens are good – which they were, and André and Caroline became happily married.

My father's life had been an eventful one by the time he met my mother. Serving in the First World War with the French infantry, he had been wounded in the head, the bullet remaining with him until his death. In the inter-war years he had raced a Daimler into first place between Paris and Berlin, and after the death of his first wife he had also brought up his son Jean, just three years old when his mother died. He found happiness again with Caroline Hunter, but it was not to last, for he died of his war wounds when his second son – me, also christened André – was just fourteen. In recognition of my mixed nationality and my mother's maiden name, my passport had been issued in the name of 'Hunter-Hue'.

Shortly after my birth my mother insisted that she, her own son and her stepson be moved to my father's family house in Le Havre, where I – Welsh-born and English-speaking (albeit it with a pronounced French accent) – learned my first French words from my father.[2] As it was to turn out, these parallel linguistic attributes would fit perfectly with the recruiting guidelines of the Special Operations Executive, due to be formed exactly one month after the *Champlain* foundered.

During the evening of 18 June 1940, Jean and I listened intently in our new quarters as the ship's wireless officer relayed to the *Savoie*'s passengers and crew General de Gaulle's first words from his embryo government in exile: 'France is not alone. She has a vast empire behind her. She can unite with the British Empire, which holds the seas and is continuing the struggle . . .' I was stirred by these statements, and promised myself that I would join de Gaulle's fight – whether as a Frenchman or as a Briton it mattered not.

Further along Bordeaux's quay lay the *Massilia*, an armed auxiliary cruiser already loading political figures who wished, with Marshal Pétain's treacherous approval, to establish a political base beyond mainland France. Some of our 'new' passengers in the *Savoie* were also of that number: men and women determined to fight on, despite knowing that to do so from the uncertain sanctuary of North Africa would be a near-impossibility. The two ships, one armed and one unarmed, but both full of civilians, sailed on the afternoon of 21 June, twenty-four hours later than planned. Two days later the news that Marshal Pétain had signed an armistice was broadcast, and the day after that we anchored off Casablanca.

The news of the armistice was the final catalyst that convinced me to join de Gaulle, but an anchorage off Casablanca's sultry harbour was not the ideal springboard – either personally or geographically – for a probationary junior trainee purser who wished to see action. So, with no opportunity for reaching British shores via Gibraltar – just a tantalizing 180 miles to the north-east – my fight for France would have to come from within, and that meant a return to the occupied north. It was to be a dispiriting wait until that moment.

I was young, determined, resourceful and driven by the impatience of youth, but just when I needed my freedom most my future lay in the hands of others.

July in Casablanca is no time to be incarcerated in a liner with only overhead fans to keep air circulating – for that is all they did: they certainly did not cool it. Through three long and hot months we were all imprisoned, sweltering, aboard the *Savoie*. My duties were, as before, those of an assistant purser, with particular responsibilities for first-class passengers. This time, though, I was not looking for promotion and the job satisfaction that I had sought earlier. I wanted to be away from all that. I wanted to fight.

Our passengers, and those of the *Massilia*, were also becoming increasingly disheartened as it slowly became clear that they had been duped by Pétain, who wanted no government in exile.

They were not easy days. The politicians, now imprisoned in the armed cruiser on Pétain's orders, began to direct their grievances towards their own leaders – and rather less towards the Germans – for not allowing them to carry out what they believed to be their patriotic duties. Our own passengers felt the same, but were perhaps less militant.

Meanwhile the *Savoie*'s ship's company struggled on through the sweaty nights and humid days, while I planned and fretted between my long hours on duty. I could have attempted an escape to Spain and thence to Gibraltar, but that plan was riddled with uncertainty. I could, more easily, have applied to be returned home, for I was (if I cared to admit it) legally too young for merchant-marine, let alone military, service. One thing, though, was certain: La Compagnie Générale Transatlantique was now wary of employing anyone from a country with which its new masters were at war, and it was well known within the company that I was of British birth. The directors probably knew I was under age as well. But I worked hard – if perhaps without my earlier enthusiasm – and that was all that mattered, so I was kept on.

It was not the same for my half-brother, Jean: French by birth and parentage and the holder (until it was lost off La Rochelle) of a French passport, he was old enough for war service and, if rounded up by the Germans, was liable to be sent to the Channel coast as a labourer building the anti-invasion defences. Whatever lay ahead for us half-brothers it had to be something more positive than festering in a steaming liner throughout a North African summer. Normandy continued to beckon strongly.

But it took three months of badgering away at the shipping-company officials before permission was reluctantly granted for us to leave the *Savoie*. Then, while our destination was not Gibraltar, it was at least France, and I was happy to take my few chances from there – from anywhere but a stationary ship a quarter of a mile off the Casablanca waterfront.

Deep-down grateful for this tiniest of mercies, we were placed on a ship bound for Marseilles, from where we were escorted by armed French police to the railway station; then in a locked compartment we began the long repatriation north to our mother and stepmother. This was no triumphant Train Bleu journey home for shipwreck survivors, but an uncomfortable and slow plod towards a future that neither of us could guess at – a point forcibly emphasized at the demarcation line between unoccupied and occupied France, where we were handed over by our escorting and Vichy-sympathizing gendarme without ceremony and with considerable bad grace on both sides, as though we were prisoners of war being exchanged and not French Mercantile Marine officers.

For the second time in recent months I returned to Le Havre, but this time to a town badly damaged by German bombing and with little or no public transport. Fearing what we might find, we walked the short distance from the station to our mother's house, which was ominously empty and shuttered. We made our way, swiftly now, to the gendarmerie, where the police were of no help. On, then, to the *hôtel de ville*.

'Were is Madame Hue?' asked Jean nervously.

'Guer!' was the unhelpful reply.

'Where?'

'*Guer, en Bretagne.*' We had never heard of Guer.

Mother was safe, but had been evacuated to escape the German bombing of the port and was now living in an unknown village, 160 or so miles to the south-west, in the *département* of Morbihan, near the boundary of the neighbouring *département* of Ille-et-Vilaine.

No doubt she had read of the sinking of the *Champlain*, but a telegram sent from Marseilles had probably not been forwarded, so we had no means of knowing if she knew we were safe. It was therefore even more important that we wasted no time in reaching her. Selfishly, too, we needed to return home to re-establish myself as an under-age youth and for Jean to resurrect his bona fides as an electrician. We could not exist for long without formal work, as the alternative was the Channel coast – from which we knew there would be little chance of escape. Meanwhile our standing as shipwrecked mariners was endorsed by new papers from the shipping company's Le Havre office.

Later that day and without difficulty we hitched lifts to surprise our mother with kisses, hugs and a few luxuries we had managed to bring. It was a wonderful, tearful reunion, helped by much Calvados and promises that we would both find work in Guer. Jean, able-bodied and fit, did find employment as an electrician, which was the nearest thing to a reserved occupation and recognized by the occupying forces as of importance both to them and to the civilian population.

For me the future was not so easy. I was anxious to work in whatever way I could, for I had not 'escaped' Casablanca to twiddle my thumbs in the country, but I was young and without relevant training. Up to now, being British by birth had not hindered my work on the international liners, but in German-occupied France formal employment was nigh impossible without declaring my nationality. Every employer, no matter where his loyalties lay, would want to delve a little deeper for fear of being caught harbouring an Englishman, or even a Welshman!

Despite this serious handicap, neither my mother nor myself was daunted, for we were both certain that I would somehow find a job. It was our new landlady – a staunch patriot – who, unexpectedly, came to the rescue. An indomitable retired headmistress, she had never taken 'No' for an answer – and especially never from her ex-pupils, one of whom was the local viscount, le vicomte Bouexic de la Drienny, an owner of land which included three large forests.

'Come with me, André,' she ordered – 'we're visiting the chateau.' And off we set at a determined pace.

'This young man needs work,' the landlady fronted up to the nobleman. 'You must give him some!'

More concerned with obeying his former mentor than with risking the wrath of the Gestapo, he answered with a swift 'But of course, Madame', and after little further discussion I was quickly 'tucked away' as a lumberjack – whether I liked it or not.

I did like it, although with a few reservations. The work meant money of course, but I viewed it only as a useful stepping stone towards satisfying my prime ambition. In the meantime I plotted my fight with the Nazis by learning every yard, every glade, of Guer's local forests and the near-secret tracks and clearings that bisected and joined them. Hearing tales of the growing resistance movements across the countryside, I knew that one day we would have to fight across our own ground and consequently a prior knowledge would be invaluable.

For nearly a year, through the wet autumn and bitter winter of 1940, then the spring and glorious summer of 1941, I worked among the trees of Brittany – often living rough, but all the while gaining in stamina and strength until I knew that my personal preparation was over. It was time for action.

'What do you intend doing with all this knowledge of the woods and forests? Why is it so important to you?' Mother would ask. I had no answer then, but knew that one day there would be one.

'I've been getting to know Monsieur Touzet,' I announced one evening.

'Ah yes, Charles Touzet. A good man. He'll come up with something, I'm sure.'

And he did. Early one evening, shortly after I had first mentioned Monsieur Touzet's name to my mother, a firm knock rattled the front door. Caution was necessary, but a brief recognition through the letterbox soon had the chain and bolt removed.

Charles Touzet, a retired member of the Guer railway station with whom I had been purposefully striking up a friendship, entered the house. Mother poured a glass of Calvados. 'Would you like to join the station staff?' he asked after a first sip. 'It can be fixed.'

The suggestion was not a surprise, for I had been waiting for something like this but had never dared to make the first move.

'Yes,' I said without hesitation and with a quickening of my pulse. I knew nothing of trains nor how I could use them for my own purposes, but the Germans did use them – extensively.

'Then you must wait a little longer. I'll contact you when things are ready.' Touzet finished his drink, and with a kiss on my mother's cheek he left.

Two long days passed in the woods with no sign of the new job. I became pessimistic. Then another sharp knock on the door startled us.

'Tomorrow you must visit the stationmaster,' ordered Monsieur Touzet. My heart leaped, but he slowed the pace. 'Be warned,' he continued, 'there is now a German in charge who knows nothing of trains. The French *chef de gare* will ask the questions. Don't appear too keen or the German will be suspicious.'

The following morning I bicycled the few hundred yards to the railway station,[3] leaned my bike against the wall, wiped the toe of each shoe on the backs of my trouser legs, and knocked on the station's office door.

'*Entrez*!' I went in.

There was no interview. In a bored voice, the French station-master asked a few questions, not one of which required even a half-truth let alone a direct lie. I assumed that he was going through the procedure just to keep Charles Touzet happy – then he would dismiss me and return to his coffee.

'Name?' I told him.

'Age?' I didn't lie, although I was now old enough for war service.

'Address?' I gave my mother's house. He showed no sign of recognition.

'Previous occupation?'

'Ship's steward,' I said, leaving out the months in the woods. The Frenchman looked across to the obese German sitting by an open fire. They nodded at each other.

'Write your name here . . .' the *chef de gare* commanded, pushing a hastily drawn-up contract – of sorts – across the table towards me. He paused as I spelled out my name in capitals, '. . . and sign – there!' So, with a flourish, I became an employee of the French Railways. My wartime career, indeed my life's work, stems from that moment.

Guer Gare, SNCF, was – then – the terminus of a branch line that wound for fifteen miles north-west through gentle, wooded country from the village of Messac: a village straddling not only the river Vilaine but also the main railway line from Paris to, eventually, the Brest naval base.

The Guer line supplied the large French military camp of Coëtquidan–Saint-Cyr under two and a half miles from the railway station. As the Germans had forged westward, this massive training complex with its large barracks and repair facilities became a prime military base. Nowhere throughout Normandy and Brittany could its equal be found both as a rest centre for officers and soldiers, especially for those fighting on the Russian front, and as a prime repair-and-rebuild depot for tanks, lorries, guns and general military stores damaged or worn out in battle.

Once restored to operational efficiency, men and equipment would be dispatched back towards the east and the front lines. No tank nor artillery piece could, with ease, travel by any means other than train, nor could men be so easily transported in large numbers. Petrol was precious, coal less so: Coëtquidan–Saint-Cyr relied totally on Guer's railway station and branch line.

When they 'arrived', the Germans had decided, wisely, that they should not depend on Guer terminus's affable French stationmaster, so this undynamic but professional man was forced, on pain of instant dismissal, to accept a portly and arrogant German as his overseer. This uniformed Nazi – a functionary who considered himself the true stationmaster – exercised all the pomposity he felt necessary for such an exalted position. Holding no sympathy for his ousted predecessor, the German required the real stationmaster to remain in situ purely for his knowledge of the railway system – and to do all the work.

One of the many trappings to which the German considered himself entitled was a servant. It had therefore been easy for the ex-railwayman Charles Touzet to persuade him that a young, keen French lad – me, to be exact – would do nicely.

The German 'stationmaster', whom I dubbed Bahnhof Guer the Younger, managed the station's military affairs from a separate building. He liked his status and the comforts that it brought – little luxuries that would remain for his enjoyment and ease so long as the trains arrived and left on time, with their cargoes intact and safely unloaded and reloaded.

Meanwhile he revelled in the social cachet that came from a passing acquaintance with the officers of the army base, who, for their part, humoured the bureaucrat and pandered to his ego with ill-disguised contempt. But they also recognized that much depended on Bahnhof Guer the Younger's efficiency, and he knew that too. Nevertheless, to the officers of Coëtquidan the stationmaster remained a man to be kept in his place.

It was to this German administrator that I now reported at the beginning of each day to clean and polish his office and, in cold weather, to light his log fire. Once everything was to his fussy satisfaction, the rest of my day was spent in menial duties around the marshalling yard. Gradually, after much pleading, I was taught how to drive the engines and shunt the wagons into order before their return journeys to the east. Thus the first quarter of each day was dreary, but the remainder, as time went by, became more fun. However, I was still not fighting the Germans.

'Take things slowly,' Charles Touzet advised. 'There's no hurry.'

The war that was to have been over in months was showing signs of dragging on, so I bided my time and, as faith in my work grew, so did the number of confidences with which I was entrusted – for the German was also a lazy man. To keep the station running smoothly and his military masters happy, he needed to rely on Frenchmen to carry out many of his functions, and to ensure their untroubled assistance he was obliged to divulge certain information.

Slowly I had access to facts that would be priceless to the British, if only I knew how to transmit them. Large groups of men and tanks travelled to the east at irregular intervals; they were unprotected and vulnerable, and I was one of the few who knew the exact timings and in what numbers they were dispatched. On the other hand, I saw the manifests only the day before departure and immediately before marshalling the wagons into the correct order for their journey. German dependence on my discretion was slowly building; it would be a pity to destroy it.

My patience, only just kept under control, at last paid off.

'André,' Bahnhof Guer the Younger beckoned from among the empty wagons, 'please come to my office.'

I was puzzled, for he never used my first name. I was also frightened, for nor did he ever leave his comforts for the mud and awkward tracks of the yard.

'Can I trust you?' he began, once back in his familiar surroundings.

'Yes, sir.'

'Good,' he said, closing the door behind me and lowering himself ponderously into the deep armchair behind his desk. 'Each week I receive a list from the military quartermasters of all the repaired vehicles, guns, machinery and soldiers ready for return to the east.' I nodded. 'From these lists I make a load manifest and allocate the correct number of wagons.'

I could guess what was coming, for I knew that this had become too humble a task for a 'stationmaster' on first-name terms with colonels and majors, especially as the station's peacetime clerk had, 'without a thought for the inconvenience to me', recently been dispatched, by the Germans themselves, to serve on the north-coast fortifications.

'You have neat handwriting, and you know enough German to copy accurately. So, here are the lists of equipment and men due out by train from Guer in seven days' time. I need two extra copies.' He pushed a low pile of military documents across the table. I nodded hesitantly, anxious not to show excitement.

'I'd rather work with the trains – shunting and loading,' I said, yet knowing exactly what the British could do with a copy of each manifest.

'You will do as you're told – here's the first lot. Make sure they're neat and accurate.' And with that clear invitation to take part in the war the 'stationmaster' walked out, leaving me exhilarated at this sudden windfall.

Apart from Coëtquidan's officers and the German 'stationmaster', only I would know the details of all serviceable matériel and the numbers of men about to be dispatched from Guer, bound for Rennes, Le Mans, Paris and thence to Germany and the front lines.

I sat alone in the office copying out the two extra manifests. Men's names, ranks, numbers and units plus the serial numbers of tanks, guns and vehicles, all with their individual destinations, were transferred neatly on to fresh pages while the German laughed and drank in the *bar tabac* opposite. I knew from my cleaning duties that jackboots clacking distinctively on the stone floor and the laboured breathing of an overweight, elderly man returning from a café heralded fifteen seconds of warning, and that after that precious quarter of a minute the office door would swing open to admit a haze of tobacco and cognac fumes before the German lowered himself deep into his ample chair.

Manifests came irregularly over the next few weeks, and each was copied twice. Trains departed safely and arrived safely at their distant destinations; I cleaned the offices; I marshalled and shunted; and in the evenings I drank with my farming and forestry-working friends. I listened to their stories as intently as ever, for over the weeks they had become increasingly spiced with tales of parachute drops and clandestine military training which I longed to take part in, but I could not jeopardize my position. In the meantime I remained, outwardly, a willing, biddable young worker, eager to please.

After the third or fourth manifest I decided it was time I sent Charles Touzet an innocent-looking note, with the result that his now familiar knock once more shook Mother's front door. I explained my new job.

'I was hoping something like this would happen,' he said, 'but this is better than I dared believe was possible.'

'This is good news, then?' I fished.

'Couldn't be better,' Charles replied. 'I'll speak to a friend in the morning and arrange a meeting.'

He put down his empty glass. 'Do nothing out of the ordinary,' he said, struggling into his coat. 'We need time to let the Boche[4] confidence in you set solid. In due course others may make contact if they think they can make something of your information.' I must have looked crestfallen, for he tapped my shoulder. 'Don't worry. I'm sure we shall be able to use you – but we must be careful.'

'Thank you, *monsieur*,' I replied.

'In the meantime, make the occasional mistake. Spill ink or something, so that the occasional messed-up copy in the waste-paper basket won't look out of place.'

The next evening Charles came again to the house. 'Oscar wants to see you in Rennes at the weekend,' he said.

A shiver of excitement ran down my back. 'Oscar wants to see me,' I thought. 'Oscar! Me!'

I had heard of Oscar and admired him from a distance, but knew only that he was working for France and not that he was Captain François Vallée, MC, of the British Special Operations Executive and running SOE's 'Parson' circuit centred on Rennes – a town twenty-five miles to the north-east of Guer.[5]

Nor did I know that Oscar had parachuted into Brittany on 17 June 1943, to be joined on 24 July by his radio operator, Edouard (whose real name was Georges Clement), and that by the middle of August they had raised a number of sabotage teams within the Ille-et-Vilaine *département*. Awaiting orders and supplies from London, Parson had yet to undertake any operations, for fear of local reprisals, but it was certainly ready to pass on information that could be useful to the RAF.

Charles Touzet had met Oscar that morning in Rennes, and briefed him on the possibilities that unexpectedly existed at Guer railway station.

'Ask André to come and see me,' Oscar had told Charles.

We met, the three of us, as innocent friends at a prominent café after Charles had told me all that he knew of Oscar so that our meeting would appear natural and between old acquaintances. Coffee and wine were ordered. We drank and laughed in the sun, then after an hour or so Oscar called for the bill before we parted with warm handshakes. The charade was natural enough, with no notice being paid by the few Gestapo officers teasing the waitresses. Ten minutes later and by two different routes – both unwatched as far as we could tell – we were sitting over a Calvados in Oscar's apartment in the Boulevard Magenta.

'We need the information that you're being given. Every time there's a load due out you will make an extra copy of the manifests and give it to Monsieur Touzet. What happens to it then will be no concern of yours – it's better that you know nothing.'

Unsurprised at the request, I agreed, for what was one extra copy of a manifest? A small deed to undertake in order to call myself a member of the French Resistance. I did not know it, but I was from that moment also an embryo member of the British Special Operations Executive. I returned home full of pride and trepidation. Could I really get away with it? What would happen to me if I was caught? Who, should I break, would be dragged down with me? Was I worthy of the trust they had so readily placed in me? I was excited, but I was also nervous.

I didn't start my 'new' work right away, for it was just possible, Charles and I agreed, that we had been followed and been seen talking to a man in Rennes. If, as the result of the next manifest, 'something were to happen', Gestapo minds might start adding random snippets of information together.

At the station there was no mention of where I might have been or what I might have done over that weekend, and there were no complications with the two extra 'legal' copies; nor were there any obvious tricks being played to test my integrity. The trains left on time, fully and correctly laden, and reached their destinations as planned – or, if they did not, the delays were far from Guer and unconnected to any office boy.

Eventually the time was right. As often as necessary I now copied the salient details of each manifest on to paper which I hid in my lunch haversack and handed later to Charles Touzet – whose regular visits to my mother's house were laughed off, by those who bothered to notice, as being 'social'.

Sometimes, as I had previously done by way of a smokescreen

for the future, I managed to spoil a copy, giving me the excuse to make an extra. To add to this subterfuge, I would leave crumpled-up copies in the waste-paper basket overnight – and it was my job to dispose of the contents each morning. The apparent inability to make two good copies straight off would occasionally earn my 'clumsiness' a mild rebuke, but never suspicion. At other times the detail was easily remembered, or would fit on to tiny scraps of paper slid behind the cigarettes in a packet of Gauloises.

The first train whose manifest I had illegally copied was reported, a week later, to have arrived safely at its destination. I showed no surprise, but inwardly I was hurt and puzzled. Did 'they' not know I was risking my life for a scrap of paper?

All I did know was that 'my' information was 'helpful', but in what way was kept from me, and I never asked. Whatever Charles and Oscar did with it was their problem; for me, I knew that I had begun what I had wanted to do ever since my shower had been so rudely interrupted by a German mine.

Oscar must have been satisfied too, for he now entrusted me with a second task – and one that I was even happier to undertake. His Parson circuit needed a new parachute dropping zone further west than Rennes, perhaps even further west than Guer. 'Could you find a suitable place?' I was asked.

'I certainly can,' I replied via our mutual friend, and took another step closer to my ambition. I also needed to begin a list of suitable and like-minded young men in my area who could be relied upon if the moment came.

The cafés were fertile recruiting grounds,[6] and so it was from within this milieu that I initiated a private trawl for similarly in-clined, but so far unemployed, resistance fighters. In no time I knew who was likely to form the nucleus of a resistance movement which might eventually, I hoped (but did not tell Oscar), sabotage the rail link between Guer and Rennes. Nor did I tell the likely candidates that they were on my list, for I was anxious to be regarded simply as an employee of the railways. I also listed those who would not be suitable.

Although the final selection of a dropping zone was Parson's responsibility, it was to be in what I was already, and presumptuously, beginning to regard as 'my' area. Of course I knew little of SOE or of its relationships with the French Resistance, or of its growing network of agents in occupied France, but I did know that British aircraft dropped vital supplies on request – and I wanted some! After days of careful research I chose the local *boucher* to help me.

One of the diverse responsibilities foisted upon this enthusiast was the control of parasites in cattle. Properly conducted, this activity could offer the perfect alibi for travel, so, each evening and at weekends, we trudged and measured our blameless-seeming way around the fields between Guer and Malestroit to the south-west and between Malestroit and Ploërmel to its north. Although many sites suggested a second visit, we knew we had not yet stumbled upon perfection – and men's lives would depend on perfection.

'I have to check a farm of about 120 hectares called La Nouée en Sérent belonging to a Monsieur Pondard outside the village of Saint-Marcel – just beyond Malestroit,' the butcher announced one evening after my railway work was done. 'I think you should come with me. Twenty-seven kilometres to the south-west. Lovely flat fields. And Monsieur Pondard has five pretty daughters – and two sons.' I agreed to accompany him.[7]

'This is André Hue,' the butcher announced to Madame Pondard after a Gestapo-free drive. 'He's helping me with the parasite control. May we walk across your fields?'

Madame Pondard knew nothing of the real reason for the inspection of her husband's land, nor of our keenness to study the long, open space that lay a few hundred yards to the north at the end of a semi-sunken track with dense woods to the west and *bocage* of thick bushes and low scrub to the east. About nine hundred yards long and half as wide, it had crossed the butcher's mind some weeks before that it might be precisely what we should be looking for. In fact neither of us knew precisely what we *were* looking for, but I was pretty confident that when I saw the right place I would know that it was the right place.

We paced its length and breadth; we studied the entry and exit routes; we looked for suitable woods, copses and spinneys in which we could hide containers, and we trudged the paths and tracks. Later we would record the local landmarks to aid the pilots in the moonlight.

The river Oust (rivers and waterways were the pilots' favourite landmarks for night navigation) lay a couple of miles or so to the east, while the field itself ran south-west to north-east. I knew from the maps that the Oust was the first major river an aircraft would cross if flying due south from, say, Saint-Brieuc, which is an easily identified coastal town after a Channel flight for it lies at the head of the deeply indented Baie de Saint-Brieuc. Continuing south, the aircraft would meet the river after a further thirty-five miles, then turn thirty degrees to port for another twelve and a half miles until a large reservoir eight and a half miles north-north-east of the farm was recognized beyond the port cockpit window. Given the prevailing weather, the pilot would then turn left and down-wind before the final upwind turn to cross the river at a right angle just as the dropping-zone lights came into view to the south-west. It seemed that the search was over.

'We must give it a name – I'm sure all landing grounds have a code name. What do you think?' The butcher didn't think.

'Right,' I replied to his unhelpful shrug. 'I shall call it La Baleine, because of its long low hump – just like the whales in the North Atlantic.'

'La Baleine it is then. Now we'd better look for parasites before anyone gets suspicious.'

At home I told Charles of my find.

'Check it with Emile Guimard. I'll invite him over from his farm.' I didn't know Emile Guimard. 'He'll be useful for the future,' Charles continued, 'for he knows all the contacts between here and the north coast. In fact he's the final link in this part of France for the escape route to England, and if he's happy with La Baleine he'll tell Oscar.'

Although not perfect (none were!) La Baleine was to be considered the best potential dropping zone in the area by the pilots, and from our point of view the field was unobserved from the roads and major tracks around the farm and, of great convenience, it was surrounded by a sprawling patchwork – network even – of rambling woods and brakes. Best of all, Monsieur and Madame Pondard were known to support the resistance movement in all its guises.

Back in Guer and always anxious for snippets of news, on the few evenings that I was not helping the butcher or assessing gossip in the cafés I often crouched with Jean over his employer's illegal wireless set, with the volume turned so low that we could hear it only through one ear each pressed to the loudspeaker resting between us.

To begin with I did not know what I wanted to hear, and anyway I was certain that the part I was playing was of such little significance that the BBC would ignore it. Yet suddenly one evening I straightened up, my mug shaking in my hand, spilling coffee across the carpet. The English announcer was halfway through his bulletin: 'Royal Air Force fighter aircraft this morning attacked a goods train between Rennes and Le Mans in occupied France. A significant number of the enemy's tanks and artillery are believed to have been destroyed.'

'André,' Jean said, switching off the set with one hand while sweeping hot liquid from his trousers with the other, 'wasn't that a train from Coëtquidan? How do you suppose the British knew?'

'I haven't a clue,' I replied casually, knowing that a manifest had been passed to Charles just four days earlier and that it had been a particularly important load.

Bicycling to work the next morning, I was unable to suppress a flock of butterflies disturbing my stomach. Would the 'stationmaster' see a connection? Would he accuse me of involvement? I carried out my duties as nonchalantly as possible until my boss arrived for work as usual and, also as usual, smelling strongly of stale brandy and nicotine. If he suspected anything he showed no concern – and I wasn't about to raise the subject. Once his office was tidied and dusted I sauntered out to the marshalling yard with no sign that he had even noticed my presence – as usual.

After that I listened intently to the BBC every time that I had passed a manifest, but to begin with there was nothing. Then, with the passing days, attacks began again and became more frequent.

As though to divert suspicion from our area, some trains were attacked beyond Paris and some were left unscathed, but all had started from Guer.

Nothing could be pinned on me directly, but as I sat tight I worried – until the day my worry was justified. On that morning I noticed, out of the corner of my eye, the 'stationmaster' picking his way delicately through the weeds and across the tracks. He seemed to be in a hurry, and as he approached I could see him shaking – with fear or anger I could not tell, but it was not with laughter. I continued shovelling coal into the firebox of my shunting engine.

'Hue,' he said in his appalling French. I looked down from the footplate. 'Please come to my office.'

I stepped thoughtfully from my locomotive and stood facing him, wiping my hands slowly on an oily rag. He turned and waved his arm for me to follow his portly shape as it waddled back to cleanliness and warmth. My mind was racing, my body tensed for instant flight or fight.

As I entered the office behind the considerable bulk of drab uniform and leather belts, for a moment or two the ample girth obscured all else inside the room. Someone closed the door firmly behind me. I looked round, startled, and into the faces of two senior German army officers. I turned back to the 'stationmaster'. His drawn pistol was aimed at my stomach.

'You are not carrying out your duties correctly,' he growled. I sensed the officers behind me nodding in agreement.

'But, *Herr Chef de Gare*, you have made no complaints.'

I was cut short by a voice from over my shoulder: 'We have complaints!' I turned round. 'You will work properly or you will work on the north coast.'

I turned back as the 'stationmaster' continued, 'You are nineteen years old now – *ja*?'

'*Oui, monsieur.*'

Having flexed his muscles in public, the *chef de gare* had no further use for me, and I was suddenly dismissed with a wave of the pistol before it was replaced in its holster. Outside I paused momentarily to hear my boss being shouted at in German. I didn't understand the words – nor the reason behind them – but anger has a universal intonation. I decided to keep a low profile.

My luck had held – just – but that evening I returned to the family flat concerned more for the safety of my mother and elder half-brother than for myself. If 'things' became awkward they could leave within the hour, but I (or in reality Oscar) had yet to receive the first air drop of arms, equipment and explosives on to La Baleine, and to me that was worth the risk of staying.

While I worked diligently but boringly, I heard from Charles that the RAF liked La Baleine; they liked the ease of navigation and the absence, as far as any of us could tell, of anti-aircraft batteries. Spurred on by this new development, I persuaded Oscar to send a request for supplies. Having nothing positive to offer, I had yet to form my team; but now, with confirmation that an exploratory drop would be carried out on to La Baleine as soon as conditions were right, I called a meeting of potential 'recruits' in the well-frequented Café de la Place.

My friends knew something was up, and at last I could tell them what.

'You all know that there's a resistance movement centred on Rennes,' I began. Although they probably didn't know, they nodded excitedly. 'Well, now we have a movement centred on Guer.'

Someone called for more Calvados, while others leaned inward over the table to hear the details. I explained the future as I saw it.

'We all know each other. We all share the same views. We would all recognize an outsider.'

'Yes.'

'We must keep it that way,' I said, before committing myself irrevocably to their trust and integrity by involving them in my biggest secret. 'In the meantime we can expect our first supply drop soon. I don't know the exact date: all I've been told is that it will be during "the next moon"!' There was silence while they looked at each other then back to me.

'How will we know when that is?' someone broke the spell.

'The BBC will pass a message early during the evening of the drop. Only I will be given the code. Until then we must avoid being seen all together. Now let's drink to our success. *Vive la France!*'

'*Vive la France!*'

'*Vive le RAF!*' We broke up just before the curfew descended.

Precisely two weeks after the 'interview' with the German officers and a week after the meeting in the café I sat hunched, as so often, over Jean's illicit wireless.

'The seagulls are swimming . . . Mary has a blue jacket . . .' The cultured BBC voice intoned dozens of similar messages to like-minded organizations across Europe. 'The geese are flying tonight . . .'

'That's us,' I said unemotionally to my half-brother. 'We're in business. Come, I must warn the others.'

It had been a boisterous October day, and rain squalls were still chasing each other across the countryside with no sign of a let-up in the conditions. 'And yet, and yet,' I convinced myself, 'there are just enough clear periods between the flying clouds to have persuaded the RAF that it has to be La Baleine's turn to enter the war.' The elation was overwhelming. 'Just let this go right,' I prayed, 'then I can carry out my own sabotage without needing to copy manifests.'

With infinite care I rounded up my team. Slowly the members made their individual ways down the road that leads towards Vannes; then, once over the river Oust, they entered the village of Malestroit in dribs and drabs, to sit drinking coffee in the cafés. The reception party was gathering, but remained apart. It was a long wait while the rain hammered on the smoke-stained windows between sudden shafts of light from the lowering sun.

The Germans had not yet been alerted to clandestine operations in the area, as most took place further to the east and north. For us, enemy patrols were still few and far between. 'But', I thought, 'probably not for much longer.'

Controlling their trepidation but not their excitement, my diverse selection of resistance trainees waited for me to make the first move. Then, on a pre-arranged sign, the message spread from café to café. Slowly we paid for our coffees and sauntered off as though for home. Through the shadows we walked, silently: off the main road, under the railway bridge, turning right down the lane, over the hedge, before reaching the hamlet of Saint-Marcel, skirting the eastern edge of the Pondards' farm.

We gathered to the north of the darkened farm buildings. Ahead, to the west and into the night, lay the long, open strip that had been 'checked for parasites'. At the far end, five hundred yards away, were barns – the limit of La Baleine – and to their right were more farm buildings, sometimes visible when the moon shone between the racing clouds.

Oscar had taught me how to lay out the lights. I turned to my second in command's now-blackened face. 'Got the torches?'

'Yes.'

'Right, take each man and place him as I showed you – the bottom of the L downwind, right here at the eastern end. The aircraft will come over this first. When the pilot sees the offset light out of his starboard window he knows he's over the beginning of the dropping zone's centre line. The four men with the lights, space out every hundred metres, starting with the first one right here. The last one should be by the barns at the far end.' I took another man by the arm and pointed to the right. 'Fifty metres away, at a right angle – the arm of the L as I showed you in the café.' I felt him nod in the dark. 'OK?'

'OK!'

'Right, off you go. *Bonne chance.*'

The final minutes passed as though each was an hour. Then, above the wind in the surrounding trees, the unmistakable, wonderful noise of a multi-engined aircraft entered my life for the first time. I flashed my signal down the line of torch-bearers. The guide path lit up, each weak beam facing back towards me and upward into the sky at a shallow angle. The engine noises came closer, then, with a deafening roar and the hint of a fleeting black shadow against the moonlit clouds, they faded quickly, leaving in the silence silhouettes of parachutes and containers swinging gently down from five hundred feet.

No fuss, no mistakes – no Germans. The lights were quickly doused as men fought billowing silk to prevent the heavy containers dragging across the grass. It was all over in seconds, and our first drop had been a success.

The team crowded round, hardly believing what they had been involved in. Up to then it had been my dream, the dream of a nineteen-year-old youth, but for them until that sublime moment it had been merely a midnight adventure. Now it was real for all of us, and the serious work was to begin. This was for us, if not for the pilots, the most difficult of phases, for we could not know whether the enemy had seen or heard anything. Were they, even as we congratulated each other, setting up their ambushes? No reports came from the web of lookouts, but no one was infallible. Were they preparing a full-scale assault on us while we were at our most vulnerable? Would they catch us in flagrante delicto, our arms full of parachutes and containers?

Before the self-congratulations could start and the cognac be tasted we had to collect the widely dispersed containers and bury them, a task that involved five hours of searching and two of digging. It was an exhilarating experience, heightened by knowing what was in the containers, and yet one balanced by the approach of dawn. All had gone to plan, and with no sign that either the Germans or even the *Milice* had noticed. We dared to believe that we might, at last, be in business.

Tired and worried once the adrenalin had been reabsorbed by our physical exertions, we made our way back to work along the web of local paths and woods that I had so meticulously reconnoitred over the months. In and around Malestroit various *camions* were coaxed back into life to take those from Guer home along Route D776, while others mounted bicycles and mule-towed carts. All we needed now were targets. We had our own favourites, of course, but London – via Oscar – had a wider view and a fear of Nazi vengeance that our limited experience had yet to appreciate. In the meantime we would organize ourselves and train ourselves, then train again and again – and no doubt reorganize ourselves again.

No enemy patrols hindered our return. I shaved and, appearing as though I had slept the sleep of the guiltless, reported for duty on time, ready to sweep and dust. No eyebrows were raised and no questions were asked, but I was glad when the day was over and I could assess the night's work, send a report to Oscar, and sleep.

But my joy at reaching home that evening was tempered by new family concerns, for that morning the Gestapo had hauled Jean in for interrogation. Despite his being the blameless face of the Hue brothers, the Germans were taking a closer interest in his work, with its easy access to many buildings both official and private.

'I'm also one of the few young men still in Guer who's fit,' he said.

'So?' I replied, not sure where this was to lead.

'They're short of labour for the north-coast defences.'

'You're worried, aren't you?'

'Yes. But, if I leave, the Boche may put pressure on Mama and you to find out why.'

'Never mind that. You must go. Tomorrow morning, after the curfew. If you're already worried then it's already too late,' I emphasized. 'Charles Touzet could provide papers saying that you're unsuitable for work on the coastal defences, but I think you should go now.'

Even if his mind was not made up, that of my mother was; and so, with our blessing, Jean left the next day for Rennes and eventually Paris, where he found work as an electrician in a cinema on the Champs-Elysées. Neither of us was to know if the other was still alive until well after the war.

The time of my own departure from Guer was unexpectedly taken out of my hands after one more train and one more attack. What was to be my last day in Guer began as normal with cleaning and tidying followed by a short bicycle ride to the furthest end of the station yard for a spell of wagon-marshalling. Here I left my bicycle leaning against the perimeter fence as I always did, in case there was a need to return to the station buildings during the day.

It was the autumn of 1943, and the morning was a shunting morning – a practical task I enjoyed, and one for which I was now qualified. With a staccato clanking and crashing of empty goods wagons, I brought a line of trucks into a siding close to the station buildings. There, even over the puffing and hissing of my engine, I could suddenly hear shouting and the unmistakable hollow sound of jackboots running across cobbles.

Despite the close proximity of the German military, Guer railway station was mostly a quiet place. The Germans tended to visit only on 'cargo' days, and the next one was not for another week, so I stopped to have a view of this kerfuffle. Four staff cars had stopped untidily outside the 'stationmaster's' office, their passengers already rushing inside, gesticulating and bawling.

I was not used to witnessing such theatrics, and certainly none had ever taken place with such apparent urgency. I felt fear mounting, convinced for no good or obvious reason that I was the cause of the fuss. Anxious to do nothing that might turn a possibly innocent occasion into a drama, I stepped cautiously on to the tracks, undecided what my next move should be or even if I should be making one.

There was then one other teenager working at Guer station. My friend Durandière was also employed by the SNCF, and, as I watched the last of the uniformed Gestapo men disappear through the office door, he appeared furtively from the opposite end of the building.

Checking that he was well hidden, he caught my eye from fifty yards away and quickly bent his right arm up from the elbow while making a downward cutting movement across it with his left hand – 'Get the hell out of here. NOW!' Even at that distance I could recognize the Gallic message and see the fear in his wide eyes.

It was the signal I had been dreading for months, yet one that my rational mind had kept telling me would not come. I could think of no hard evidence that would support any serious accusations against me, and yet there had been a warning of sorts when the officers had said they were not happy with my work. Clearly they had had their reasons to say that, but did not know precisely why. Maybe they had simply wanted to frighten me into making a mistake.

I climbed back to my footplate and, cursing the noise that locomotives make and the distance we had to travel, I puffed my way to the end of the yard, from where and with considerably more haste I pedalled my way furiously through the lanes to Charles Touzet's house. My worldly possessions at this time were a bycycle, the clothes I stood up in and a haversack with my uneaten lunch.

'Charles,' I panted, 'I've been caught out.'

'I'm not surprised, my friend,' he replied soothingly. 'You must get to Rennes and hide there for a day or two.'

'Will you tell my mother?'

'Yes, and Durandière. I think he should leave as well.'[8]

'I'll need new papers.'

'That's not difficult.'

'I'll go straight to René Bichelot's house. Remember him?'

'Of course.' Charles remembered the dental-student acquaintance of mine. 'But is he not wanted by the Gestapo?'

'He's too clever for them. I'll be safe for a day or two.' I was not sure that that was true, but I had to start somewhere.

By the time I reached Bichelot's flat the next morning, however, I was considerably ill at ease. Not only was I in a town which I did not know, but Bichelot was a wanted man whose *pension* witnessed many comings and goings. Increased activity, no matter how mundane, always came to the notice of the Gestapo – and particularly in Rennes, where they had established an area headquarters.

My concern built rapidly over those first few days away from Guer, especially when the news was confirmed that I was wanted by the Gestapo for questioning.

'I'm not doing much good here,' I announced after a week of inactivity made worse by the presence, in the cafés and in large numbers, of both uniformed and plain-clothed Gestapo.

René was doubly worried that he, a fugitive in his own right, was harbouring another. He suggested that I went to Messac, a few miles south of Rennes, to work with Emile Guimard.

I recognized the name. 'The man who checked La Baleine for Oscar?'

'Of course. Emile takes the pilots I give him to the north coast. Then, when there are enough, he has them collected from a beach near his farm.'

'Tell me more,' I said, beginning to realize that perhaps I should have gone straight to Emile in the first place.

'He arranges safe houses, false papers, and motor boats.'

'That's more like it,' I said with a renewed enthusiasm. 'I'll contact Monsieur Guimard tomorrow.' And, with that decision made, I was soon back on the road, hitchhiking to Messac and continuing my circuitous route towards action.

One of Emile's secure houses lay a couple of fields from Messac. Once safely in the kitchen, he suggested that I might like to start by helping to gather intelligence on the defences being built by the Germans on the Channel and Atlantic coasts.

Giving me no time to think, he warned, 'This is dangerous work, due to the restrictions placed on all "non-essential" civilians in the area. However, we do need to know what's happening. Will you do it?'

'Yes!' I replied.

'I thought you would. While we wait for your papers to be produced I'll need to keep you out of harm's way.' I guessed this meant back to the woods and smiled, especially when he mentioned that the local landowner was yet another viscount. However, instead of heading for the woods as a lumberjack, I was taken to the chateau's kitchens, where indoctrination as a part-time cook began under a fierce housekeeper: between us it took less than five minutes to discover that I was better with a handsaw than with an egg whisk!

The viscountess – much younger than her husband and not, like him, gently going senile – was full of vivacious energy, all of which she channelled into being an active member of Emile Guimard's network. With her willing acceptance of shot-down airmen into the chateau (where they were easily spirited away among the many rooms, secret passages and alcoves), it was easy for me, working in her *cuisine*, to listen in to the 'lessons learned' and hear at first hand of the tricks required to evade capture. I fitted effortlessly into the routine – or lack of it, for every day brought new and different challenges – and felt that I was even closer to fulfilling my aim. But I had been close before, and was not so foolish as to believe that this was the final leg of my journey.

Escaping airmen, filtered via René Bichelot, arrived at irregular intervals. Although SOE did not employ him in this task, pilots would be taken to the nearest member of the resistance movement that the farmers knew – and all the farmers seemed to know René, such was his reputation. Once René was satisfied that an escaper was genuine and not a Gestapo plant, he would pass him on to Emile and one of his widely dispersed chateaux, houses and farms where airmen would wait until the next shuttle across the Channel.

My task in this 'pipeline' was now to conduct the pilots in their ones and twos from wherever René had them hidden into Emile's northern network to await departure, some for Spain and some direct to the UK.

Those destined for the shorter, less arduous but far from hazard-free route travelled either by motor gunboats (MGBs) from a north-Brittany beach or, if of high value, perhaps via a trawler out of Concarneau to rendezvous with a submarine lying offshore in the Atlantic swell. The journey via Spain was considerably more fraught.[9]

Farms were the preferred option for the escape pipeline, if there was ever a choice, for the men could work or hide in the fields by day and stay out all night in the summer – and in winter too if necessary. The difficulties increased, however, as the escapers moved progressively closer to the heavily controlled coastal zone, where special 'safe-conduct' passes were required – and supplied by Aline Jestin, a resourceful employee of the Rennes prefecture who had earlier ensured that my own journeys had been trouble-free.

But if moving one airman was awkward enough in a city, where gaggles of men are commonplace, moving half a dozen through the countryside produced its own problems, for large bodies of unknown men were conspicuous in a place where everyone knew everyone else. No matter how loyal the locals might have been, tongues did wag and the *Milice* listened. This phase of each operation provided unique challenges, particularly as we began to rely more heavily on outside help.

Often this help would come from Félix Jouan and his van. Félix was the miller in the small town of Bédée, about thirty-four miles south of Saint Malo and the other side of Rennes from Messac. He had an excuse to travel widely, although the fact that his *camion gazogène* was registered in the Ille-et-Vilaine *département* did not always help, as the coastal zone was prohibited to most people by day and to everyone after the start of the evening curfew.

Village priests, too, would supply more than pastoral care. 'I've arranged with the Germans for my church football team to be "awarded" an away fixture against them,' said one cleric when hearing of six Americans I was trying to get to the coast from Paris.

'Brilliant,' I agreed with what I hoped was uncharacteristic sarcasm. 'But we also need to get my "team" there, and it's many miles.'

'Please, I've asked that as a special favour we be allowed to send a deaf-and-dumb squad with the fit team, and your six will be part of that. No arguing,' he held up both hands – 'it's all fixed, and I even have some genuine disabled to go with them.'

As the 'deaf-and-dumb' trick was as old as the hills in escaping folklore, and about as implausible as a Breton who did not smell of garlic, I was worried. But approval was given, suitable shirts were swiftly procured and issued, and both teams – the genuine and the disabled – were loaded at dawn the next day into the church's charcoal-burning, steam-driven lorry.

With strict instructions to keep their mouths shut, this unlikely crew, with me the anxious coordinator, set off for the coastal region of north Brittany, a staggering one hundred miles away. Everything was going well until we were faced by a steep hill with which the *camion* simply could not cope.

'Everyone out,' ordered the priest. 'Now push!'

We did as instructed, thoroughly blocking the road with our snail's pace.

'*Schnell! Schnell!*' screamed the driver of a German lorry as he braked behind us with his equally full load of soldiers, all of whom now began shouting encouragement in pidgin French.

'We'd be faster if you helped,' shouted back the priest.

'You're right, father,' the German driver replied before turning to his passengers: 'Help this priest and his colleagues.' And with that and light-hearted but one-sided banter the enemy soldiers lent their weight.

Struggling and sweating up that slope, I tried to appear noncha-lant while constantly keeping an eye on the ditches on either side for the best avenue of escape. Nobody noticed my concern, and the motley convoy made its steady but very slow way to the summit.

Had our ruse been foiled the airmen would have become prisoners of war, I would have faced a summary trial and the firing squad, and the priest and his 'home team' would have been imprisoned.

Thankfully, common sense held and the 'teams' were able to part company from their helpers with a subdued '*Merci*' from me, the priest and the genuine footballers, while the 'deaf and dumb' waved vigorously. Thinking they had helped cement local relations (as they were under orders to do), the Germans drove past shouting further encouragement out of the back of their accelerating lorry; many hours later our own *camion* managed to reach its destination of Guimaëc, just a mile or so from the English Channel.

Since the duplicated railway manifests, it was not only the Gestapo who wanted to interview me: apparently the French Resistance had been keeping an eye on me. Now, although I did not yet know it, my name was being mentioned in the London headquarters of the Special Operations Executive. With the Allies' proposed return to mainland Europe less than a year away, SOE had for some time been drawing up plans to boost the size and modus operandi of the resistance movement, particularly in Brittany and Normandy, in order to prevent German reinforcements reaching the coast once the invasion was under way. The men they wanted to organize and coordinate this phase of the war had to be from that rare breed, Englishmen who spoke French as their primary language.

In November 1943, back in the Messac chateau's kitchen (where I had returned after delivering my 'footballers' to the north), I was surprised by a summons from the viscountess. Waiting in her salon was a man I did not know.

'André Hue?'

'*Oui*,' I replied, hesitant at admitting my identity to a stranger.

'I'm from Emile. I have a message that you are to go to England. The SOE – you know of the SOE?'–

'Yes.'

'. . . have made arrangements for you to cross the Channel with the next batch of pilots.'

'What for?' I asked. 'I'm doing a good job here.'

'You'll do an even better job with training.' I agreed with the logic, and nodded as he added, 'The Resistance have arranged to get you to the farm near Guimaëc where you took the foot-ballers. It's close to Emile's own farm. There you'll meet two other resistance workers also in the pipeline: a young girl and a young man, each of about twenty years. They too are going back for training.' He knew a great deal about our work, but I still could not identify him.

Unsure whether this was good or bad news, yet certain that if the viscountess said the visitor was genuine then he was genuine, I returned to my work deep in thought. I guessed, through Oscar's periodic messages, that I was a marked man, and if SOE wanted me then that was a move forward not to be questioned. After all, I was British and therefore could not refuse. And nor did I want to. I slept well, fully prepared for whatever lay ahead.

Escaping – or, more accurately, evading – was never a precise activity running to a fixed schedule, and time passed slowly while arrangements were submitted, checked and agreed. So slowly, indeed, that I returned to the woods as a lumberman chopping the winter fuel, while my prospective colleagues, the girl and the young man, cooked and tended cattle respectively. It was the best that could be arranged should the German-sympathizing police of Finistère – or the Gestapo, or the *Milice* – decide to swoop. Plans that I should spy on the coastal defences were laid aside, and deep down I was not sorry about that.

Emile not only ran an escape network from his north-Brittany farm, but now also led the expanding Maquis based on the Pondards' farm, known locally as La Nouette, one of whose fields I had named La Baleine. Helping Emile with his huge area of responsibility that stretched from Vannes in the south to the Channel coast in the north were General Allard and a number of retired colonels, all of whom were acceptable to de Gaulle as his personal representatives in Brittany. I listened intently to these men and their voices of reason and experience.

Evader though I might have become, I still regarded myself as 'on duty' during this waiting period, a status I was able to reinforce while trimming logs in a clearing one late-autumn morning of 1943. Above the trees the sound of an aerial dogfight was suddenly sharp and loud. I leaned on my axe transfixed by the first such fight

I had seen, and looked up in time to see a British aircraft spiralling down, smoke and flames streaming aft from the root of a wing. Near by, in contrast, the pilot was swinging slowly and safely beneath his parachute. Dropping everything, once hidden from the possibility of prying eyes, I ran to report what I had seen to Emile.

'I thought I should check with you first,' I gushed, out of breath. 'Because of the *Milice*.'

'Quite right – but we're safer here than further inland. Near the coast the *Milice* leave everything to the Boche. But don't get caught.'

'I won't.'

'Good lad. Now get back there,' Emile ordered. 'Tell the farmer what you've seen. Tell him you've come from me. Get him to agree to hide the pilot, then find the pilot and tell him to stay put until we collect him.' I nodded. 'With any luck we'll get him back in the next batch, your lot, by Christmas. Now hurry, before he does something stupid.'

I ran back to carry out his instructions. The farmer, Emile's friend, did not query the outline plan, so I hurried off to start my search. It didn't take long, as the pilot was hiding, not very convincingly, in a haystack.

'Welcome to France,' I shouted at the soles of a pair of flying boots sticking out of the straw. As there was no answer I continued, 'And welcome to the escape pipeline.'

'That was bloody quick. It's a trick,' a muffled voice growled.

'It's not,' I laughed, 'and with any luck', I went on, playing my part with enthusiasm, 'we'll get you home for Christmas, or at least for the New Year.'

Sliding to the ground, the pilot remained grim-faced at this news, delivered by an apparent scruffian, yet, puzzlingly perhaps, one who spoke good, if heavily accented, English. On his feet and seeing that I was unarmed, he slowly drew his service revolver.

Unamused, uninjured and wearing the uniform of a wing commander, he pointed a loaded barrel at my face. 'You can bloody well get me back sooner than that,' he growled again. 'I haven't been married a year yet, and I promised my wife I'd be back to celebrate our wedding anniversary – before Christmas.'

Undaunted by either this onslaught or the revolver, I felt the need for a little realism. 'If that's your attitude then you can make your own way home. Not many pilots land straight into the escape pipeline. Goodbye!'

I turned to leave the field.

'Sorry!' the wing commander shouted after me.

I turned, 'If you are, then for heaven's sake don't yell.'

Shocked and disorientated after the third unexpected change in his fortunes within an hour, he slid his weapon back into its holster. Now contrite and cooperative, he said quietly, 'OK. Lead on, young man. Sorry about that.'[10]

Waiting for the right conditions often meant a lengthy period of forced inactivity. The lack of a moon was essential for getting out of France by boat as much as moonlit nights were vital for getting in by aircraft. Also important were a calmish sea, a steep beach to reduce surf, no minefields immediately offshore, a lack of navigationally complicated rocky outcrops, benign tides at the appropriate time during the night and, obviously, a lack of prying eyes from a shore battery. While benign tides – meaning, if possible, neap tides – were important, they also had to be rising tides at the moment of embarkation or disembarkation, so that footprints would be quickly erased. A prominent landmark on the cliff, or even a distinctively shaped cliff itself, was equally important, to aid an MGB skipper's terminal navigation. German coastal-convoy activity, with its escorting destroyers and E-boats, was an unpredictable hazard that also had to be accounted for. All these factors did not come together every night, nor even every month.

Late on 26 February 1944 my long wait since 1940 came to an end when the three of us 'farm hands' were summoned to a neighbouring house to be ushered into a capacious hide dug beneath the dining room. Already sheltering in the gloom were René Bichelot's six American pilots, plus others from Britain and France. In the semi-darkness I recognized two or three of them and, with a laugh and a handshake, the maritally frustrated wing commander.

Once the full load had been gathered, we listened to Emile Guimard's detailed briefing.

'Any questions?' No one spoke. Everything was clear and concise.

'Right, now do as I tell you. We move off in ten minutes.'

We donned our darkest clothing as instructed, although, without luggage, this meant no more than some of us turning a jacket inside out. We pulled our socks over our shoes to deaden our footsteps; removed luminous watches and anything that could be accidentally dropped to be discovered as tell-tale evidence of our illicit night-time activity – hats were forbidden unless stuffed deep into pockets – and, finally, jumped up and down to see if we 'rattled'. We didn't, and were declared fit for this trickiest stage of the escape journey.

Beckoned by a guide to follow, we tiptoed one behind another for a quarter of a mile, shuffling in a snaking queue through the darkness. Our intermediate destination was the Baie de Lannion (although we were not told that) and the beach that lies a mile or so west of the coastal village of Locquirec and under the prominent headland of Beg-an-Fry. A darkened motor gunboat, we were told, was lying one and a half miles offshore to a coir anchor rope – out of sight and out of earshot.

The procedure for beach exchanges was as well rehearsed as had been the approach to the cliff edge. While the outgoing team waited at the western end of the beach, an incoming team was being landed, unseen, at the other end.[11] It was imperative that neither party knew how many, or especially who, was being transported in either direction.

Once the MGB was empty of the new arrivals to France, its two specially designed surf boats were paddled along the seaward edge of the slight surf towards our end of the beach, while we desperately craved the comfort of a Gauloise or two.

At last, for we had actually been unaware of what was happening just a few hundred yards to the east, we could make out the silhouettes of the two small craft a few yards offshore. A crewman moved up from the water's edge, noiselessly and quickly. Passwords were exchanged.

Divided equally into two boatloads, we were beckoned to the tide line and, once full and settled, the craft were urged gently into deeper water. Though we remained in the greatest danger, the relief of tension was marked: all being well, in five minutes we could take that first deep drag of nicotine and, if the rumours were correct, swallow something hot and well laced with navy rum.

But the journey was not yet over, for a thick, all-embracing fog was creeping in from the sea as silently as the craft had done, adding further drama to an already suspense-filled night.

'Where the hell's the boat,' whispered the sailors as they paddled offshore with feathered blades. It was an anxious moment in which I and my companions could play only a passive role. The naval officer in charge risked a two-second flash of light to seaward. Its beam glared back at us from a million tiny droplets.

We waited. The need for a cigarette was becoming acute. Another risky flash of light to seaward; then the low rumble of supercharged diesel engines wafted faintly across the water. A minute later, through the opaque darkness, the wonderful silhouette of an MGB[12] nosed a few more perilous yards closer to the beach.

'Thank God for that,' breathed the lieutenant. 'I thought we might have had to switch jobs, and I would rather you came with me than me return with you!'

The rumours were true: as we were led quickly below and out of the way, each of us was handed a steaming mug of 'kie' – the naval version of Ovaltine, liberally spiced with 'pusser's rum' – and a packet of ten Player's Navy Cut.

The captain, Lieutenant Peter Williams, DSC, RNVR, wasted no time in turning his boat's head for the open sea under slow-speed, auxiliary power, until we felt rather than saw the stern dip as the throttles for the main engines were pushed fully open. The embarkation had taken longer than expected, but with a top speed of twenty-eight knots and a journey of almost exactly one hundred nautical miles we expected to be safely in British waters before dawn. Huddled together like spillikins in the cramped crew's quarters, we knew nothing of the dangers as we slept or smoked.

And so, early on the morning of 27 February 1944, and after a four-hour dash, I landed in the country of my birth for the first time for many years. I would leave again in just five months.

As I stepped on to the *Westward Ho!* – a 460-ton paddle steamer that served as the MGB's depot ship – and turned to wave good-bye to the captain on his open bridge, it struck me that I knew nobody there. I did not even know where to go, nor whom I should contact. All I did know was that my life was no longer in my own hands.

2. Headhunted

Tired, filthy, unshaven and hungry, but with my socks now comfortably inside my shoes, I stepped from the naval picket boat on to the pontoon below Kingswear's railway station on the east bank of the river Dart – opposite the Royal Naval College. The narrow gangway, sloping up from the water's edge, led towards the ticket office and with luck, I thought, a kiosk selling hot coffee and sandwiches. The sustenance meted out on board the *Westward Ho!* had been welcome but not enough.

Apart from that immediate need, my life from here on was a blank, for I had no idea what to expect, whom to meet, where to go – or how to get there.

I wasn't used to blanks, and to add to my discomfort there was no hot drink and certainly no food. An unaccustomed homesickness enveloped me. Where was the smell of freshly baked bread, of hot croissants, of real coffee? War or no war, this was not like home: despite being subjugated by an occupying power, France was still able to maintain some semblance of normality.

I looked around for a sign that I might have been expected.

'Monsieur Hue?' A woman approached from a parked staff car.

'Yes,' I replied, surprised to be important enough for such a greeting.

'Please come with me, sir,' she invited. Inadequately prepared – and dressed – for such a welcome, I followed meekly, worried that there had been no formal identification.

'Where are we going?' I asked hesitantly, as she waved two railway tickets at the ticket collector. By luck – or was it planned, for it was not unknown for the train to be kept waiting for returning agents (although the reason for such delays was never made public) – a train was waiting and, relaxing into a reserved compartment, I realized that civilization takes many forms. Not being worried about the Gestapo was one of them.

'SOE's Patriotic School,' she said, smiling. 'I'm afraid it'll take some time, and I have to escort you the whole way.'

'What on earth is that?' I asked.

She explained. Situated at Wandsworth, within the Greater London area, the Royal Victoria Patriotic School (London Reception Centre) was a mandatory two-day screening process run by MI5 for all those coming out of occupied Europe. Every member of SOE, no matter how often he had returned nor how senior he might be, was required to be identified and debriefed as a first precaution against German infiltration or brainwashing. Despite speaking English with a French accent, I was easily identified, thanks to an uncle and aunt brought from Swansea for that purpose, and with those initial formalities successfully negotiated I was moved to a flat in Baker Street – close to number 64, SOE's headquarters – where an officer had been detailed to entertain me to dinner and to break me easily into England's wartime restrictions with copious wine. To repay this 'duty entertainer' I recounted a less formal version of events in the Morbihan area of Brittany, hoping to add flavour to the sketchy messages received from other agents. But nothing I said actually altered my new circumstances.

'You will be confined to the flat until "legalized",' the officer explained enigmatically at the start of this irritating restriction. For so long I had run my own affairs, but now my every move was to be dictated by someone else. Nevertheless, the restrictions would have their compensations: a comfortable bed and regular food – starting with a 'full English breakfast' the next morning.

On the second day an army officer arrived carrying a smart new suitcase and a sheaf of official-looking papers stating that André Hunter Alfred Hue was now a second lieutenant on the General List of the British Army. To prove the point, he unpacked, with a theatrical flourish, a khaki battledress blouse with a single 'pip' on each shoulder; matching trousers, brown shoes, and a khaki shirt and tie completed the uniform.

After the briefest of instructions on how to salute senior officers and return those from other ranks, I was ready to meet Colonel Maurice Buckmaster, the charismatic, colourful and occasionally controversial head of the French section of SOE since 1941.

From him and his staff I received orders covering my 'employment' over the next few months. Little of the future beyond that was hinted at, but as a fluent-French-speaking British citizen, and now army officer, I knew that I would eventually be returned by parachute to the Morbihan *département* of Brittany 'towards the middle of 1944'.

The Morbihan was, after all, where I had been helping the local, but largely ad hoc, Maquis and its associated escape routes. It was a countryside with which I was familiar – and one which would come to prominence once the Allies returned to mainland Europe, for it lay between the north-coast landing beaches and the major German garrisons controlling the Atlantic ports.

In the meantime I was off to Scotland for SOE's 'Group A' course in sabotage and its associated military disciplines. Before that, a few more days' leave in London preceded a meeting with my new colleagues; then we set off to start our tour of SOE's training schools under the close eye of a conducting officer.

The school for which I and my friends were heading by train lay off the road and railway line that twist westward for forty miles between Fort William and Mallaig. This was, and remains, a wild and unforgiving country of steep glens, fast rivers and long lochs. It is perfect terrain for hard physical work and explosives training well away from prying eyes and areas of population.

Conveniently – and not by coincidence, since the early reconnaissance had been carried out personally by General Gubbins: the SOE's executive director and Colonel Buckmaster's 'boss' – the cover story for these five-week courses was that we were 'commandos': an acceptable ruse, for the 'real thing' were being trained over similar country to the north and east of Fort William. It was presumed, correctly, that as potential saboteurs we needed a considerable amount of toughening-up – and we certainly got it. While the land is more rugged than that found in Brittany, the principle of 'train hard for an easy war' was well applied. It was here, based in one of the country houses around Arisaig, that I, my predecessors and my successors learned the skills necessary for our future. It was here, too, that we were introduced to the ubiquitous plastic explosive – a substance so safe that bullets will not detonate it, though the fastest cup of tea in the world can be brewed by using it as fuel. Pliable like plasticine and easily moulded, it makes the ideal weapon for a saboteur – or terrorist. The secret was knowing how little explosive to use to achieve any given objective, rather than an ad-hoc application of a kneaded mass of the stuff in the hope that the bigger the bang the more effective the attack. Even with demolitions the skill of a surgeon is needed, not that of a bulldozer driver.

All the commando skills were taught: 'silent killing'; fighting with the Fairburn–Sykes knife, known colloquially as the commando dagger; stripping, assembling (blindfolded, in quick time) and firing the silenced British and enemy sub-machine guns and pistols; working with small boats for raiding tasks, sabotage and demolition work – and all the while fieldcraft, map-reading, hard physical exercise, and the Morse code.

Apart from the basics in Morse, I preferred to stay well clear of this discipline by leaving it to the acknowledged experts – of which in 1943 there were too few to support all the agents and circuits that needed them. I tried, but my heart was not in it and I had neither the patience nor the latent skills necessary. I preferred to organize and resist in practical terms, rather than sit in a room receiving and sending coded messages.

SOE's Special Training Schools (STSs) were dedicated to the preparation of men for active resistance work, using French-speaking British commissioned and non-commissioned officers as instructors. Occasionally a student might act as an interpreter, for many other nationalities had to be catered for.

Down from Scotland, the now-fit embryo agents headed for the New Forest in southern England and the less physically but more mentally demanding work of 'Group B' training. Instruction in the ways and means of clandestine operations now faced us, including the personal skills required of a successful agent in a foreign land, plus a working knowledge of the German army. 'Know your enemy' was the new motto. Above all, we were taught the 'import-ance of looking natural and ordinary while we did unnatural and extraordinary things . . . "He that has a secret should not only hide it, but hide that he has it to hide." [1]

To prevent our fitness from tailing off, two hours a day of physical training, silent-killing exercises and unarmed combat were added to the daily routine, as were 'live' exercises in resisting interrogation (known, and feared, for their absolute realism). When all was finished to the satisfaction of Colonel Buckmaster and his instructors, the week came that, while some dreaded, all looked forward to – the parachuting course at Ringway, a few miles outside Manchester.

Then, with a huge smile, I could write 'What a week!' in my diary before proudly stitching parachute wings to the left chest of my battledress blouse.

Ground training had dominated the first two days at Ringway before the thrill of two day and two night drops using dark-cream-coloured parachutes. At least one drop from the converted Stirling bombers was with heavy leg bags, which we were taught to lower during descent on a long length of line. This allowed a greater personal load to be carried yet a comparatively soft landing – with, at night, warning of the approaching ground.

The overall training package was not yet over, for we now had to complete a detailed course in intelligence, with many practical schemes thrown in to test us when unawares: only then would we be considered safe and reliable in every aspect of modern underground warfare. These realistic approaches – attacks and escapes against real targets such as mainline railway tracks and, notably, the Manchester Ship Canal – were conducted without the local authorities being informed, and were designed to test us to the limit.

We would be observed and sometimes approached clandestinely and covertly, never knowing that these 'locals' were in fact 'trained seducers' anxious to exploit any weakness in our cover stories and to cajole out of us information that might reveal the real purpose of our nefarious deeds. Our alibis would be strained to the limit by both the military and the civilian police, but those of us who kept silent, or were able to stick convincingly to our cover stories, were on the way to passing the course.

Throughout, I had it drilled into me incessantly that my new occupation was to be an aggressive one: I was to eat, sleep and dream of exploiting every possible means of attacking the enemy with whatever was available. All was grist to the common desire for 'victory at all costs'. Every personal danger and difficulty was subservient to that aim.

Towards the end I was briefed in very general terms on my duties in occupied France, post-D-Day. Little came as a surprise, for much of it was what I had been planning on doing before coming to SOE's attention. In my notes I wrote that I was trained to:

A. Carry out acts of sabotage and demolition behind the enemy lines. Including the fostering of resistance movements to that end. Once trained these groups will carry out their own share of work, acting upon our orders, and saving precious time.
B. Obtain information about the enemy and his intentions.
C. Assist the escape of aircrew, French VIPs and SOE agents from occupied areas either by MGB or submarine or, in due course, light aircraft.
D. Deceive the enemy of Allied intentions, and inform SOE of any suspected enemy moves or concentration of troops in our area. This might endanger the whole of a group, for a member of the team captured will be submitted to torture and, in severe pain, could confess the location of a group to the local Gestapo.
E. Be responsible for the safety of the group and take all necessary steps to see that they are well covered and protected. A minor lapse in detail could give us away. The safety of all depends on ensuring that nothing is left behind or unchecked. The safety of a WT [wireless telegraphy] operator, our only link with London, is to be our main concern. This man has to be well protected. We must do our best to see that everything is done for his safety.

(A member of our group captured by the enemy means that the entire group has to move as fast as possible to a new location, unknown to the prisoner.)

With training complete, I returned to Baker Street and the 'waiting house', supervised by the indomitable Mrs Fraser: a remarkable woman, who looked after her young men and women with motherly concern and pride. She knew our problems and worries and, although she saw some of us leave and then, months later, return for rest or intensive debriefing, she saw many more of us leave never to reappear.

Here I was issued with my 'personal operational equipment', which, contrary to my expectations, contained no weapon or piece of equipment which might compromise my cover as a 'local Breton', for, I was now told, it was not as Second Lieutenant Hue that I would be returning. This was in stark and dangerous contrast to other teams, who would be uniformed members of the Allied armies, by whom they were issued with a remarkable array of the most modern weapons. Although I was now an SOE officer, and dressed in the uniform of an officer on the British Army's General List, I was issued with nothing more than a magnificent set of false papers and ration cards: of the up-to-date style, stamped, and endorsed by the genuine-seeming signatures of the appropriate local officials from the area in which I would be operating and from the areas in which I had – as far as the enemy were concerned – been living.

This new persona of mine was finally brought to life by a complete wardrobe of genuine French utility clothing with authentic trademarks and labels stitched into the proper places.

I was not issued with the standard escape kit, which contained a purse with £12, a silk map to the scale of 1:1,000,000, emergency rations, a water bottle and a compass. As a 'genuine' Frenchman I had no reason to carry what would be incriminating evidence if caught – nor, incidentally, was I presented with the statutory seven days of rations. As my commanding officer put it, although all SOE work was special, mine was particularly special – but in what sense I was never told.

Fully equipped and trained, but not yet briefed in detail, in late May 1944 I travelled – under the control of SOE staff – to a holding camp near Fairford airfield, close to Cirencester and some eighty miles from London, to join French companions, unknown to me until this moment, with whom I was to face the Germans. As this forbidding establishment was one of the departure points for the invasion of occupied France, it was heavily guarded by military police: once entered, the way out of it was usually via a parachute.

It was here, safe from scrutiny and the public, that the final stage of my sojourn in the UK was conducted. It was also the place where I would learn the date and location of D-Day, with no chance of informing anyone other than those with whom I was to drop.

When it came, my personal briefing was delivered by General Gubbins himself, and I at last received detailed orders confirming what I had long been expecting: as an SOE officer, I was to establish my own circuit – Hillbilly – in the Morbihan area of north-west France and, using my local knowledge and SOE links via my own wireless operator, give every assistance to the French Special Air Service and the local Maquis. Initially I was to 'take charge' by organizing the Maquis and preparing the ground for the arrival of Free French forces in the form of 4 SAS under the command of the one-armed, legendary Colonel Pierre-Louis Bourgoin.

My real name was 'André Hue', my training name was 'André Hubert', my operational name was now 'Fernand', my circuit was code-named 'Hillbilly', our SAS base area (one of two) was nicknamed 'Dingson', my name in France was already established as 'Alfred Havet', and in one swift move I was promoted from second lieutenant to captain – still on the General List but 'accredited' to the Parachute Regiment. Most people were to call me Bob!

The Maquis into which I was about to be dropped was, as I knew it would be, centred on the Pondards' farm, La Nouette, to the west-north-west of Saint-Marcel – about two miles towards the village of Sérent. One of that farm's fields was 'my' La Baleine dropping zone.

Although most French troops were not destined to take part in the initial Normandy landings, there were exceptions, two of which were advance parties of the 4th French Parachute Battalion (SAS). The plan, I was briefed, was for this 4th Battalion to be split between two base areas, one to be called Samwest, initially established in the area of the Forêt de Duault some seventeen miles south-west of

Guingamp, while the second, Dingson, would be centred on the Pondards' farm at Saint-Marcel, where the commanding officer, Bourgoin, would establish his base.

It was to this second area that I was now accredited and with whose advance party I would drop.

At last the realization began to dawn in my youthful, excited mind that those desperate, almost amateur, operations before repatriation, the dash across the Channel and the unremitting training routines had not been in vain: there was now a firm purpose, and it was about to be revealed in detail.

General Gubbins stopped his briefing to invite an aide to usher in two young French officers, who stood stiffly to attention and saluted.

'Captain Hue, this is Lieutenant Marienne of the French 4 SAS, the commander of the advance party for your Dingson base, and Lieutenant Deschamps of Samwest's advance party. You'll be jumping together.' We shook hands, Marienne and Deschamps relaxed, and the three of us sat as General Gubbins continued, 'Now, I expect you'll want to know when, where and what we expect of you.'

We nodded.

'Each of you', the General pointed at the two Frenchmen, 'will be in a party of eighteen. But, to ensure a better chance that at least one officer from Dingson and Samwest makes it to your respective Maquis, we will split you into four teams across two aircraft. So you Marienne and you Deschamps will travel in the same aircraft to both dropping zones, while your seconds in command and their teams will do likewise. That way we hope to ensure that at least one team for each area is successful.'

We saw the logic and nodded in silence.

'Now,' the General continued, 'you will be dropped well before dawn on D-Day, and, what is more, you will be dropped "blind", to ensure absolute secrecy.' My disquiet about parachuting into a darkened field with no reception committee to guide us and to help collect and transport our containers must have showed, for the General quickly explained the reason. Considerable anxiety was felt that any premature warning of the arrival of teams such as mine would risk the loss of surprise over the date of the invasion.

Myself, my wireless operator and Marienne, accompanied by his Sergeant Major Raufast, two wireless operators and three men, would leave from Fairford airfield one hour before midnight on 5 June 1944 and drop on to a previously unused dropping zone alongside the wooded hills of the Landes de Lanvaux a little south of Saint-Jean-Brévelay. This new dropping zone was about twelve miles west of the Maquis.

'You will receive the coordinates shortly, but nothing can be allowed to connect your drop – should it be witnessed – with Saint-Marcel.' The General was adamant, and I had no good counter-argument!

Once on the ground, my first task would be to guide Marienne to the Maquis – commanded now by my friend of the Brittany escape pipeline Emile Guimard, known as Jim – and divide it into smaller groups. To begin with we were to monitor and report German troop movements and train departures from Guer, so that SOE could orchestrate their trains' destruction. Teams of maquisards, advised and trained by the French SAS, would immediately execute their sabotage duties and so prevent as many German reinforcements as possible from reaching the Normandy coast.

Within a week of D-Day, the main party of 4 SAS under the command of Colonel Bourgoin would be dropped on to La Baleine with not only his own arms, ammunition and stores but also those with which the Maquis was to be armed.

The General continued, 'The Colonel's orders will be to sever, as far as possible, all communications between Brittany and the remainder of France and to raise a full-scale revolt in the area. To do that he will take under his control the Maquis centred at Malestroit – your Hillbilly circuit – and the Maquis to the north-north-west, centred at Guingamp, which is in part covered by the Racketeer circuit. The two centres are almost exactly sixty-two miles apart, so that 4th Battalion will have a very wide area to cover. You should also know that a number of Jedburgh teams[2] will be operating with both Racketeer and Samwest.'

Marienne and I grinned at each other like naughty schoolboys before the General brought us down to earth with a reminder of just how many enemy troops there were in the Atlantic ports and just how important it was that they were not to reinforce those about to face the Allied invasion: it was a serious task, and one not made easier by the uncontrolled enthusiasm of the maquisards.

'Captain Hue,' the General went on, 'you and your Hillbilly circuit will have an uphill task coordinating and controlling these Frenchmen so that Colonel Bourgoin has something useful with which he can augment his SAS teams.

'Eventually', we were told, 'Colonel Bourgoin's Dingson and Samwest base areas will connect with the breakout from the beach-head and guide Allied forces to destinations in the west, while at the same time supplying intelligence on enemy dispositions and strengths.' And with that prognosis we were dismissed by the General.

Marienne and I sat late that night discussing the forthcoming operation, and through that process we began to get to know each other's strengths and weaknesses.

Once we had dovetailed our orders it was clear that there were some details still to be clarified, such as chains of command, frequency of drops and availability of arms, and that these could only be discussed in person at SOE's headquarters. I asked for, and was granted, a meeting with Colonel Buckmaster at Baker Street, which meant a departure from the secure camp.

As I was now privy to the time and place of the invasion, I would be escorted day and night to prevent any roaming through London's places of wartime entertainment – which had, of course, been a factor in my request.

The first few hours to London in the staff car were cool and silent. No doubt my escorts were as displeased at their escorting an apparent foreigner as was the 'foreigner' himself, but by the time of our arrival at SOE headquarters we had begun talking and laughing.

After a successful meeting with the Colonel, during which the outstanding points concerning departure and the landing reception (or the lack of it) were settled, as were my other anxieties, all was on a friendly level: indeed, so much so that my escorts now began to supply me with as many cigarettes as I wanted – anything to prevent me from buying them myself in a shop.

In case any other matters arose, it was suggested by Colonel Buckmaster that I should remain in a quiet, 'sanitized' house in town for a couple of days. This would have been fine had it not been for my faithful guardians not only sharing my bedroom (with one sleeping next to me and the other by the door) but also accompanying me to the bathroom!

As it was, the next day I was summoned back to the Colonel's office, where Maurice Buckmaster felt it necessary to re-emphasize a number of points about communications. By noon I was ready for lunch and a drink – a suggestion taken up with enthusiasm by my escorts, who, bored with the whole episode, had already ordered a table in a small restaurant they considered well away from SOE's usual milieu.

However, it was clearly not far enough off the beaten track, for as we entered this discreet establishment a shout of 'André!' stopped the three of us abruptly. Fully trained though we were, we paused long enough to be noticeable, before I was quickly steered to our own table. By coincidence, a couple of my former colleagues from the course had also chosen that same watering hole – and for identical reasons. Embarrassed, and trying to ignore them, I could only continue with the deception of non-recognition – despite all five of us being members of the same organization.

Pleased to have had the opportunity of discussing things in person with Colonel Buckmaster, I returned to the secure camp in Gloucestershire on 3 June 1944. There, over a few quiet drinks, I said farewell to the guardians I had come to know well over those intimate days. We had become firm friends, and parted at the camp's gate with the mutual hope that we would meet again. They left me to my barbed-wire cantonment, a hard bed and last-minute details to check.

During the next two days there was plenty of time to think of less fortunate friends who had had to wait days, often weeks, until the call from France came. Not only did local conditions in the objective area have to be right, militarily and meteorologically, but the phase of the all-important moon had to be correct for accurate navigation. Often when conditions on the ground were suitable the moon was contrary, and vice versa. Thus was coined the expression that was to become a harbinger of frustration: 'Sorry, old boy, we'll have to wait for the next full moon.'

This waiting for the next moon! Many days could be spent staring at the moon as it waxed, was then hidden by cloud, and then waned until no use for another week; then, when it was present, agents prayed that each evening would bring the order to board the bus for the airfield, longing only that the take-off would be authorized.

On this occasion neither the weather (within reason) nor the moon mattered, for we were going in regardless. Come what may – and the delay to D-Day caused by bad weather is well documented – the invasion of France by the Allied forces would take place.

But trepidation continued to fill those two days – trepidation and excitement, for dropping 'blind' meant no reception committee to guide in the aircraft and no assurance from the ground that the enemy was absent.

We were fully aware of the risks of such a decision, and for my part I accepted the added hazard that, while dropping in civilian clothes would make it easier for me to establish the necessary contacts before leading the uniformed SAS advance party to the Maquis de Saint-Marcel, if caught I would not be made a prisoner of war but would be shot after interrogation.

We were driven the short distance to the airfield to be issued with – and to check – our parachutes. Sheets of strongly driven rain swept the airfield, but there was no mention of any further delay to the landings, so, individually satisfied with the fit of our equipment, we returned, still under escort, to the camp for a last meal in England and quiet farewells to others waiting for their own calls-forward to different areas of France.

Just before eight o'clock that evening we received, with huge relief, a message that we would be leaving camp at ten o'clock for a slightly earlier take-off than the originally planned eleven o'clock departure. In the event, our call-forward occurred at nine o'clock, when, after the short drive, we were greeted at the airfield by the female ground crew offering mugs of strong tea and packets of cigarettes. The French parachutists in particular found themselves the centre of attraction from both air and ground crews, while I, being the only one in civilian clothes (and French 'utility' ones at that), was strangely stared at. 'Are you really going to war dressed like that?' I was teased.

Our pilot entered the hangar to watch us for a moment or two as, surrounded by girls, we laughed and smoked. Then, above the light-hearted banter of men facing danger, he drawled casually but authoritatively, 'Time to go.' Above the cheers, he shouted, 'Get your chutes on. We load the aircraft in five minutes.'

Assisted by the girls, we struggled into our harnesses and, once checked and lined up in the reverse order for jumping, Marienne's men shuffled across the windy tarmac towards the waiting Stirling while, unexplained, he and I were driven the short distance in a staff car. Settling uncomfortably into the canvas straps of the lightweight 'jump seats', none of us was sure that the weather conditions were suitable for amphibious operations, let alone parachuting – but the delay had begun to take its toll of nerves, and, wind or no wind, we were glad to be on the move. While we faced a difficult time, it was unlikely to match that faced by those thousands in their tiny craft already well into their journeys from all along the south coast of England.

Taking a look round before the lights were switched off – my first chance to study my companions' faces since our crocodile procession across the airfield – I burst into laughter, for every cheek and chin on either side of me was covered in layers of lipstick, smudged across the dark camouflage cream.

The door was slammed shut, the lights dimmed, and almost immediately a deafening roar enveloped us as the aircraft's engines were coaxed willingly into life and 'run up'. The plane shook violently; any more conversation was pointless. A lengthy and bumpy ride to the end of the runway followed, then a pause for the engines to reach full power, a slight jerk as the pilot released the brakes, and our aircraft was speeding down the runway, engines screaming.

In less than a minute we were airborne and taking station on the other aircraft who would accompany us, first to the Samwest landing zone and then on to ours. An hour or so after gathering height and speed we flew over a part of the great D-Day armada, which, if I squirmed sideways in my seat and against my bulky kit, was just visible through a window. In the dim red lighting inside our aircraft, we looked at each other and, smiling, took out flasks to toast the beginning of the liberation of Europe.

Crossing the French coast, we were subjected to the popping of flak shells as the German gunners probed away. Holding on tightly, we watched the explosions burst harmlessly below and, although for a few minutes we held our breaths, we soon passed inland and into light cloud. Then, after those terrifying moments – terror balanced by the exhilaration of witnessing the passage of the main assault – the pilot began his descent to the Samwest dropping zone, which lay about thirty miles in from the coast at Paimpol. The trapdoor in the aircraft's deck was opened while the pilot circled to get his bearing, and almost before we had time to feel the cold from the blast of air the stick of nine men had gone and we were climbing back to a suitable altitude for the final fifty miles towards our own rendezvous with the war. We imagined the similar scene taking place in the other aircraft, then a second blast of air heralded the penultimate phase of the flight – the approach to our landing zone – as the specially constructed circular hatch in the cabin floor was opened to reveal France rushing past, a thousand feet below.

'Get ready. Dropping in ten minutes. Check your equipment,' the dispatcher shouted above the added noise of the wind. Two of us squeezed towards the open hatch and wriggled into place, dangling feet buffeted by the slipstream.

Marienne was jumping 'number one' and myself 'number two', so for the next few minutes we sat calmly together, our thighs touching and our feet swinging above the fields. Beneath our boots the woods of Brittany came closer until, at five hundred feet, the aircraft was lined up and levelled off. Then, suddenly, we were over the dropping zone and a fleeting glimpse of an open field swept past; but the aircraft banked and circled as though uncertain of its final course. All were ready, keyed-up, anxious to get on with it, desperate for the final command – it had been a long three hours since the farewell kisses.

When they came, the instructions were quick and precise.

'Running in.'

'Action stations.'

'Number one – GO!'

That was all I heard. Marienne's body disappeared down and aft. Mine followed, almost alongside him, then number three's boots hit me on the head. A cool rush of wind, a slight pull – a pause – and my dark-cream parachute opened with a reassuring crack. To the left and below Marienne's chute swung slowly, while others billowed open to my right and above. Forty-five seconds were all we had for 'sightseeing' before hitting the fast-approaching ground – just enough time to catch a glance of equipment swinging astern and below the aircraft.

My return to France began in an unfamiliar potato field. Within a minute I had gathered my equipment and begun to make my way towards the SAS lieutenant.

'Marienne,' I whispered loudly into the dark. The reply was muttered and unintelligible, for the Frenchman was in difficulty. My concern increased as I made out his body straddled across a small wall.

'Are you all right, Marienne?'

'Nothing broken. Just a bit dizzy. Be all right in a few minutes.' He gathered his breath. 'Why the hell do farmers build walls in the middle of their fields? And then why do people choose them for dropping zones?' Marienne's faith in aeronautical navigation seemed unshaken.

'They don't. This isn't the right bloody field!' I replied. 'God knows where we are – or which direction we go from here!

'And', I added, 'where the hell is your second in command's stick?'

'If they're lucky they'll have been dropped in the right place.'

'Let's hope so – and that they can find their way to La Nouette.'

I let him catch his breath as the others made their way to the pre-planned rendezvous in a corner of the field, which, by coincidence, seemed to bear a passing resemblance to the one we had been briefed to expect – apart from the low walls. None of that mattered now we were on the ground: the priority was to conceal the few containers and get away fast. When it was safe, we would return to collect our gear, if we could identify the place again (one of the troubles with dropping blind).

'OK,' said Marienne at last, but still in pain. 'I'm fine. Let's join the men.'

'You're hurt, aren't you?'

'Let's just get on with it.'

The two of us made our way quickly towards the others, until shortly the whole team was mustered, present and ready for the next move. If not in the right place, at least the drop had been tight.

I turned to Marienne. 'Supervise things, will you? I'm going to take Sergeant Major Raufast and look for the special packages. I think they fell a little further to the south-west.'

Marienne nodded as Raufast and I trotted off, while others began gathering in the parachutes and containers.

Two or three fields away we found the 'special' cases, including my personal kit and 9 million francs.[3] All were intact and lying in a cornfield beyond a thick hedge. The parachutes were detached, and everything was stuffed quickly into bushes.

But our elation at a safe landing was short-lived, for as we made our way back to the potato field a long burst of automatic-weapon fire, followed by single rifle shots, stopped us. This unexpected noise of battle came from where we had just left Marienne. Adrenalin shot through my veins.

'There's a ditch to our right. Quick,' I whispered to the Sergeant Major, and as we wriggled flat on our bellies the louder crack of grenades indicated a fierce ambush and retaliation. Hesitantly, we crawled towards the original rendezvous until we could just make out the shadows and shapes of men. They were not French SAS.

'Halt! Hands up!' The cry from close ahead came suddenly out of the darkness.

The Sergeant Major went for his grenades, but so soon after landing was not the time to be killed in a firefight.

'I'm going to try bluff first,' I whispered. 'Stay in a fire position and keep me covered. We may be cornered, but I think I can work it out.'

Four enemy soldiers now advanced, shouting with a trace of panic, '*Deutsche*? *Deutsche*?'

I moved forward carefully. '*Non*,' I replied. '*Je suis Milice française* – working with the Germans.'

'*Deutsche?*'

'Raufast,' I said quietly in French over my shoulder. 'They're not Germans. I think they're Russians. They want to know if we're Germans.'

'*Deutsche? Deutsche?*' The challenge increased in urgency.

'*Nein. Nein*,' I replied again, thinking quickly. '*Milice française.*'

'*Milice française?*' repeated a now-visible Russian, waving his weapon uncomfortably close to my stomach.

'*Oui, Milice française.*' Thanking God that I had lived in France, I lowered my hands and told Raufast to do the same as he scrambled slowly to his feet – 'So they can feel that we're on their side.' These were White Russians fighting on the side of the Germans.

'This is a German camp,' the one who appeared to be in charge said in poor French.

'What!' I exclaimed louder than I intended at this unexpected news.

'*Ici un camp allemand.*' The Russians were calmer now. 'We have seen some parachutists come down, and are having a go at them. We've already killed four.'

If true, this was bad, and I stifled my concern with difficulty. In civilian clothing and with Raufast's uniform indistinguishable in the dark behind me, we had to make a positive move before certain discovery.

'Raufast,' I said quietly and deliberately over my shoulder, 'follow me. Do not run. We'll try and make the other side.' Turning back to the Russians, I cheerfully wished them luck: 'Well, I hope you have good hunting.' And, with a wave, I began to walk nonchalantly back into the dark. Other Russians, sensing the casual exchange, watched our departure without suspicion.

Once out of sight, and feeling the Sergeant Major's rising impatience, I murmured, 'Raufast, don't run whatever you do.'

'I think you've just saved my skin.'

'It was nothing.' I didn't mean it.

'Maybe, but it was good acting.'

'We're not out of this mess yet. If I find the idiot pilot who dropped us in a German camp I'll murder him!'

We stopped in a secluded area of the field to assess our situation; a convenient ditch gave welcome cover and protection. Although firing continued, it was imperative that we make one more attempt to join the others, for without my local knowledge – especially as we were not starting from a known position – Marienne and his men would soon be lost; and even I had so far failed to recognize any familiar landmark. We waited, but there was no sign that the firing was dying down.

The battle – for such it had now become – was raging on three sides, making contact with Marienne impossible. And our ditch was not a hiding place but a target, for the Russians must now have deduced that we were not *Milice*.

'Raufast, run like hell when I give the signal,' I urged. 'If we don't get out of this now we never will.' And with that we leaped from our cover for a nearby wood and the welcome security of substantial trees. An occasional, unaimed, rifle shot followed us, but it was desultory stuff.

'Keep running,' I panted.

We ran for thirty minutes, thankful for our Scottish training, and at one point stopped briefly to catch some breath. I gasped, 'We must join the Maquis as quickly as possible, so that Emile Guimard can send an armed search party.' Raufast nodded in the dark as I added unnecessarily, 'The sooner the better, but even if we'd been landed where we should have been it's nineteen kilometres towards the east-south-east.'

We had been expecting that, but – with no inkling of how far off track the actual dropping zone had been – we were, both metaphorically and literally, in the dark. By allowing for an error of just one mile from our intended starting point, and providing we kept roughly to the lie of the Landes de Lanvaux, I knew I should cross two major roads a few miles to the south-west of Saint-Marcel. It was rough navigation, but, equally roughly, it tied in with my original plan.

Feeling a little more secure, we walked on towards a deserted-looking farmhouse that loomed out of the dark, but a dog's bark discouraged us so we pushed on for a further two hundred yards and a main road.

Dawn brought a welcome mist in the valleys and a warming sun above, and after more miles of dodging along hedges and banks another small farm lay ahead. We studied it until, risking exposure but trusting that the occupants in such an out-of-the-way place would be sympathetic, I made my decision.

'To the farm, Raufast. I could do with some coffee.'

Dirty and bleeding from minor cuts, we entered the cattle yard to face a defiant and grim farmer shielding his wife and children.

'Who are you?'

'This gentleman', I pointed to my companion in his filthy, but French, uniform, 'is Sergeant Major Raufast of the Free French forces, who has just parachuted into France, and I am a British officer who came with him.'

'I don't believe you. Go away,' the farmer replied suspiciously, squaring up to us.

'Did you hear a battle last night?' I asked carelessly.

'Yes.' He couldn't have done – at least not ours – but I let that pass.

I explained what had happened, and as I spoke I detected a hint of understanding. I tried my luck for a second time. 'What we would be grateful for is food and coffee, a wash, and then perhaps you could tell us where we are.'

The farmer appeared a little less belligerent. 'You're near the village of Pleucadeuc.'

Thank God! I knew the place – a few miles south of Malestroit. My navigation hadn't been that far out, though we had travelled further than necessary, but then it was probably just as well we hadn't gone straight to the village.

Sensing an increasing goodwill, I continued with my overriding priority: 'Would your wife be willing to go to the restaurant in Pleucadeuc and tell the owner that Bob is here and that I would like to see him as a matter of urgency?'

The farmer now replied without hesitation, 'It will be done immediately', and, after a short and hurried conversation out of earshot, the woman left on her mission by foot. It was not the best solution, nor would I know until the wife's return which organization she would be summoning – the Gestapo, the *Milice* or the Maquis.

Settling uneasily with coffee, Raufast and I recounted all that we knew of the Allied invasion force: that it had, at last, landed in Normandy and that, with luck, it would shortly be in the area.

After years of waiting the farmer was reluctant to believe the news, so I pointed to the family's wireless. 'Turn it on,' I commanded. Encouragingly, it was pre-tuned to the BBC's French-language frequency. With the announcer confirming all that I and Raufast had said, we were given unambiguous approval.

Breakfast over, I explained that I did not wish to involve the farmer in any more danger than he had already incurred by his wife's assistance.

'We'll hide in the fields until her return,' I assured him. 'If the police or the Germans turn up to search the area there'll be no incriminating evidence, and she could always explain that she was summoning them to have us arrested.'

Grateful and relieved, the farmer pointed out the best place and, with thanks, we moved out to a hedge from where we could take a close look at all visitors to the farm.

Our wait was not long, for about two hours later the farmer's wife returned, followed at a discreet distance by a middle-aged Frenchman whom I recognized instantly. With no need for closer scrutiny, I broke free of the bush to accost him. '*Bonjour*,' I said. 'I require two hundred dinners with white wine.'

'Did you say two hundred dinners with red wine?'

'No, with white wine.'

'I see. Cider?'

'You are Monsieur Pommerel?'

'Yes. And you are Bob?'

'That's right.'

We shook hands vigorously before I brought Monsieur Pommerel quickly up to date with events in Normandy, and locally, over the previous twelve hours.

'I'll take you to my house,' he said when I had finished, 'and from there a car will take you to the Maquis HQ.'

The Sergeant Major, still under cover, was called over. 'Raufast, you stay here. I'll get you picked up later today.'

Unstrapping a money belt from my waist, I took out two

thousand francs, gave the farmer a thousand for his help, and asked that the remainder in the belt be hidden until sent for. If nothing else it was a sign of trust. It was also a precaution, for I knew I could trust nobody until absolute confirmation had been achieved, and if I was about to walk into a trap I wanted nothing incriminating on me. In my civilian clothes, with my knowledge of the area and with French as my first language, I hoped that, *in extremis*, I could bluff my way out of most things in occupied France.

We parted with Gallic gestures of friendship and gratitude, and after a forty-minute walk I arrived at Monsieur Pommerel's Pleucadeuc house, where a Citroën was waiting. Two men were sitting in the back. I climbed between them, delighted to see that one was Morice Chenailler, the head of the Force Française de l'Intérieur in the Morbihan area and a colleague of my old friend Emile Guimard from the days before my repatriation. Emile and this man had been the last to say goodbye to me six months before.

'How is Jim?' I asked Morice once settled and using Emile's Maquis *nom de guerre* that had been given to me in London.

'Who?' A worryingly frosty response.

'How is Emile?' I tried again with his real name, puzzled and on my guard.

'Look,' the older guard barked gruffly, 'during the last three months the French *Milice*, acting for the Gestapo, have been playing funny tricks with us, and until we get to our camp you're getting no information.'

The strain of being dropped in the wrong place, escaping death at the hands of a Russian patrol, a long, fast march and, finally, being mistaken for a Gestapo agent was too much for such a brief spell in French territory. I knew that Chenailler knew me, and so did the other bodyguard, but clearly they were not going to admit anything until I had been personally greeted by Jim himself.

The journey from Pleucadeuc to Saint-Marcel is four miles, but the flight, the run, the lack of rest, the tension and the failure to make conversation forced me into an instant and deep sleep while the car meandered through the narrow farm lanes of the Morbihan.

'Wake up. Come on, wake up, *mon brave*!' I was being pushed from left to right by my escorts, and opened my eyes. The bright morning glare forced them shut and sent me back to my dreams. How my stiff and tired limbs would have been improved immeasurably by a cup of tea, a few aspirins and some quiet music!

'We have arrived,' I was told.

'Where?'

'Le Maquis de Saint-Marcel.'

This time I woke properly and fully – my long journey was over. I looked past the driver's head to see that we were surrounded by trees and had stopped alongside the start of a narrow forest path. Beautiful, secure trees I thought, and glanced at my watch. Just over twelve hours ago I had been kissing the ground-crew girls; now I was fighting for my freedom. With one guard in front and one behind, I was escorted quickly and in silence down the overgrown, secluded path, ducking beneath and between thick bushes.

Then, with no warning, the path opened into a wide clearing filled with probably thirty Frenchmen. All were armed, and all were watching me with suspicion. Each man carried either a Sten gun, a pistol or a rifle; hand grenades were clipped to belts and shirt pockets. There appeared to be no shortage of weaponry, as I caught sight of more powerful Bren guns half-camouflaged behind trees and bushes.

A maquisard with an authoritative air came forward. 'Monsieur Guimard will be here in a few minutes. In the meantime, make no quick movement.' Faced with such opposition, even if supposedly friendly, I wanted to give no one the opportunity of testing his marksmanship: the target would not have challenged a child.

'Thank you,' I replied. 'May I sit down?' The maquisard nodded, and I sank to the grass to light a cigarette as calmly as I could, irritated at the charade in which I was playing the lead role.

After a few deep puffs I looked up as a rustling through the forest's undergrowth came closer. I stood, tense, conscious that thirty armed men's eyes were following every move I made. Emile swept into the clearing, and we stood staring at each other for some seconds.

'Hello, Emile.' I felt I should take the initiative. 'You have a remarkable way of greeting old friends.'

A startled Emile stared for a moment longer. 'Bob?' he said. I smiled and nodded. Then he grabbed my shoulders at arm's length and stared while a smile grew on his face. 'André, it's you!' and we clasped each other in a full Gallic hug. '*Merde alors!*' Emile swore loudly over my shoulder. 'I am so sorry, I didn't know you were back. And I knew no Bob, so we had to be careful. And I too have changed my name – to Jim. Come.'

He led me to the edge of the clearing, the armed men making way for us, and there we stood smoking the rough French tobacco with which I had been issued in London. 'I wasn't told you were coming, and as we're having a little difficulty with the French *Milice* my men can take no chances.'

With my identity restored, the driver and guards joined in the handshaking as though anxious to make up for their earlier abruptness. Chenailler added his apologies: 'We had to be careful, so couldn't say too much when we met you. And,' he stood back to study me, 'after all, you are wearing some very interesting clothes – too authentic for someone claiming to have come straight from London!'

I smiled, but was anxious to get on with business, for Marienne was still missing along with his men and equipment – and had not the Russians reported four dead even before the fight had reached its climax?

'Jim, I must have a talk with you as quickly as possible. I'll explain when we get to the HQ.'

With the guards now turned companions and with the maquisards staring at us, we made our way from the clearing to the Maquis de Saint-Marcel's headquarters at the Pondards' farm.

After more kissing, Madame Pondard echoed Chenailler's views about my clothes, but Jim explained all as she poured coffee and prepared a second breakfast.

Between mouthfuls, I précised the situation as I saw it. 'Jim,' I started, 'last night I was dropped with a team of Free French SAS *parachutistes* . . .' and I continued to recount events since landing in the potato field.

When I had finished, Jim offered good news: 'Before you say more, you should know that Marienne's second in command, Lieutenant Déplante, is here, safe and well with his men.'

'Thank God for that – he must have had a better pilot!'

'Probably. Now I'll call in some of my officers; they can take their platoons and find Lieutenant Marienne and his men and bring them back here.'

While a maquisard was dispatched, Jim deduced that we had been dropped in a potato field about two hundred yards south-west of the German observation tower outside Plumelec and possibly about a mile from where we should have been.

'Had we known where and when,' he continued, 'we could have been on the alert to help you. We could have marked it for your pilot without anyone seeing.'

Several officers now arrived, to whom everything was explained again, and once each had agreed an individual search area they set off to collect their maquisards. Runners were dispatched over a wide area to warn farmers and to ask for help in providing a safe haven should any men turn up.

Alone with Jim again, I continued, 'Give me your present situation and I'll pass on to you London's operational orders. Meanwhile, it may save time if you call in the remainder of the officers.' Then, while we waited for them to gather outside, Jim explained the local position.

'At present the Maquis is centred here in about eight hundred hectares, some six kilometres by road from the town of Malestroit. As you know from before, the land is managed by Monsieur Pondard and his family. He has put the farm at our disposal as a headquarters, while his girls liaise with other Maquis. This area is in the centre of twenty-five square kilometres of forest with plenty of bush, one very large field and several smaller ones. Most of this part of Brittany is wooded, with scattered farms and fields here and there.

'This particular farm has one main path that leads towards the main road between Saint-Marcel and Sérent. This path is over 800 metres long before it joins a minor road which is another 1,000 metres to the main road – the D10. Otherwise we have only small paths leading to the two roads, one south of the Maquis – the D776 – and the one to the north I have mentioned.

'Sentries are posted on all these paths, and, while this area is on the same level as the nearby towns and countryside, there is a small hill about half a mile to the south of the farm from where you can see all the surrounding land without being seen yourself.

'The problem is, we are too many here – I'll come to that problem in a moment – and too close to the local villages and towns and, while everyone seems friendly and supportive, just one traitor could destroy everything. If we're attacked we could always withdraw to the south and west and hide in the vast network of the Landes de Lanvaux woods. Food would be supplied by the farms – as it is right now by the Pondards.

'Apart from the numbers of men, we only have one dropping zone, La Baleine, so it's not all entirely satisfactory. There are a couple of other areas worth considering.'

I butted in for the first time: 'What we need is at least four dropping zones and ten small Maquis supplied by a few farms, so that traffic is cut while dependence on the local shops is reduced to the absolute minimum.'

'Agreed,' Jim replied. 'But let me finish, then you'll see the full picture and we can discuss how best to make it more efficient.'

I waved with my cigarette for him to go on.

'We have about eighteen hundred men here. Some, but not many, are armed. We have three doctors and nine nurses. We can call on about another fifteen hundred men, but there's no point having those extra men until we have weapons for them – it reduces the accommodation and feeding problems. Because of the amount of food we need as it is, we can't be supplied by just the Pondards' farm, so we're supplied by carts – and those increase the chances of detection. However, we do have fourteen lorries and twelve small cars, sufficient petrol has been stockpiled and hidden, and there are drivers for all our vehicles, plus some to spare. So we're not badly off for men and transport: it's just that it's all together – in the same place.

'For some reason we've had no drops during the past five months or so and are beginning to run short of military supplies and money. We've had a wireless link with the UK, but it's been pretty tenuous. We've been waiting for you, but of course we didn't know when you were coming.'

Again I nodded for him to continue.

'In the immediate area there are two German divisions – one armoured and one infantry. Their headquarters are at the camp in Coëtquidan-Saint-Cyr, which you know well from your experiences at the Guer railway station. There are also about two hundred Frenchmen in this area working as *miliciens* for the Gestapo. On the other hand, we're greatly helped by our police and the mayors. Our local population is very friendly. Nearly every family has a member in our Maquis.

'Our chain of command is a loose one. The Force Française de l'Intérieur de Morbihan comes under the command of Colonel Morice Chenailler, who is in touch with other groups covering the whole of Brittany. I'm his number two for this area. Grouped around Colonel Chenailler are retired officers of the French army, including General Allard, whom you met before going to England. By various means we get our instructions or orders from the French High Command in London or from the British High Command via your special services. Our group of senior officers, who all run their own Maquis throughout Brittany, meet informally on occasions and, through runners, we keep each other posted on what is happening or what we should do or think of doing when we're ordered to engage the Germans.

'It may be a loose system but it works, for we can't have regular meetings in case we've been infiltrated by the *Milice*.'

With our mutual briefings over, Jim called in his remaining twenty officers. I was introduced to each one, and after a few minutes of greetings we were led towards a large barn where I opened my own briefing.

'Gentlemen, early this morning the Allied forces landed on the Normandy beaches. The invasion is progressing satisfactorily.'

The applause was overwhelming. I looked at these French officers, smiling, shaking hands, their eyes bright. They had waited four years for this news, and now, within minutes, the whole of the Maquis would know. Through the windows I could see happy smiles and women crying.

When the congratulations and kissing had stopped, I was able to continue. 'I don't know how long it'll be before this area is liberated

– possibly two months, because of the strength of the German army around us. So from now on we have a good share of the work to do.'

For the third time that morning I ran over the events of the previous twelve hours and offered a résumé of the future.

'During the next few days a battalion of Free French Special Air Service will be dropping here and in the Duault area to join those who came with me. Here they will be split into four-man teams to sabotage German lines of communication. You will provide men to help and guide them and, on completion of each task, bring them back here to the Maquis so that they can be resupplied ready for the next task. Between operations they will be available to train our recruits.

'We will organize their reception and accommodation, and until we stop asking we are going to get drops every night from ten aircraft and possibly more. We will receive weapons, ammunition, food and possibly jeeps, mines, grenades, radio equipment and anything else we ask for – especially money. The SAS will train and instruct our maquisards in the use of the weapons and equipment.[4]

'The Maquis will be split into groups of one to two hundred men, each group responsible for its own area. Every Maquis officer here will command a group. In each group there will be three men from the SAS. Our jobs will be to mine the main roads, blow the bridges used by the Germans, ambush German convoys, and provide intelligence for the Allied Supreme Commander. In the team that dropped with me last night there were three wireless operators and their sets. Let's hope that they're all right.

'When Colonel Bourgoin arrives he will be in charge and will take over from me under the agreements reached between the French and the British.

'This, gentlemen, is our task. Thank you.'

3. Maquis

Jim ushered his officers out of the barn, then returned, shutting the wicket door softly behind him. I was uncertain whether or not I had impressed his men, and his quiet return suggested not: he was, I was sure, about to tell me so in confidence – and forcefully. The Allies might have made a good start securing a beachhead to the north-east, but mine had been rather less stirring: I had landed among the enemy, still had men missing as a result, and could not confirm by wireless that we were ready for that night's drop. The omens were not good, and I guessed that Jim and his teams had seen through my optimism and bravado. As he said nothing, I used attack to defend myself.

'Now, Jim, I want you to arrange tonight's reception committee – and at La Baleine this time. It must be in place from 2200 hours, along with sentries covering the dropping zone for 360 degrees. I want an observation post manned day and night from now on, and if they see any men dropping outside La Baleine they must help them. They will also monitor any German movement in the general area. However,' I added, 'without a wireless set to confirm we are ready to receive it the drop may not happen.'

'It'll be arranged.'

'Thanks,' I said meekly.

Jim smiled. 'I'll get things started.'

'Thanks,' I said again, as he gathered up various sheaves of paper and prepared to leave. 'Your men seemed well armed I must say.'

'Bob, you saw only thirty or forty armed men out of a total of eighteen hundred who have no weapons at all – enthusiasm, but no weapons.'

'Then that has to be my first priority.'

'They'll be useless unless it is!' he said with a wry smile, and left me to ponder this vital fact.

Alone for almost the first time since arriving in France, I thought slowly through the past hours. The most important men were missing: Marienne and the wireless operators. News travelled fast – that much I already knew – and yet there had been no reports of their capture or death. With a bit of luck they would walk back into my life at any moment – and, with further luck, in time for a wireless operator to send the signal confirming the night's drop.

There were also questions exercising my brain, mostly concerning the pilot and someone else's signals on the ground. No lights should have been placed for us – we were supposed to have been dropped blind – so had the pilot seen lights and, being perhaps a little lost, thought that the French had decided to take the initiative? I was never to know, but setting out decoy lights was certainly a trick sometimes played by the Germans when they heard aircraft circling overhead, and if that had been the case with us it was a trick that had almost worked. Little long-term harm had been done – although the rumoured casualty list was of course bad, and we had heard that our containers had already been driven away in a German lorry – but the episode had frightened the daylights out of me.

The barn door rattled open, and Jim swept in. 'Everything is under way, including a small team to collect Raufast. Another team has rounded up two more of your men.'

'That now makes just four of us safe. Not good, Jim.'

'I know.'

'Marienne and all the wireless operators are still missing.'

We sat in silence for a few moments while we lit cigarettes.

Waving smoke away from his face, Jim changed the subject. 'When would you like to visit the camp?'

'Later, perhaps. I must wait for Marienne.' I was concerned, and didn't want to be anywhere else should he turn up. My optimism, though, was waning fast. 'I'll give him another couple of hours.'

'OK. In the meantime I've given orders for a fatigue party to set up a tent for you and Marienne – among the trees, close to mine.'

'Thanks,' I said, but my mind was elsewhere.

Jim didn't give up. Easing me out of my worries, he went on, 'The runner will show you where when you're ready; right now I think it's time for a very late lunch.'

Lunch! Despite the early breakfast at the Pleucadeuc farm and Madame Pondard's later one, I was starving.

Jim stood. 'Come on. I think you need it.' He was right, and I followed him meekly to the farm's kitchen, where I was greeted by a pot-pourri of 'French' smells, a large fire (despite the month of June) and a long wooden table at which the three eldest Pondard girls – Anna, twenty-three, Geneviève, twenty-two, and Henriette, nineteen – dressed in summer dresses and woollen cardigans, fussed among us with plates and glasses as they 'decorated' it for the meal. French food, and plenty of it, was followed by real coffee and smooth Calvados as we talked of the landings.

A crescendo of cheering from the farmyard crashed through the open windows. We leaped for the door, with Monsieur Pondard leading the mêlée.

'Raufast!' I shouted over the farmer's shoulder. 'It's good to see you.'

The Sergeant Major was surrounded by the small team of maquisards that had escorted him from Pleucadeuc, and now others surged forward from their various hiding places to shake the hand of the first Free French soldier they had seen. Tears of pride welled in the Pondard family's eyes as the three elder daughters each kissed Raufast on both cheeks.

Holding out my own hand through the crowd, I asked inadequately, 'How are you?'

'All right, thank you, sir. I'm glad you're safe too.'

'Excellent,' I said, then turned to practicalities. 'Got the money?'

Raufast unstrapped the belt from his waist. 'I wouldn't leave this behind.'

Good news continued with the arrival of one of the wireless operators – plus his set – and so during the afternoon of 6 June I was able to make my first contact with London. Although we could do no more than confirm that at least five of Marienne's stick had survived the drop and made it to the Maquis, I felt I could begin to relax. If the others had been killed or captured, we would have heard through the Maquis intelligence network. I did not know that Marienne had already been in contact with his battalion headquarters.

Eventually Marienne and five men were escorted into the farm's complex of buildings and barns, where he confirmed that one of his team was dead and three wounded. Nevertheless, as we stood for a short while shaking hands, comparing notes and mourning our lost companion, we were generally enthusiastic over the course of events.

'Sir –' a wireless operator grabbed me by an elbow. 'Signal from London,' he said, and handed me a scruffy piece of paper – all that he could find until he unpacked his message pads.

The message was short, simple and exciting: 'Tonight's drop confirmed. Two aircraft. Ten men.'

'Excellent. Thank you. Please hand this to Monsieur Guimard.' I waved the paper over the operator's shoulder. 'Jim, you'd better read this. We're in business.'

From the farm's back door Monsieur Pondard shouted above the chatter of excited men. 'The girls have made sandwiches and the water's boiled.'

Marienne and I sat at the kitchen table hugging mugs of coffee while he recounted his story.

'After you left with Raufast, I took the others back on to the dropping zone – which, as you know, was not the right one – and started collecting our kit and the containers. Then, as we made our way back to the rendezvous, a long burst of automatic fire came very close to us and I saw a crowd of Germans crawling into firing positions –'

'I think you'll find they were Russians,' I interrupted.

'Russians?'

'Yes. I'll explain in a minute.'

Puzzled, Marienne continued, 'Well, whoever they were, they came running towards us. We immediately dropped the kit, took cover, and got engaged in a firefight. Then it was suddenly obvious that there were too many Germans – Russians – so I issued the order to evacuate the area and gave all the men a grid reference for a second rendezvous. Of course most of them didn't have maps, but I reckoned there were probably just enough if they stuck together so there was a good chance that we would all meet up.

'But getting out of the dropping zone wasn't easy, for the enemy had had time to get on to both our flanks. The only way we could do anything was to run across the fields. We did – splitting into ones and twos to make the targets more difficult in the moonlight – and it was then that four men were hit.[1] One was killed, and we couldn't recover him. Eventually we managed to regroup in some cover, but from there we were forced to go slowly, as every now and then the enemy took a crack at us. But we did now have an advantage of distance. Eventually we made it to the new rendez-vous, where I collected two or three other men who had been waiting safely.'

'Bloody lucky, if you ask me,' I offered.

'Yes, which is more than we said about you at the time, as we saw you and Raufast for a few seconds when the Germans – or whoever – started taking pot-shots at you after we'd scattered across the field. Until we arrived here we thought you were both dead, and when I managed to get a message through this morning I even informed your Colonel that I thought you'd had it!'

I grinned, imagining the scene in the Baker Street headquarters. Now it was my turn, and I began with an explanation: 'The Germans who ambushed you were White Russians.'

Marienne was unmoved. 'They were still bloody dangerous!' he said laconically. 'And they now have all our supplies.'

'Including my uniform and most of the francs,' I added – 'I'd only a limited amount in my belt when we jumped.'

I explained where we had been landed, but could throw no light as to why. Then I continued, 'I also thought that you'd all been killed, or at the best made prisoner. I wanted to send a message to London, but of course I couldn't – which is just as well, for I would probably have said what I feared.'

Marienne smiled. 'Well, at the moment SOE still think that you're dead and they know I'm alive.'

'Odd, though, as I sent them a sitrep this morning – so they'll have had conflicting information. At our four o'clock schedule they made no specific mention of me – so perhaps they still do.' Marienne smiled as I went on, 'And there were no regrets on the seven o'clock message either . . .'

'That proves it then,' Marienne said – 'they've just written you off without further thought.' He laughed: 'I always knew you were expendable!'

'Now,' I began in rather more earnest, 'we have over eighteen hundred maquisards grouped around the Pondards' farm and woods during the day, with nearly as many again living at their homes. That's too many, especially as most are not armed. The Boche, and especially any of their sympathizers among the people of Saint-Marcel, will notice the traffic in food and supplies that's taking place no matter how well we're trying to conceal it. It's madness: we must split up into small groups across the countryside.'

He nodded his agreement.

'What I suggest we do, Marienne, is keep everyone here until first thing tomorrow morning. I'd like as many as possible to see what happens at a drop which, God willing, happens where it should.'

I turned to the maquisard runner hovering with his back to the fire, teasing the girls with stories of doubtful authenticity about life in a Maquis, and we followed him for about a hundred yards as he led us beyond the farm's outbuildings and across a small field to where, under the cover of thickly planted apple trees, our tent was pitched and ready. Rough scrub formed a rudimentary camouflage cover that was certainly good enough to deflect a casual glance should enemy eyes get that close. As clean as we could make ourselves from hot water brought in two enamel bowls, we then made our way back to the farm kitchen, where Monsieur Pondard and Jim were sitting by the fire. Madame and the girls were preparing supper; all were drinking the local cider poured from heavy stone flagons.

'Welcome. You must drink and eat with us – I've sent food to your team, Marienne, and the maquisards always look after themselves, although we do supply most of the basics.' Monsieur Pondard pushed two tall-backed chairs towards the fire.

Jim, now happy with cider, wine and unfamiliar but welcome rum from our flasks, was, I hoped, ripe for conversion. 'Jim,' I began, 'we've agreed that you must move most of your men out of here.'

'I'll think about how many to move overnight – if you don't mind. Perhaps we can discuss all that in the morning.'

'Of course.' I didn't want to rush things, but was glad that we were all agreed on the principle.

We dropped the subject, and for an hour we mulled over less fundamental problems until at eleven it was time to pull on warmer clothing against the comparative chill of a June night and make the fifteen-minute walk to the far end of the dropping zone that I had chosen all those months back with the butcher from Guer.

As we reached the downwind end, where the lights at right angles to the centre line would be lit, the officer in charge of the night's drop greeted me in the dark. 'There are two battalions of four hundred men each covering a wide area round the dropping zone this evening. The reception committee is on the strip with torches and men waiting to gather the containers as soon as they land.'

I thanked him and, grabbing him by the arm, led Marienne away off La Baleine's centre line. The chill was creeping through my meagre clothes, and I needed a cigarette. 'If we sit in the bottom of this ditch do you think we could smoke?' I asked.

'No, I don't think we should,' Marienne replied quickly before I had a chance to strike a match.

'I can't see why not: we've got two battalions around us in a wide area; we're under cover.'

'Bob!' Marienne was firm.

Before we had time to argue over my craving, the officer, who had followed us from the middle of the field, knelt down at the edge of the ditch and held out a packet of Gauloises. He must have heard our muttering, for he said, 'Of course you can smoke! We have sentries posted on all the main roads and paths, at the entrance of Malestroit, and at various other main points. We have our own private telephone link, so if just one German or a patrol comes within five kilometres of us we'll know exactly where they are and what they are doing. We all smoke here when we get drops.' Which I knew was a comment born of bravado rather than truth, for they had had no drops in many months. He continued, 'The forest is so large that nobody would see us unless they came very close from that direction – and from the other, of course, they would have to pass through the farm.'

By this time I was puffing away, thankful for common sense.

Pleased with his arrangements, the officer finished with a flourish, 'We also have two three-tonne lorries and a fatigue party of about a hundred standing by waiting for the aircraft.' I wasn't sure if this wasn't overdoing things, but circumstances had changed since I had last witnessed a drop and I felt it best to keep quiet and simply observe. The officer in charge excused himself and slipped silently away.

I was lighting my third cigarette when one of the wireless operators crept along the ditch, softly calling my name. 'Captain André,' came a whisper through the dark.

'*Oui, ici.*'

He handed me a message form torn from a pad. 'Just in from London, sir. From your Colonel.'

I struck a match and read Colonel Buckmaster's latest communication. 'Very happy you are not dead. Saved two pounds on flowers so I will now buy you lunch on return. Tonight's drop includes two suitcases of replacement clothing for you, wireless sets, automatic weapons, petrol, welfare and possibly one jeep with each aircraft.'

I knew that 'welfare' meant more money.

Slowly, through the night air, came the unmistakable drone of heavy aircraft. We stubbed our cigarettes and stood stiffly. Off to our right and downwind we could just make out the Morse letter B for Baker being flashed in the direction of the rising noise: dah dit dit dit, dah dit dit dit, the silent beam of light faintly visible as it slanted skyward along the length of La Baleine. The men with torches pressed the 'on' switches.

Quite suddenly and with one roar after another, two large shadows swept low overhead as the Stirlings made what I considered to be an unnecessary dummy pass, presumably to check wind and headings. Then, as the noise faded and reappeared in a great circle, we were witness to a breathtaking sight that few of us would forget, and as men drifted silently down we could only stare upwards, mouths and eyes wide open. The aircraft turned across and downwind in a wide arc and began their run in for the drop of containers; as the newly arrived men were quickly rounded up and hustled to the edge of the field, other maquisards 'marked' each container as it left its aircraft's bomb bay. The lorries were waved into the field, where eager hands hurriedly bundled parachutes and lifted containers on to their backs.

We thought it was all over, but a fourth roaring crescendo had us staring upward again as, in salute, the two Stirlings conducted a fly-past at two hundred feet and were finally gone. For the second time that evening I wasn't too sure that that was a good idea, and made a note to make the point to SOE headquarters. Any unnecessary activity over La Baleine increased the chances of the wrong eyes noting our position.

Marienne turned to me: 'That's it, I guess. Let's get back to the farm and meet your new friends – my companions from the 4th Battalion.'

'OK,' I replied. 'A good drop – no jeeps, but, with any luck, plenty of weapons and my uniforms.'

We retraced our steps, but this time through a large throng of maquisards and ten newcomers who filled the farmyard. Pushing our way through the excitement, with Marienne shaking every hand thrust towards him, we waved to the uniformed French SAS soldiers to follow us into the barn that doubled as the Maquis de Saint-Marcel headquarters.

As each man entered through the wicket door he stopped at attention, saluted, then thrust out a hand while Marienne read off the names like a school roll-call.

Their leader was Second Lieutenant Taylor of the French 4th Battalion SAS, looking as scrupulously clean and smart as his men, as though they had all just stepped off the parade ground – which in effect they might have done, for they had had a good flight with no difficulties crossing the French coast.

Taylor had brought with him my personal mail and verbal orders. There was plenty to do, but before work took over – and we all certainly needed sleep as well – we briefed our new arrivals on 'the story so far' over mugs of coffee and glasses of Calvados served by the three eldest Pondard sisters.

Once our tale had been told, the girls were asked to leave – without taking the Calvados bottles – so that Lieutenant Taylor could deliver his classified messages. Although the girls were wholly trustworthy, their presence always brought a meeting close to collapse – a fact that Taylor had already discovered.

'Captain André,' he began, 'you told London that there are over two thousand French organized into a Maquis just north-west of us – in addition to those that are here – but that it's rather disorganized.' I nodded, for that information had been part of my first signal back to SOE.

'It is the intention', Taylor continued, 'that one of the SAS 4th Battalion's companies will drop into Samwest's area – somewhere to the south-east of Callac – to train them into a fighting Maquis. You will be pleased to know that the advance party that came with you arrived safely. They will also be supplied for demolition, sabotage and ambush operations.'

'If I'm right,' I replied, 'the other Maquis covers from here to the coast and then to the west. In other words, that's the north and west of the Morbihan plus the whole of the Côtes-du-Nord and Finistère. And I guess that, if we get kicked out of here by the Germans, we'll join up with them, and vice versa.'

'Yes, sir, that's right.'

'Anything else?' I asked, for there was clearly more to come that could not have been risked in a signal.

'First of all there will be a drop tomorrow night, and then the next night Colonel Bourgoin is due with a hundred men.'

'Excellent.'

'The Colonel would like to know, before he leaves England, if you can receive gliders.'

'We'll need to take another look at the dropping zone tomorrow morning,' I replied. 'It's long enough, but we need room to get them out of the way once they're down.'

I turned to Marienne. 'I'd like to have a conference with you, Taylor, Jim and the French Maquis officers tomorrow morning. I agree in general with what's going on here, but there are certain points that I'm not completely happy about that must be sorted out before Colonel Bourgoin's arrival.'

'I'll arrange it for eight o'clock.'

I turned to the latest member of our team. 'Taylor, you must get among the Maquis – Jim will brief you on how it's organized and how it's about to be reorganized – and be prepared to start training the officers and men in the various tactics while shaping it into an efficient unit.'

'Yes, sir.'

'Marienne, after tomorrow's meeting I want you to visit the Maquis, organize the defence, and improve the guard. After that, take a look at the airfield for gliders.'

'Right. And I suggest that more sentries are posted: our chaps could take over some of those duties, or at least supervise them.'

'Agreed. And the drop we had this evening should all go to Taylor's company' – I looked across to him and we both nodded – 'to bring it up to strength as a fighting unit with the necessary number of maquisards, and the same with each delivery until his company is fully kitted out and armed. The rest of his own men will be with us shortly.'

'Now, Taylor –' I turned back to the young second lieutenant – 'I expect you'll need some sleep,' and without waiting for an answer I called for the runner from the barn. 'Please take the Lieutenant and his men to their tents.' And with that they were gone.

A little later we made our way to our own tent for our first full night's rest since England. Sleep, though, did not come quickly.[2] Memories of the tension during the previous days in England and France kept my mind busy as, unaided by conscious thought, it recalled our own dramatic events while pondering too on those of others. I was also worried about so many men in one concentration, especially as so few were armed.

4. 'My Grandmother will Smoke a Pipe with You Tonight'

Waking at dawn, for a few seconds I was unable to place myself exactly and fumbled for a cigarette, knowing that, although it wouldn't clear my head of the previous evening's Calvados, nor tell me where I was, I could at least pretend to be alert.

Marienne – snoring, it seemed to me, from left to right, as a drill sergeant might call out the pace on the parade ground – was oblivious to the world. I picked up a shoe to hurl at his peaceful face.

'Good morning, sir!' The duty wireless operator's head was bending through the tent's entrance. 'Message for you.'

I dropped the shoe. 'Is it good news?'

'Yes.'

'Then it's from my girlfriend?' I didn't have one.

''Fraid not.'

I was wide awake now and reaching for another cigarette. 'OK. Let's have it.'

'"For Bob,"' the operator read: '"ten aircraft tonight; fifty men. Cash and wireless sets with Colonel night of 10/11 June."' He handed me the slip of paper.

'Fine, thanks. Confirm receipt and add, "Last night's drop successful."'

'Yes, sir.'

'While you're here, how are things with your department?'

'Fine. We lost one set, but recovered two. We've got all the codes, and are set up in the pigsty.'

'And the pigs?'

'Don't ask! But it's a good site for us.'

'OK. I'll come and see for myself after breakfast. I'll also arrange for sentries to keep prying eyes away from your work. It'll be an out-of-bounds area to everyone but the officers and you three operators.'

He ducked out of the tent muttering, 'Thank you, sir.'

With Colonel Bourgoin's arrival imminent, I knew he would want to start immediate offensive action against the Germans. While teams had already been busy on small-scale operations such as the destruction of telephone lines and, more impressively, the cutting of the railway line between Vannes and Auray some twenty-five miles to the south-west, we were not yet setting Europe as much ablaze as Churchill would have wished.

Fifteen minutes before the meeting, Jim and I took a detour to the pigsties to confirm my orders and to see if the number of sentries I was suggesting was correct for the lie of the land. We also quickly agreed an outline reorganization of the Maquis.

Back at the barn, all had settled down and a hush greeted us as we stepped through the entrance.

Everyone knew that this was to be the formal beginning of what had been planned, prepared and, on occasion, practised for: operations up to this moment had been only spasmodic and uncoordinated.

I took my place in front of men perched on straw bales or squatting on the cold, packed-mud floor. In front of me were eight Maquis battalion commanders, four of whom were, in theory, responsible for four hundred men each, stretched – again in theory – as far west as the coast at Vannes and as far inland as Guer. The other four commanders had yet to be given their responsibilities – and their full complement. The senior of the Maquis doctors, Dr Mahéo, was also present, as were two 'civilians' employed on intelligence duties in Saint-Marcel and the local villages and towns. While the 4th Battalion might be about to take over responsibility for both Samwest and Dingson, these two bases were spread between a number of smaller Maquis – ours being the larger. On the other hand, my actual circuit – Hillbilly – was responsible for the whole of the Morbihan *département* and much of Ille-et-Vilaine. Altogether at that stage there were probably over twenty thousand maquisards under arms in Brittany.

'Ready, men?' I started.

'Yes!' The collective enthusiasm in that one word was palpable.

'Right. The first thing that must be settled is the distribution of our members. I've discussed this with your commanding officer Jim, and he's agreed in outline.' The look of enthusiasm subsided a little, but the realities of war had to be spelled out. I was talking to men who had not experienced even a light skirmish, let alone a full-blown enemy attack. So far they had been playing a young man's parody of the real thing, but now they would have to grow up – and quickly – and learn that being a soldier is not a school-playground frolic.

'If we are attacked by the Germans, they will not only kick us out of here with ease, but in doing so they will inflict very serious casualties. We are not here to be attacked – even if we could hold our own. We are here to take the war to the enemy, so that he cannot reinforce Normandy. But we will also, when the time comes, pave the way for the advance westward of American forces to the Atlantic ports.'

I hoped the Maquis officers could see that I meant business: the trouble was I was still in civilian clothes that were almost too authentic, and, frankly, I did not look the part and felt rather foolish. Nevertheless, I went on, 'The men of this Maquis will now be divided into eight independent battalions of about 225 men each; each battalion is to be further subdivided into four companies, each of 56 men. The battalions will be numbered 1 to 8, and I will leave it up to Jim and your commanders how best to sort all that out . . .' a nervous titter echoed forlornly around the large and barely filled barn – they still didn't like this meddling – '. . . by this evening!'

I continued, 'We are due air drops almost every night until we are fully equipped, trained and operational.' That was better news, and genuine smiles confirmed this. 'For instance, tonight's drop will consist of ten aircraft.' I could see backs straighten. 'We will receive approximately twenty-five containers, fifty more French SAS *parachutistes* from Marienne's 4th Battalion and two jeeps.'

This was more like it, and there was plenty more to come. 'No. 1 Battalion will post itself on the north and east sides of the dropping zone; No. 2 Battalion will take the south and west sides, with both battalions in position by ten o'clock at the latest. They are to send a report when they are in those positions.

'No. 3 Battalion commander will send all his companies to patrol in a large sweep around the perimeter of the Maquis, while No. 4 Battalion will provide two companies for the reception committee and to carry the stores to the places reserved for them outside the farm. The battalion commander is to report to Marienne when everything is ready for the reception.'

I asked each of the officers in turn, 'Any questions?'

'Everything will be ready, Bob.'

Turning to the other four battalion commanders, 'Tomorrow night Nos. 5, 6, 7 and 8 Battalions will take over those duties and, where necessary, the weapons, until everyone has his own personal rifle or sub-machine gun.'

I stifled excited whispers. 'The next point I want to make is that Colonel Bourgoin, the commanding officer of the 4th Battalion Free French SAS, will be dropping here sometime in the next couple of days. He only has one arm – the other one is still in North Africa,' I ignored the giggles – 'so he is no stranger to battle. I know him personally as a brave and gallant officer.'

I now turned to the doctor: 'In each drop you will receive two packages with which to start building up a small hospital. I would like it within the Maquis, but separate from the farm buildings. You may like to look at a spot I've chosen a few hundred metres from here. Jim will show you, and if you're happy he'll make arrangements for sentries and suitable protection.'[1]

'Thank you, Captain. I received good bandages and good carving knives this morning. Now all I lack are good patients!'

'And what we lack is a good doctor!' someone shouted.

After the laughter had died I faced the doctor again. 'I fear your wish will be granted all too soon. Which leads me on to another aspect. Too many of the Maquis are talking in the villages, and it has even been reported that some are walking the three kilometres home to Malestroit with their weapons in full view. One day we will be infiltrated, our location – and, of more importance, our defences – will be compromised, and we will not find that amusing.' I studied the wry smiles, but remained unconvinced that the seriousness – the delicacy – of the situation was yet understood.

'I do understand the thrill of showing off your weapons to your girls –' welcome smiles – 'but from now on nothing military leaves the Maquis, or – and I tell you this with absolute seriousness – you will be caught and shot by the Boche and no questions will be asked.'

And on that sombre note I called the meeting to a close, just as the welcome smell of coffee began drifting across the farmyard. Jim and Marienne joined me in the Pondards' kitchen, where we listened to the news from England; Marienne wrote a signal for dispatch to London;[2] I sent a runner – without his rifle – into Saint-Marcel to buy a couple of shirts; and Jim began, on paper, to redistribute his men across eight equal-sized battalions.

I had chosen La Baleine with only air drops in mind, but now it was to be upgraded to an airstrip, if we judged it suitable.

'Come on,' I said, putting down my empty cup and smiling my thanks to the Pondard girls. 'Jim, Marienne, let's go and look at the field from a new perspective.'

The field, as it always had been, was first class: about nine hundred yards by four hundred, with small bushes at one end and barns at the other. We walked its length and breadth, studied low-level approaches that would be needed by an aircraft landing and taking off, and dug our heels into the surface. There was little to prevent a glider landing or a light plane taking off.

'With a couple of days' work we could make it a first-rate airstrip,' I said, and turned to Jim. 'Could you put, say, fifty men on to the job: cut down the few bushes, level out the larger bumps – make it reasonable?'

'Easily!'

'Good. Now, just for the record, let's look at the smaller fields.'

As we walked, Jim told me that a year earlier the Germans had ordered all farmers to plant long poles in their fields every ten yards and to make sure that their ends were especially sharp. 'They had visions of chaps like you landing on them,' he added unnecessarily, 'and when they made their inspections they could see how well we understood the word "collaboration". I didn't think it useful to explain that, every night there was a drop, squads of men went into the fields to pull the poles out again, only to replant them before dawn. We burned the poles last winter for fuel: the Germans simply couldn't check every field in Brittany and Normandy.'

For another hour we walked across the Maquis. Sentries were now more alert, doubled up and not standing around smoking and making a racket that could be heard for miles. Once on our rounds we heard a German convoy on the main road south of the Maquis, and made our way in that direction. From behind cover we had a good sight of young men – sixteen or seventeen years old – and elderly men, probably over forty.

Jim watched the expression on our faces. 'Their best types are in Russia. But don't be deceived: they have two divisions here which would be far too good for the untrained maquisards. I reckon that a thousand of our chaps would only have a 60 per cent chance of holding off five hundred of theirs.'

With a mid-morning mug of tea beckoning, we headed back to find Lieutenant Taylor waiting.

'There are two men from the north-Brittany Maquis wanting to see you,' he said, 'and I have the message that will confirm tonight's drop. It will be put out on the BBC at 2115 hours.'

'What is it?' asked Marienne.

'"Ten friends will drink fifty glasses of red wine with you tonight."' We smiled. It didn't really matter what was said, provided it was personal to us and could not be confused with similar messages for other reception parties.

Taylor then added, to my delight, 'Good news, sir – I've found your cases and put them in your tent.'

In the farm, the two leaders of the northern Maquis were standing by, each quenching with cider what appeared to be a considerable thirst while staring, with some envy I thought, through the windows at our own maquisards unpacking the last of the most recently arrived containers.

'Good afternoon, gentlemen,' I said.

One offered me a curt *bonjour* before looking directly at the uniformed Marienne. 'During the last two nights,' he said, 'we have had teams of men dressed like you saying they were French SAS men from England who had dropped in our area for, so they explained, demolition jobs and to organize our Maquis.'

'That's quite correct –' Marienne started, but he was interrupted.

'We've been caught out too often to believe them without proof, so we've brought their identity cards and have come to see if you can confirm their identities without seeing those cards.'

'Yes,' I interrupted, 'I can.'

The two men looked anxiously towards me – a 'French' civilian, and a scruffy one at that. They looked back at Marienne, who explained, with what I hoped was mock disgust: 'This,' he laid a hand on my shoulder, 'this *officer*, is Captain Bob of the British Army. At present he looks like a tramp, because he was not greeted kindly on landing – and his clothes were lost.'

Hesitantly our two visitors held out their hands, and while I shook them in turn I decided to move on quickly before further doubt erupted in their understandably suspicious minds. 'One', I said, 'should be a Lieutenant Deschamps. There is also – or there should be – a Squadron Leader Smith, with white hair, a Captain Leblond and a doctor called Sassoune.'

For the first time smiles began to replace frowns. 'The first three names are right,' said one of the Maquis. 'We don't know this doctor – he's not turned up yet, but maybe he will sometime.'

'I hope so,' said the other: 'I think we may have work for him.'

'Look,' I continued, 'why don't you stay and watch tonight's drop? That should remove any final doubts you might have. Taylor will look after you, and we'll meet again at the farm later.'

They were happy with this idea, and so, nodding to Marienne to show them round, I left them to it, picked two maquisards who had been detailed as duty runners – or, to use British army parlance, batmen – for the day, and asked that a couple of buckets of hot water be taken to my tent.

And – oh bliss! – the London team had done a wonderful job: clean battledress, clean shirts, shoes, boots, ties, underwear, civilian clothing with, among the personal touches, two pipes, my favourite French tobacco (someone had done their homework), my preferred French cigarettes (both of which were still available in our area – so avoiding a mistake often made by those arriving), chocolates and sweets. 'What more could a man want?' I thought, and with that my final prayer was answered by the arrival of the hot water.

It was good to feel clean again and to have a British army uniform. If caught in civilian clothes I would immediately be shot as a spy: uniform should, in theory at least, offer me a modicum of protection. Nevertheless, I packed my civilian clothes in one case ready for visits to the town and for any reconnaissance work that might be necessary. After all, I reasoned to myself, I was in every practical respect a local – I had known no home other than the north of France and the French Mercantile Marine. I knew, though, that that would not get me far during a diligent Gestapo inspection.

After a silent thank you to the staff for my new-found persona and a promise to take them out for a good dinner on my return, I stepped through the tent flap properly dressed, smoking good tobacco in a new pipe. The two northern Maquis officers were happy to have some confirmation, visually at least, that I was indeed a British officer. And yet . . . There remained, I felt, a last trace of suspicion deep in our visitors' minds.

'Gentlemen,' I tried to reassure them, 'for you to be certain that we are French and British SAS officers there is one simple – and final – proof I can give.'

'We're convinced,' they said unconvincingly. 'But if you insist!'

'Write a message – any foolish thing you like – and I'll send it off to London this evening. They'll get the BBC to broadcast it at 9.15 tonight to confirm tonight's drop.'

This seemed to delight them, and as I scribbled out our daily sitrep they sat in a corner laughing over a blank piece of paper.

'What would you like to send?' I asked when I had done my own writing.

'"My grandmother will smoke a pipe with you tonight,"' they replied.

'That's fine,' I said, and called for the duty runner.

By nine o'clock that evening we were seated round the fire with the wireless tuned to the BBC, and by 2115 I had started to watch our guests out of the corner of my eye.

'Sun will shine at midnight . . . Rufus has a black dog . . . Eleven bottles of brandy will be spilt . . .' Fifteen messages, sixteen messages: I could feel the Maquis leaders becoming anxious . . . 'My grandmother will smoke a pipe with you tonight.' The eighteenth message. I switched the machine off, and in silence the Maquis officers raised their glasses in my direction. We were in the clear!

Equally relieved, Jim left to tell the four battalion commanders that the evening's entertainment was 'on'. He returned a few minutes later: 'It won't be until 2230 or 2300. We might as well wait here in comfort.' And so we did, by a log fire and with rather more Calvados than perhaps was sensible.

'Perfect night,' Marienne whispered once we were settled in a ditch.

It was indeed: dark enough, but with a clear view of the country-side's salient features. Another longish wait followed, then, as before, came the slow realization that the silence was being gently broken by the faintest of low-pitched hums until, a few minutes before midnight and gradually at first, the noise intensified. Then, quite suddenly, one after the other, five four-engined aircraft swooped down to dropping height, from which level over seventy-five containers and men floated down. Then, as quickly as they had come, they were gone, leaving us with the usual mix of pride, excitement, confidence in the future and satisfaction with present events – but, as always, a fear that we might have been spotted.

That night, though, the departure of the first five aircraft heralded the arrival of a second wave, until we had received loads from ten planes in all.

The brief silence after the last aircraft left was short-lived as men scrambled across La Baleine shepherding and guiding fifty men and collecting 120 containers. Parachutes were bundled up separately, for, although jealously sought-after by the local women, their possession could – and often did – lead to Gestapo reprisals. In our Maquis all parachutes were given to the doctor for use as blankets, outer bandages, slings and tourniquets. Of the promised jeeps there was no sign.

The senior battalion commander in charge that night slid up to us to make his initial report: 'Four chutes didn't open, and I think a few men landed in the trees at the end of the dropping zone.'

'Yes, thanks. I heard the containers crash, and I guess we'll have a couple of broken ankles.'

'I'll get a more positive report to you as soon as possible,' he said, and disappeared back into the night.

On our way to the farm we overtook teams of four carrying

containers to the main pathway, where they were dumped ready for removal by lorries; others carried parachutes, with an air of a South of France carnival about the whole scene. Our two lorries trundled past, laden with men, containers and parachutes. In the farmyard, yet more containers were being stacked, and men – new arrivals to the war – were standing around smoking and talking excitedly. None, especially those maquisards who lived locally, would ever forget this drop of ten aircraft: a sign that their job was important and possibly vital. More aircraft might fly over in future drops, but this was the first 'big one', and it brought with it convincing proof that, after all the years of uncertainty, after all the doubts and worries over the apparent invincibility of the Nazis and their odious cruelties, the Allies meant business. And if the little Maquis de Saint-Marcel was worthy of such effort, what must be happening elsewhere across occupied France?

Men reached down from the tailgates to shake my hand; men carrying heavy loads stopped to congratulate me. I explained that I was merely an 'organizer', a 'fixer': it was their presence and willingness that had made it all possible.

I hurried on to the farm's main building, where, I was informed, the two newly arrived officers of the 4th Battalion were already drinking Calvados and teasing the Pondard daughters.

Captain Puech-Samson and Lieutenant Déplante, to whom I had said goodbye only a few days earlier – it seemed like a year – were warming themselves in front of the burning logs.

'Good trip over?' asked Marienne.

'Yes,' replied the Lieutenant, 'and, in particular, a very good drop – although I think a couple of my men may have landed off the edge of the field.'

'What happened to the two jeeps?' I began after my turn to shake hands was over.

'Sorry, Bob –' I was glad he remembered my change of name in France – 'at the last minute it was decided not to send them today but with the Colonel in two or three days.'

'Good. Until we get sorted out they'd probably be a luxury anyway.' I knew such decisions were not of Puech-Samson's making, so I changed the subject. 'How is the Colonel?'

'Fine. Raring to come across – whenever. All I know is that when he does jump he'll be number one in the stick.'

'Good. Anything else?'

'He'll be bringing a few dollars in a container.'

'I hope it's more than a few!'

'I think you'll find it will be.'

Marienne, ever practical, butted in, 'It'll be no easy job for him jumping with one arm: we'll need to help him the moment he hits the ground.'

That seemed to be the clue for our northern-Maquis guests to make their thanks for the display, and once they had gone we turned back to the fire and the Calvados.

Sergeant Major Raufast swept in. I handed him a glass. 'What's the news?' I asked.

'Two broken legs – not bad, I suppose, out of fifty.'

I replied, 'It's still two too many.'

'Bad luck,' chipped in Marienne. 'I'll visit them as soon as the doctor's strapped them up.'

Once the newcomers had been briefed on the 'story so far', I turned to the immediate future. 'Our first priority is to unpack the containers, clean and check the weapons, and see if we can build up one battalion to full fighting strength. It'll be amazing if the Boche aren't aware of the night's activities, so we must be on our guard.'

'All sentry posts have remained doubled up in case of a counter-attack, and all off-duty men are sleeping fully clothed and with their rifles,' Jim explained. 'With what we already have in camp I think we can now build four battalions.'

Marienne wasn't too sure: 'I'd prefer two crack battalions to begin with, and well-armed, permanent, strongpoints round the Maquis with at least twenty Bren-gun positions.'

We all nodded our agreement. Ideally all battalions should be brought up to strength simultaneously, but without enough training teams that was not achievable. Additionally, as Déplante informed us, four small teams were due to be dropped to us the next night for demolition duties on local railway lines, using one of the battalions as guards and guides.

Coffee and Calvados over, everyone left for their tents while

Marienne and I visited the wounded. Déplante had done so earlier.

'Six weeks in plaster, then they'll be fine,' the doctor said as we shook hands with the unfortunates, lying as comfortably as was possible on beds made from parachutes.

The doctor – happy now that he had been presented with the first of his 'good patients' – was proud of his work, but the patients themselves were rather less than keen on their plight. Somewhere in southern England a pilot's ears were burning. While the casualties cursed and moaned, we did our best to console and cheer, but a broken leg after all the training and at the beginning of such an operation was beyond our soothing.

5. Treachery and Death

I had only been asleep an hour, or so it felt, when through a dream someone was trying to wake me: a hand was pulling and pushing at my shoulder. I lost the battle and opened an eye.

'Wake up, sir!' A hushed voice shattered the last of my subconscious. 'We've seen them.'

'Who?' I groaned. 'What?'

'One of the teams,' the runner whispered with patience.

'Where?'

'About twenty minutes ago we heard an aircraft, and thought nothing of it until it began to circle some way off. Then suddenly four men and a container were dropped.'

I jumped out of bed, grabbed at my pile of clothes, and stretched across to wake Marienne. A few minutes later we lifted the tent flap and shuffled into the pre-dawn gloom. The duty major of the 'watch' battalion met us at the farmhouse: he had already dispatched a patrol to make contact. While this was good – and expected – news, my attention was diverted by three *demoiselles Pondard* pouring coffee, clothed only in their nighties and dressing gowns. I kissed each one in turn to recognize their thoughtfulness, only to receive a hefty dig in a rib from Marienne for my good manners.

Sounds of a second aircraft prevented further banter as we rushed outside to see if we could identify anything useful. Off to the east – the nearest railway line ran north–south a mile or so in that direction – we could just make out the shape of a heavy bomber and then another, but by then parachutes had appeared beneath and behind the first. To my muddled mind – or had I not heard Déplante correctly? – this was all a day early. Nevertheless, it was positive stuff, and as we wondered at their target a fourth aircraft flew low and without warning over La Baleine before banking to the south and disappearing.

A runner appeared from the darkness and spoke hastily to

Marienne, who then turned to me. 'Four aircraft – three teams dropped. I've sent search parties to find the second wave.'

'Right. Not much we can do standing here. Back to the coffee.'

'Back to the girls is what you really mean!'

A red flash lit the roofs and chimneys as we crossed the farmyard. We stopped and turned as a loud, rumbling explosion rolled over the land.

'One railway gone, Bob.' Marienne was more animated now.

Twenty minutes later, over coffee, two more explosions rattled the curtained windows. 'Three gone,' intoned Marienne. 'Now for the fourth.'

'This is good, but I hope they get out of the area quickly before the Germans start swarming.' Looking at my watch, I added, 'It's five o'clock – I'm going back to bed.' Although the explosions were in our area, they were out of our hands: they were someone else's operation, with us as bystanders.

But our beckoning beds remained cold for, as we crossed the yard, for the umpteenth time that night another slow four-engined aircraft made yet another low pass over our position. 'Not good for our security,' I thought as it headed round for La Baleine.

'Who the hell are they? I wonder. Come on . . .'

'We're too late. The duty company will bring them in.'

We watched from a distance as four men and one container floated down – to be met, we were told later, by not such an enthusiastic welcome as earlier arrivals had enjoyed: the maquisards were already becoming blasé; drops had quickly become routine.

Ten minutes later the duty sergeant reported that this latest team – of whom we had had no warning – was due to blow up the railway line about three miles from the Pondards' farm. As this was in our immediate tactical area of responsibility, and as the countryside around the railway line was almost certain to be buzzing with enemy, I sent instructions that the operation be delayed for twenty-four hours.

Beds were found for this fourth demolition team, and once Marienne and I had satisfied ourselves that they were well looked after we turned in. We were washed and breakfasted by seven, and staring at 120 containers stacked close to the barns. Men from the duty company had started to unpack rifles, carbines and pistols, handing them down a chain to others who quickly stripped, cleaned and reassembled the weapons. Bren guns, PIATs – hand-held anti-tank guns – and mortars were repacked into their carrying boxes but ready for near-instant use.

Satisfied that all was well – and morale was certainly high with this latest tangible expression of confidence in our Maquis – I sat to compose my daily sitrep, which included a report on, and our thanks for, the latest drop; the names of the two wounded; details (as far as I knew them) of the four teams most recently to have arrived in our area; and a request to know the targets and success rate of those three that we had not yet met.

By coincidence, just as I finished, a runner panted into the barn and staggered to a halt in front of my trestle table.

I looked up. Our two, self-appointed, civilian intelligence men had urgent news for us and were waiting in the farm.

The one who seemed to be in charge, Alexis Babin, began excitedly as soon as we were round the table with coffee. 'Since those three explosions early this morning,' he gushed, 'the Germans have gone completely mad!'

I nodded. Nothing unusual so far.

'They're like bees, all over the countryside – interrogating, beating up people, arresting people for no reason. No one close to the explosions is safe.'

I nodded again, and let him continue – indeed, I could not have stopped him had I wished to. 'Your teams blew up three railway lines and, believe me, they did a good job.'

I believed him, but I wanted details.

'The Boche have got their Gestapo and the *Milice* with them. Colonel Hauffmann is in command, and that's serious.'

'Tell me about Hauffmann in a minute. Where were the lines cut?'

This stopped Alexis. He relaxed a little and looked at his companion, who shook his head slowly. 'Don't know exactly. I just know where the arrests are taking place, so that'll give us a clue.'

'Quite so. Not a problem. I'm sure we'll learn soon enough. Now, tell me about this Colonel Hauffmann.'

Alexis took a long suck at his coffee and swilled it round his mouth as though savouring the first of a new vintage. 'Hauffmann', he began with a near-snarl, 'has been in charge of the Gestapo in Brittany for two years, in which time he has arrested, tortured and killed God knows how many young French men and women. He's living in Sérent,' Alexis waved an arm towards the west, 'just a few kilometres away, in a small hotel with his mistress – who happens to be the owner – and a young barmaid.'

He paused to let me take in these unpalatable facts.

'What else is he up to?' I pressed.

'Oh, you know, the usual stuff – black market, robberies and killing Maquis men. We've got enough evidence to make a good case against him – if we're ever in a position to do so.'

I poured more coffee while summoning the runner from his seat by the fire. 'Tell Jim I'd like to see him as soon as is convenient.' A few minutes later he was with us.

'This Colonel Hauffmann,' I asked: 'What do you know about him?'

Although he didn't, like Alexis, begin with a snarl, Jim's eyes blazed. 'He's a crafty, dirty brute who's arrested and tortured several of my men and girls. For the last four months we've been trying to capture or kill him and, though I don't know what else Alexis has been telling you, I expect you'll have discovered that so far we've failed.'

'Yes, and he seems to be on the rampage again as a result of last night's activities. Which is hardly surprising,' I added.

'He never goes out without a strong bodyguard. In the hotel he lives on the first floor, and could hold the staircase for some time – certainly long enough for his men to arrive. But he'll have to be stopped sometime.'

'The sooner the better,' I said. But I knew we all understood the inevitable retribution that would follow.

For ten minutes Jim recounted some of the more unpleasant atrocities committed by Hauffmann, all of which were confirmed by further snorts of hatred from Alexis and his companion. 'He's a devil,' Jim concluded.

'Well,' I suggested more with black humour than in earnest to others round the table – for by now we had been joined by a number of Maquis officers anxious for gossip – 'let's vote on the death sentence! All those in favour . . .'

Not surprisingly, the motion was carried by seven votes to two, with Marienne and me casting against.

'Gentlemen,' I smiled, 'while I totally share your views, you know we can't commit what in effect would be murder – unless . . .' I paused to look into the eyes of everyone round that large table, 'Hauffmann were to be killed in a genuine military battle.'

There was a silence I had not known before, while a sense of unease drew a spasm of adrenalin through my veins. I was a Briton: it was not my kith and kin who were being tortured, raped and killed.

'Make him a prisoner – yes!' I pursued my argument. 'But killing him would bring us and your friends and relatives down to his level of bestiality, and there'd be travel restrictions, tighter curfews, searches.'

'These all happen now – we've got nothing to lose,' a battalion commander opposite me chipped in. I knew he had strong personal reasons for wishing Hauffmann dead, but I still had to support the rules of war and reason.

'I understand the position – and yours in particular, Major – but it's not our job. We're soldiers, not judges. A military court must decide his fate at the end of the war, using all the evidence we'll have.'

There was a long silence, but this one was calmer as, slowly, they nodded their assent.

'Keep an eye on him,' I said to Alexis. 'Things may change.' I wasn't sure how they could, but I did not want to appear too negative over such an emotive – and dangerous – issue. If I had known, if any of us had known, what was in store we needn't have fretted. 'I'll come and see you this afternoon to place our intelligence-gathering on a more formal footing.'

'Excellent,' he replied, and nudged his companion to his feet. 'We'll get back now and see what's happened in our absence.'

Outside, the men of No. 1 Battalion were behaving like children with new toys, and, as each section of Maquis men was armed, a team of two SAS men took them away for a professional introduction to their new weapons followed by repetitive drills and routines.

Suddenly a shot echoed round the stone buildings. We stood motionless, unable to determine whether it had been an incoming enemy round or from within our own ranks.

Breaking the silence, Marienne shouted, 'Who fired that?' in the rough direction of the shot and started running, only to collide with a maquisard charging in the opposite direction.

The man stopped and panted himself slowly back to composure. 'One of the men was cleaning his pistol,' he gasped. 'He didn't realize it was loaded, pulled the trigger, and hit another chap who was sitting in front of him in the leg.' He spoke less quickly now, and paused to catch his breath for the second time.

'All right, all right.' Marienne placed a hand on his shoulder. 'Back to your duty,' he said, and turned to me to growl, 'I knew this would happen sometime. It's not the maquisard's fault. It's poor instruction and supervision from my men.'

I sympathized, and felt that part of the blame should lie on my shoulders, for I was their adviser and had failed to check that adequate training was being given. On the other hand, the Maquis was already comparatively well armed, and everyone should have known the dangers: it was not as though they were unused to arms and live ammunition.

Marienne called for the duty runner: 'Get a message to the battalion commanders and my SAS ranks. I want to see them all here immediately.'

'Yes, sir,' he saluted, and departed on his errand. Ten minutes later the eight French majors, the French SAS officers and all Marienne's men, except the duty wireless operators, filled the main barn. Jim was the only other absentee. When everyone was seated, Marienne stood up.

'At present,' he began, 'there are 68 SAS men in the camp, and when the final teams turn up we shall be about 200 with the other 200 of the battalion in the Samwest base area. So that's about 400 trained SAS officers and soldiers available to train our 96 Maquis platoons.' He paused while his audience grappled with the unknown.

Marienne continued, 'For those of you who haven't yet heard,' a number of men nodded, still waiting to know the reason for this unexpected mass briefing, 'a maquisard was shot less than an hour ago – by another maquisard – and one such incident is one too many.'

He had the full attention of his audience now. 'Quite apart from that, the Germans will hear the shots. The only place for shooting practice is in the range deep in the woods – you all know where that is, and it's not in the farmyard. I blame both my men for bad supervision and Jim's men – you battalion commanders – for lack of supervision, and I'll be issuing new orders later in the day! But for the moment that's all – except I want the utmost professionalism from the instructors and the utmost attention from the men under instruction. Nothing less will do. Thank you.'

Later in the day we were to receive a report that sixty-five of the platoons were back in training and using their weapons safely on the woodland range. At the farm, we could just hear the forest training range in full use.

Jim, some of whose men were spread far across the Morbihan and who had gone on his rounds after the Hauffmann vote and before the impromptu gathering, returned to tell us that the three successful demolition teams had been picked up and were on their way into the Maquis with two prisoners.

'Two prisoners?' I asked.

'Yes,' Jim replied. 'I've no more details – don't know who they are or how they were captured.'

'I assume they're Germans,' I offered hopefully.

'We'll know in a couple of hours.'

'Good news,' I said. 'We've been a bit short of that today.' And I explained the events that had taken place in his absence.

'Well, here's some more,' said Jim. 'No. 1 Battalion is now up to strength and fully armed. Bearing in mind what they already had, we now have enough arms for a second battalion. The others, of course, have some weapons, but we'll need more drops to bring them up to fighting strength.'

'Excellent,' Marienne said. 'Get No. 2 Battalion on parade as soon as you can and they can start arming themselves – but remember what happened this morning.'

While Marienne and Jim sat at one end of the trestle table discussing training routines, sentry positions and priorities, I sat opposite them adding and subtracting figures on a piece of signal paper.

'By my reckoning,' I butted in, 'we should have two fully equipped battalions by lunchtime – that's almost five hundred men ready to fight as proper, cohesive units – a further sixteen hundred reasonably well armed, and a final fourteen hundred with approximately one weapon between two men.'

'And', Marienne chipped in, 'we should know later today if we're getting further drops tonight, and that could mean another two battalions' worth.'

'One further point,' Jim added – 'more in Bob's line for his sitreps. I've chosen twenty men – intelligent, perceptive guys – to work with Alexis Babin and his intelligence network to monitor German movements, intentions and strengths. That includes the bloody *Milice*.'

He went on, 'With all the contacts we have in the towns – with the police, the mayors, and in the cafés, the restaurants and hotels where the Germans congregate – and by using *les demoiselles Pondard* as our primary contacts, we should be able to establish a reliable rumour network that'll keep us up to date.'

'By coincidence, I've been thinking along the same lines,' I added, 'and I'm off to Malestroit this afternoon. I'll take this on from now onwards, so I'd like to interview your men as soon as you can get them here. But not all at once.'

It had been obvious for some minutes that Marienne was growing impatient. Now he stood up and slipped through the wicket door. Two minutes later he burst back in and shouted, 'Jim, Bob, it's time for lunch.' I was quickly learning that, after getting to grips with the hated Germans, sleep and food were his secondary priorities. 'Monsieur Pondard is sending out frantic signals that if we don't turn up soon it'll be ruined, and I'm against that.' The implacable Monsieur was doing no such thing, but we followed meekly to the farmhouse nevertheless.

'Look what's coming,' a voice shouted through the door, nearly causing a stampede. Someone grabbed a tilting bottle; someone else caught a falling glass. Outside, a signaller en route with a message was pointing, all thoughts of decoding forgotten.

Approaching hesitantly along the track were four maquisards, followed by two 'new' SAS teams, who in turn were trailed by two young French girls being held in check by a maquisard gripping a stout rope tether in one hand and a sharp stick in another: he might have been driving them to market. A third SAS team and two more maquisards brought up the rear. I awaited the explanation with interest.

As they came closer, the reason for the rope was clearly etched into a number of faces. Five or six of the men were sporting bloody scratches down their cheeks and across their forearms, and now and again they glared at the girls with no trace of sympathy. The girls were attractive: both were well-built, even buxom – or, as I noted at the time, *bien en chair*.

The posse shuffled to a halt in front of Marienne, who squared up to its leader. 'What's all this about?' he asked without humour. The SAS might have expected a more friendly welcome – but I was sure that would come.

The three sergeants in command explained, in turn and briefly, that their individual missions to blow railway lines had been a success, after which they had met, as arranged before leaving England, at a farm. Apparently all had continued to go well until the two girls had wandered, unexpectedly, into the farmyard where our maquisard guides were waiting. On seeing the SAS soldiers the girls foolishly turned and ran – but not before one of the maquisards, who knew of the willing distribution of their undeniable favours among the Germans, had recognized them.

They were a liability and, as they had spotted the soldiers in a 'friendly' farm, no risks could be taken, not least because all previous experience suggested that the farmer – and probably his family too – would be shot by Colonel Hauffmann. In short, the girls were traitors as well as sluts.

'So,' explained one of the Maquis simply, 'here they are.'

Marienne nodded.

The soldier continued, 'They fought like tigresses – as you can see. Twice they escaped. So we tied them up.'

'Did anyone else see this?'

'No.'

'But they'll be missed by their German friends.'

'No doubt,' the maquisard said with a leer. 'Wouldn't you miss them?'

The girls would have to stay with us until we could check how dangerous they really were: Monsieur Pondard would know where to house them. He scratched his head – a pronounced habit of his whenever a problem needed a solution.

'I've got a new pigsty,' he began, 'about fifty metres from the main buildings. It's clean and fairly large. I haven't used it yet – nor have the pigs,' he laughed – 'so with a couple of beds, a table and two chairs I could make it into a reasonable room. I can give them a large basin for washing, and if you have a sentry they shouldn't be able to escape.'

'What about the pigs?' I asked helpfully.

'When they arrive, we'll eat them!' he said simply. 'And what we don't eat we'll cure for the future.'

'Perfect,' we replied, and turned to our disturbed lunch.

Over the final coffee I faced Marienne. 'I'm going into Malestroit to introduce myself to the chief of police and the mill owner. I've ordered a car from one of the maquisards who has German permission to run one – and to buy petrol.'

By the time I had changed into civilian clothes – now made respectable by my maquisard batman – a black Citroën was waiting in the transport park with its owner/driver, and soon we were on the farm track that leads south-east towards the minor road that approaches Saint-Marcel from the west; thence to Malestroit along the D776. Here we were faced by a German roadblock – but, luckily, just beyond a bend, so that the soldiers could not see from which direction we had actually come.

'Are your papers in order?' I asked the driver pointlessly.

'Of course, sir. I live here. Mine are genuine!'

We slowed to a halt alongside a corporal with arm outstretched and a rifle slung across a shoulder.

'*Papiers!*' he demanded. We handed them through the open window. A cursory glance was all he managed before shoving them roughly back into the car with an unfriendly and heavily accented '*Allez.*'

And we did. My papers had passed their first casual check.

In Malestroit we stopped at the bar nearest to where I knew the police station to have been and, once inside, I asked the driver to point out the gendarmerie. It might have been moved now that the Germans were in control, and I wanted to make no mistakes that would have marked me as a newcomer.

The small, clean café was beginning to fill with late-afternoon coffee- and wine-drinkers – both German and French – and for the first time since I had left for my SOE training I smelt the genuine France. I ordered two glasses of rough local cider and took them to a table by the large window that faced the street.

Without pointing, my driver said, 'The gendarmerie is the twelfth building to the right of here – you can't miss it.'

It was where it always had been. I finished my drink, left some money to pay, plus a little extra should the driver want a second, and walked into the street.

'Could I speak to your lieutenant, please?' I said to the young policeman on guard in the foyer.

'Who are you?' He was direct but not suspicious.

'Monsieur Havet,' I said. 'I have an appointment.'

'Wait here.' He turned for his chief's office and was back in less than a minute. 'Follow me,' he commanded.

'Good afternoon, my name is Lejeune.' The policeman extended a hand across his desk. 'I was told by Jim to help you, and of course I will.'

I knew he was reliable from reports both in England and since I had arrived. 'Well,' I began, 'shortly we'll be operating full-time in this area, blowing up railways, bridges and similar targets. The Germans will react – as they always do – with searches, arrests and curfews. To do these things they will be calling on your help, and of course you must be seen to be giving it. You must help them, but I would like to be given as much as two hours' warning of their plans if that's ever possible.'

Unsurprised, Lieutenant Lejeune nodded.

'That'll save a large number of my men from being arrested. And if they arrest civilians before you can warn us, let us know their whereabouts and we'll assist as best we can. Whenever possible we'll take direct action against the Germans.'

'I'll help as much as I'm able, but I don't always know when they're about to carry out an operation. The way they work is that an officer will suddenly arrive by car and order me into it, and after that I don't usually know what's happening until we arrive at the scene.'

'I guessed that would be the case,' I said.

'But I'll try,' he continued. 'I'll get more friendly with them, appear to be sympathetic on their behalf. They may start to confide in me – particularly when the pace against them hots up.'

'I can ask for no more.' The chief of Malestroit's police smiled as I made him an offer: 'If you need men to help you to pass on information I'll have some attached to you.'

But he saw the obvious dangers: 'No, thanks. I prefer to work it out my own way.'

We stood and shook hands; and as neither of us was able to do, or promise, more at that moment I drove to my next meeting – with Monsieur Legrand, the owner of the local flour mill. Here I found that Jim and one of the Pondard girls – Geneviève – had beaten me to it.

'Anything wrong?' I asked quickly, seeing them 'out in the open'.

'No,' Jim said. 'We saw your car in town, and as I knew you'd be coming here I decided to wait for you so we could get a lift home.'

'Sorry to be so suspicious.'

'Actually, there is some news. Just after you left a signal came in. Three aircraft tonight, and another attack about thirty kilometres south of Malestroit.'

'Good,' I said.

'I've arranged for a protection party for the fourth team's delayed attack. They'll be leaving at midnight, and should be back by three or four in the morning.'

'Even better,' I said.

I hadn't been ignoring Monsieur Legrand, but when Jim got going there was seldom much that anyone could do to stop him. However, at last I faced the mill owner, smiled, and offered my hand.

Over tea, Monsieur Legrand suggested that – on paper – I should become an employee of his, and thus have authority to use one of the mill's cars. This would be a bonus, and especially so when added to Jim's 'extra' news that the mayor was arranging a set of genuine German papers for me with authentic stamps and passes and would hand them over in two days' time at a lunch in the town hall.

Legrand was to be invaluable, for over the years he had come to know almost everyone in the area through supplying flour to the restaurants and bakeries and through collecting wheat from the farmers. Now he was to be doubly invaluable to the Hillbilly circuit by giving me a freedom of movement that was to be the envy of everyone.

I recounted my conversation with the chief of police, at the end of which – and after an exploratory question or two – Monsieur Legrand asked directly if he could help establish and run an intelligence section for us: on the condition, he suggested, that Geneviève acted as the permanent link between us. I could only nod my thanks at each new offer he made. To have the fullest cooperation of the owner of the only mill in the area – and one that was relied upon by the Germans almost more than by the local French – would be a gigantic feather in the resistance cap. It was, however, imperative that he remained above suspicion, for his fall, should that occur, would be catastrophic and wide-ranging, and drag others down with him.

Later, as we turned into the farmyard, I was surprised to see a worried-looking Alexis Babin pacing backwards and forwards and hardly able to stop himself from being run over as he snatched open my door. Before I could utter one word he was talking fast.

'Bad news, sir,' he burbled – 'I've killed Hauffmann.'

I thought that this was probably good news, but said only, 'Take your time, Alexis, once the others are here.' Turning to Jim, I asked that Marienne be fetched as soon as possible.

'Damn it,' said Jim, 'that's all we need', and he hurried off towards Marienne's tent.

Once settled, I nodded for Alexis to start.

He took a deep breath and, without stopping, spoke for five or so minutes in a quiet, almost frightened, voice. 'After I left you I took five men to Sérent by car and parked at the back of a small café at the outskirts of the town. Then I posted my men one by one at five observation points and went myself to the café opposite where Hauffmann lives,' he paused to add softly, 'or was living.'

Nobody smiled. We all knew that Hauffmann was better dead, but we also knew that, welcome though that news probably was, it was likely to herald the beginning of fresh problems.

'After about half an hour Hauffmann turned up with his body-guard and was met at the hotel entrance by his mistress, who came out on to the pavement. She kissed and gave him quite a welcome. God! I ask you. In public. She's one of us. She knows what he and his men are doing. She must have guessed, too, that their days were numbered. If she has to have a German lover . . .' he couldn't find the words, '. . . why . . . why . . . why flaunt it?'

We shared the disgust that Alexis put into his words.

'Apparently this time he was not in a mood for affection – public or private,' this time we did smile – 'and began talking with great animation. I could hear everything perfectly clearly. He said, "I've discovered where all those maquisards are hiding, and those para-chutists who've been dropping in my area. This evening I'm going to see the district general and sort them out once and for all, before they have time to get properly organized. When I catch the bastards I'll get a load of satisfaction from seeing them in jail."'

Jail was probably the last place he would 'see' us. The execution squad was our more likely fate,

'He was yelling at this stage, and didn't seem to mind who heard. Then he dismissed his driver and bodyguards and told them to return in an hour, when they would take him to the local German army headquarters. As he went inside I decided that we should capture him then and there.' He looked round the table: 'Did we not agree that that was an acceptable option?' All except Geneviève, who had not been at the earlier meeting, nodded.

'Well then, we had one hour to take advantage of the situation. His bodyguard had gone, and he was about to be preoccupied with his mistress. I signalled to the others to join me at the car, where we unpacked our weapons, got into our seats, and drove up to the hotel's front door.

'There was no time to lose, as we didn't want to give him time to barricade himself into his bedroom, so, with the engine running, we ran into the lobby. He was there all right, leaning against the bar already, with his woman in one hand and a drink in the other.

'He saw us and dropped both, turned, and ran upstairs. We didn't fire. My orders had been not to do so – unless in self-defence. As he disappeared he shouted, "Come and get me you bastards – if you dare!" then roared with a laughter that echoed down from the first floor. We dared all right.'

No one said a word.

'We rushed past the two women. The one on the outside of the bar was his mistress, but there was another behind the bar. Anyway, we tried to ignore them and ran for the stairs, but the mistress was screaming her head off. She must have recognized me. I've lived here all my life, and I certainly knew her by sight.

'Anyway, I told her three times to shut up, but that only made her shouting worse, so we had to tie her up and gag her with a tablecloth. When two of my men had done that, myself and the others made for the stairs – just as Hauffmann threw a grenade. We had time to leap behind the bar to join the younger girl, but because the other stupid bitch had forced us to immobilize her she couldn't move. The grenade landed alongside her, and she was killed instantly.

'I motioned to everyone to lie quiet, and the trick worked, for slowly Hauffmann crept down the stairs. I don't know what he thought he was going to do, but he just emptied his pistol in the general direction of the bar without seeing us and ran back – we assumed to reload and wait to see what had happened.'

'Didn't he care about his mistress?' someone asked.

'He can't have seen her at that stage. Anyway, we couldn't leave the situation as it was, so, while I planned to hide beneath the stairs, I whispered to the others that they were to leave with as much noise as possible, rev the car so Hauffmann could hear it, then drive quietly round to the back of the hotel and wait. When all that had happened I ordered the girl, at the point of my pistol, to shout up to Hauffmann that we had gone and it was safe to come down. I would then try to get him. As it happened, it only partly worked out like that.'

Alexis paused, but as no one said a word he drew another deep breath and continued.

'When the five lads had left and I was hidden with my Sten gun, I told the girl to begin shouting. She called "Monsieur Hauffmann! Monsieur Hauffmann!" I heard him open his door and come out on to the landing above my head. "Yes, Marie?" he half whispered. "They've gone, Monsieur Hauffmann." "All of them, Marie?" "Yes, Monsieur Hauffmann." "I thought they would." It must have dawned on him then that his mistress was dead, for he ran down the stairs crying, "Oh! What have I done?" then dropped his pistol and collapsed on his knees beside her body. She had taken the full force of the grenade at point-blank range, and there was blood and intestines smeared all across the floor around her. It can't have been pleasant for him I'm glad to say!

'He started screaming, "I've killed her, I've killed her", with his back to me while trying to hug her back to life, but it was too late for that. So, as that was the only chance I was going to get, I stood over him and said, "Hauffmann, put your hands up!"'

'You should have shot him!'

'I know, but as I didn't actually want to kill him I hesitated, and in those seconds he'd grabbed his gun and begun to swing round towards me. He was in an awkward position, astride his mistress with his knees in pools of blood. I had no choice but to give him a burst from a metre or so and he fell alongside his lover. He died as quickly as she had – which was a pity, for I'd have liked him to have suffered!

'Anyway, the deed was done, and I rushed upstairs to his room, grabbed what papers and documents I could find – plus his identity card and another gun – and ran out of the hotel to the car. As I left I shouted to the barmaid to call the police and to tell them exactly what had happened. She was in a terrible state, but I think they'll believe her. She should be all right, and I doubt if the Gestapo will harm her.

'We drove for about an hour, left the car with a friend, and came back here via separate routes.'

Alexis sat back, exhausted from the telling and still shattered by the events. No one spoke, each calculating what the results might be, for we knew that the death of a Gestapo colonel was unlikely to go unpunished.

Marienne was the first to speak. 'Does the barmaid know you, Alexis?'

'Yes, my name and where I live. She once worked for my father.'

'Does she know the others?'

'No.'

'So at present you're the only one who can be traced?'

'Yes.'

'Right,' Marienne continued. 'We'll send a runner to your family right away, and hope we beat the Germans to it. They must go into hiding immediately. You'll have to stay in the Maquis for a few days until we see how this works out. You did a pretty good job. It's just bad luck it turned out how it did, but the way I see it it couldn't be helped. Hauffmann deserved all he got.

'You'll continue setting up the intelligence network from here for the time being. Send a few carefully selected men into town to find out what's happening – check on any curfews, restrictions, arrests and so on. Send a reliable man to the chief of police, and also to Monsieur Legrand: he can run your show for you for now, under your orders. We've had a close shave, and in future will need to take more care. We can't stop our local boys going into town and indeed living at home – everything must appear normal – but they must be extra vigilant.

'I know it's difficult for the men here to keep quiet, but I'd bet my last shirt that Hauffmann found out where we are through idle talk. You got to him in time, Alexis. Now your next job is to find out who did the talking and bring him to me.'

The meeting broke up amid muted congratulations for Alexis while I made my way to the wireless station.

'What's the confirming message for tonight's drop?' I asked.

'"Three friends will visit you tonight and drink a toast to Peter."'

'Thanks,' I said, and left for a few hours' sleep to find that a welcome change had taken place in the sleeping arrangements. Where there had been one tent, shared by Marienne and me, there was now a second tent, the two linked with a communications flap.

After a wash and a change back into uniform I returned to the farm, where at 2115 that evening the BBC relayed the message of Peter and his drinks. At 2230 we were on the edge of La Baleine: the three aircraft arrived on time, and the whole drop was completed in fourteen minutes – leaving us the stronger by fifteen men and many containers. Then, at midnight, the previous night's team of saboteurs left for its operation, allowing Marienne, Jim and I to enjoy a final cup of coffee by the Pondards' fire before trying out the new sleeping arrangements. As we left the kitchen I ordered the duty officer not to wake us unless there was an emergency. Briefings on the night's operations could wait till the morning.

Lying with a last cigarette, I said loudly to Marienne through our connecting 'door', 'What do you think of the set-up? Too many men are still going into town with their weapons – we only have two fully equipped battalions and, although everyone is doing his best, if we're attacked in this camp there'll be a shambles.'

'I was going to have a defence exercise now that we have the two battalions. Let's talk about that in the morning, but right now I'm packing it in.'

'OK, goodnight,' I said. But I had one final question: 'What do you think of this Hauffmann thing?'

'I don't like it. Hauffmann got his ticket, but the Germans aren't going to take it lying down so long as they are running the show in this part of France.'

I nodded in the darkness.

'They may be slow,' Marienne continued, 'but when they do wake up they're ruthless. They want to rule the world, and they don't like being prevented from doing so. They'll make us pay for his death, and I don't think we shall like it very much either.'

6. Enter the Colonel

The bright glare of a Brittany summer's dawn woke me gently after the first night's full sleep since our arrival, and I celebrated with a cigarette. More good news appeared in the form of Jim, bearing three mugs of tea. 'Get up, the pair of you,' he said, then changed his mind as he watched Marienne, draped in a parachute, stagger through the adjoining tent flap to sit on my bed. 'No. Don't. Hide your faces. My God! If there was a mirror here it would shatter.'

'How sweet you are!' Marienne said. 'Thanks for the tea, by the way, but why all the insults?'

'Geneviève will be here shortly with your breakfast, and I don't think it fair she should see you two in this state.'

Marienne hitched the joining flap back and slipped into his bed with a grin just as Geneviève pushed her way through the 'front door' with a tray on which were balanced luxuries almost unheard of in England: fresh eggs, white French bread, butter – 'Butter!' I exclaimed – and a huge pot of real coffee.

Breakfast – happy and relaxed – gave way to a more serious discussion as Marienne brought us back to reality: 'Jim. Any news from last night?'

'Yes. First of all, your fourth team did their job in a most spectacular manner.'

I raised an eyebrow. Results were important, but spectacular displays, in my limited experience, tended to draw attention. I was not, though, expecting what Jim had to say.

'They arrived at their railway line, but, after a reconnaissance, decided there was a more useful way to deal with the problem – and one which would also save explosive. They called on the stationmaster and asked if they might borrow some tools – especially the special spanners used by *les cheminots* when they lay or repair the track. Then, while they were unscrewing sections of track, they sent a maquisard back here for a lorry and a few men, and that's why this morning we have fifty metres of rail and a lorryload of wood, and the Germans have a track that is cut for twenty-five metres and a derailed train. And', he finished, 'they weren't molested. Everything went off perfectly.'[1]

We laughed. Someone said, 'A few more operations like that and we'll need an engine for our own branch line.'

But there was a serious side, and it was Marienne who, again, posed the question: 'That's all very well, but what are you going to do with this stuff?'

'Easy,' replied Jim. 'I'm using the rails to make tank traps. We're going to cut them into smaller lengths and sink them in the ground at an angle with cement. We can now build those Bren-gun positions you've been talking about so that they'll be properly protected. Other lengths will be used on the main paths into the Maquis.' Jim was in his accustomed state of 'full flow', helped by the exhilaration of the night's events and the part his men had played in them. 'You never know, a few more nights like this and you'll only be able to get in and out of the Maquis by aircraft.'

I asked if there was any further news.

'This morning we received reports from the Malestroit police to say that, surprisingly, so far there's been no action by the Germans after Hauffmann's death. In fact all that's happened is that the gendarmes have been told that it's their business to deal with that sort of thing. So,' he ended, 'no immediate worry.'

'Odd,' I ventured, 'considering past performances.'

'Maybe. Anyway, to more mundane affairs. A number of our men were in town again last night – showing off their new weapons. I've cancelled all leave until further notice.'

'It should have been done before,' Marienne growled. 'Then perhaps Hauffmann might not have known we existed. Anything else?'

'I can report that three battalions are now fully equipped, with the others remaining understrength as far as arms are concerned – but that should change tonight. All the containers are hidden underground, so the Maquis is beginning to look tidy again and not like a military base.'

'Excellent,' I said.

'Forty parachutes, not needed by the doctor, have been distributed to improve the men's sleeping arrangements; the men who arrived last night are with their platoons; the intelligence section is forming into something that I hope will be excellent; our two prisoners are employed sewing and repairing uniforms; and, finally, if we get a quiet day La Baleine will be levelled for aircraft to land by tomorrow. And that's about it for this breakfast-time!'

Washed and shaved, we strode round the Maquis, starting with an inspection of the two new Bren-gun positions either side of the main entrance and staggered by fifty yards or so. The left, forward, one was well concealed in the ditch and embankment and already sprouting two guns and a smiling crew. The rear position was larger and equipped with a PIAT, a large stack of projectiles and two Brens.

'Now you can see,' said Jim proudly. 'It's between these two positions that I shall dig in some rails, leaving just enough room for our jeeps to zigzag through – when we get them.'

There was a noticeable difference among the maquisards: they still laughed and joked, but now with a rather more professional undercurrent to their banter. They knew – they had had positive proof – that they were part of the whole for once and not just a sideshow waiting to happen. Added to that, their own dropping zone – La Baleine – was being upgraded to a landing zone. Fifty or so men, stripped to the waist, were levelling out bumps, heaving on tufts of grass and young roots, cutting bushes, and sweating in the noon sun.

Time was not plentiful, but they deserved a break. 'Back to the farm everyone,' ordered Jim. 'Monsieur Pondard has cooled the cider.' No further orders were needed as we followed the maquisards back to the shaded farmyard and a smiling proprietor.

'Did you realize', said Jim, studying the clear, pale liquid in his glass, 'that in this Maquis alone we drink over a thousand litres of cider a day? I know there's plenty of cider in Brittany – and we get it from a number of farms, so that's fine – but that's still quite a lot.'

We nodded dutifully. He then exclaimed, 'Meat! We have pigs, cows and horses, so that's not a problem either. But there are other things we need – such as cigarettes and tobacco, sugar, milk, coffee and flour. Did you know that we eat precisely 125 grams of bread per man per day?'

We shook our heads.

'We're helped enormously by the local farms and shops, but at present we must account for 50 francs per man per day, or a grand total of nearly 175,000 francs per day.' He seemed determined to ruin the warm summer day. 'We get a lot of things for nothing, and requisition others, but the bills are running up and I'd feel happier if I could settle one or two of them. People are being kind, but they have to live too.'[2]

Marienne broke the monologue: 'Colonel Bourgoin will be bringing money with him, so I suggest we make a list of those you want to pay first.'

'I shall also be receiving money in a few days,' I added, 'and have asked for 5 million francs. We can always return them if we don't use them!'

Geneviève's face at the open window brought us back to the present. 'We're having lunch outside today,' she announced, and with no need for a second invitation we filed out and followed her swaying summer dress to the orchard, where the sisters had erected a parachute as a sunshade over a long wooden table.

The duty wireless operator broke up our brief oasis of peace. 'Two signals for you, sir,' he said, waving a message pad.

'Read them, please.'

'"For Bob and Marienne – Colonel arriving tonight with three aircraft – containers and jeeps. Forty men with him. Colonel jumping number one in first aircraft."'

'Is that right? I thought it was in two days' time. Any chance of a mistake?'

'No, sir. We checked the message twice, and it's correct. It'll be confirmed on the BBC tonight, but we'll have an extra link with London at 2000 hours to confirm the drop.'

'And the second signal?'

'"More aircraft tonight will follow at ten-minute intervals. Good luck to all."'

'Right, thank you. Acknowledge the signals, send the daily sitrep, and tell London that you're closing down until 2000.'

1. André's mother, a Welsh woman whose maiden name was Caroline Hunter.

2. His mother later in life, in Red Cross uniform.

3. and 4. André's father, also called André Hue. The portrait (*right*) was taken in Wales: after the First World War he worked on a merchant ship that plied between Le Havre and South Wales. The other picture (*below*) was taken earlier, during the First World War, in Dunkirk.

5. (*right*) André working as a junior trainee purser on the SS *Normandie* in the late 1930s.

6. The Royal Victoria Patriotic School in Wandsworth, south London, was run by MI5 to screen returning agents. André arrived here from France in late February 1944.

7. and 8. Pre-war photographs of Guer: the town square and the railway station. It was at the Café de la Place, to the right of the tall building in the top photograph, that André later set up his own 'unofficial' Maquis while working at the station from where he passed on information.

9. André's identity card, made out in the name of 'Alfred Havet', was issued to him in the UK before his return to France on 6 June 1944.

ÉTABLISSEMENTS
NEVEU
MALESTROIT (Morbihan)
S. A. R L. 1.500.000
R. C. Ploërmel N° 7
TÉLÉPHONE 4

Nous soussignés, SOCIETE DES ETABLISSEMENTS NEVEU, certifions que Mr HAVET, Alfred, est employé dans nos Etablissements en qualité de chef de dépôt et qu'une bicyclette lui est indispensable, tant pour visiter la clientèle de la région que vue de ses déplacements dans nos différentes Usines.

Malestroit, le 10 Juin 1944.

10. A letter claiming that 'Havet' needed a bicycle in the course of his work.

11. Lieutenant Marienne dropped into France with André and was killed at Kérihuel a few weeks after the battle at Saint-Marcel. He is buried by the war memorial at Plumelec.

12. Emile Bouëtard landed with André and Marienne, and was killed in the ensuing skirmishes: it could be said that he was the first casualty of the Allied invasion.

13. The one-armed Colonel Bourgoin (*left*) landed at La Nouette a few nights after André was dropped. He is seen here talking to Marienne's deputy, Lieutenant Déplante.

14. Emile Guimard ('Jim'), whom André had first known as the organizer of the northernmost part of the escape route out of France. He briefed André when André arrived at La Nouette.

15. Monsieur Pondard in characteristic pose.

16. Fields at La Nouette (*below*). This is the extension to the landing zone, known as La Baleine, at a right angle to the strip itself.

17. La Nouette (*below*) was restored after the war, having been destroyed during the battle.

18. Madame Pondard with her five daughters. Geneviève is on the far left, and Anna on the far right. The photograph is believed to date from 1946.

19. Three of the Pondard sisters (*left to right*, Marguerite, Alphonsine and Anna) sitting on a parachute container.

20. The arrival from the air of a typical metal canister (known as Type-C) containing provisions and arms.

21. Radio operators Jean Paulin and Alexandre Charbonnier. The photograph was taken at La Nouette on 16 June 1944, two days before the battle.

22. Local maquisards in an armed jeep.

The duty operator saluted and ducked under the parachute's flapping edge.

I turned to the faces round the table. 'Just as well we managed a good sleep last night. I suggest we get the intelligence section to float about in town tonight. I want them to check on German reactions.'

As the girls began to clear away the lunchtime debris I looked across at Marienne. The war was about to start properly for us: up to now we had been preparing and playing at it with nightly sabotage excursions, but with the arrival of Bourgoin things would change up a few gears.

'Marienne,' I emphasized, 'from tomorrow morning a number of worries will shift from my back on to the Colonel's.'

'You're fortunate. You're British and attached to us with equal rights and authority as the Colonel, and of course not under his command. For you there'll be no changes. Personally I'm glad he's coming. There are too many majors and captains, and with me being a lieutenant – albeit a regular one – it's sometimes tricky to give orders.'

'I can't give Bourgoin orders when he arrives. My job is simply to hand over the Maquis in good condition.'

'So what do you do when he turns up?'

'Organize your supplies, weapons and money; coordinate the sabotage operations, demolitions and ambushes as required by the Allies. And if we're kicked out of here and dispersed over the countryside it'll be my job to do the running-about and gather you all together again.'

'Well, be all that as it may, I'm looking forward to seeing the old man again.'

The rest of the day was spent in peace, apart from an intelligence report that the Germans were now scouring the country for Babin. We agreed that the men preparing La Baleine for landings should stop their work and either rest or prepare for the long night ahead. While they did that, I changed into civilian clothes, borrowed a bicycle, and took off round the area to visit neighbouring farms.

By 6.30 that evening I was back in the Maquis – in uniform – where I found Marienne, Jim and the Pondards drinking cider in the courtyard. Dinner had been planned for eight o'clock, but we asked to delay it a few minutes until after the confirmation from London that the Colonel would be arriving. It came, or rather it didn't come, at twenty past.

The duty signaller handed me his message pad, on which was scrawled in pencil, 'Colonel's drop delayed until tomorrow night. Four aircraft tonight. Lieutenant Fleuriot in fourth to speak to Bob or Marienne.'

'That's fine,' I said, turning to the officers. 'We need more time anyway. The usual men can handle tonight's drop, and we'll keep the intelligence team floating for an extra night – and that'll do no harm.'

'*D'accord*,' said Marienne.

'How will Fleuriot speak to you?' Jim asked. 'Is he dropping?'

'No,' I replied. 'He's the battalion intelligence officer and he'll be using the S-phone. We have one here. When the aircraft's about thirty kilometres away we'll tune in the two sets and talk. It's like using an ordinary telephone, except that it's fitted with a microphone and earpiece.'

The night's drop went smoothly, and by the end the Maquis had five fully equipped and armed battalions. The news from Lieutenant Fleuriot was mixed: the Colonel's drop had been delayed, as the Maquis to our north and west was under intense pressure from the Germans. This was worrying news, but with it came the instruction to send a party to investigate and if necessary order the Maquis to withdraw into our area. 'Fine,' someone said, 'but there are thousands of them.'

Better news was Marienne's promotion to captain.

Back in the Pondards' kitchen Jim agreed to send a reconnaissance party to the north and west at dawn, and while that was being planned Monsieur Pondard disappeared to return with a bottle of champagne so we could toast the new promotion properly.

In fact Jim sent two teams out at four that morning, and by dawn all of our own defence teams were operational. Every man in the Maquis had been issued with four days' emergency rations in case we needed to take to the country at no notice, and there was agreement to lessen our immediate stocks of equipment by spreading it round local farms and in hedges and woods. This included two new wireless sets which had already – and fortuitously – been dispatched to two nearby farms.

'From now on,' I said, 'anything not required in camp will be concealed in small caches spread across the countryside or in the more isolated farms.'

We received no news from Jim's reconnaissance teams, but we did have confirmation of the Colonel's impending arrival for that night – and that he would be jumping from the first of fifteen aircraft, beneath a large red, white and blue parachute!

'I hope it is large,' Marienne commented – 'he's ninety kilos without his equipment.'

Just before eleven Marienne and I made our way to La Baleine. The wait was short, the aircraft on time, and as we searched skyward the rumble of heavy engines increased.

Marienne, grabbing my arm, waved a hand in the darkness beyond the downwind torch: 'There!' At six hundred feet and heading directly towards the dimly lit flarepath was the black shape of an aircraft. Then, with a sudden increase in noise, it passed overhead, leaving five bodies and a number of containers swinging silently beneath parachutes.

As soon as it had deployed in the slipstream the Colonel's parachute was recognized, encouraging a number of maquisards to run on to the flarepath to help the one-armed landing. But his feet did not hit the ground first, for his bottom landed squarely on the head of a Maquis soldier, down whose back he slithered awkwardly to the grass, from where Marienne escorted him to the edge of the field against the swarm of men rushing forward to grab the containers. Apart from that individual landing, it had been a good drop, with all parachutes touching down within the field's boundary. I caught up with Marienne and the Colonel, who was vigorously rubbing his backside with his one hand.

'Good evening, sir, and welcome home.' I thought that was a proper start to his entry into the war. 'Pleasant trip? Good landing?' I wasn't sure that the last question was appropriate, but felt that correct form required it.

'Hello, Bob,' he said, and as soon as we had shaken hands – he with his left hand – he resumed the rubbing. 'Glad to meet you at last. The trip was excellent, but my ninety kilos landed on a small field that consisted of the hair of just one man!' He turned to Marienne: 'Is he all right?'

'Unconscious, Colonel. The doctor already has him on his way to our little hospital.'

'Now, Bob and Marienne, the next fourteen aircraft will each drop ten containers, four men and up to twelve bulky packages. Four of the planes will drop one jeep each. Somewhere in the drop will be a container with a million francs. It'll be obviously marked, so, while I'm certain that your men are honest, make sure it gets to the HQ quickly. Not as much as we'd hoped, but there'll be more.'

That was my job, and I assured the Colonel that the money would be safeguarded.

'The packages are clothing, and they'll be dropped free in the first pass, so I suggest that you keep the dropping zone clear. There'll be 120 of them, and I think, funny though it may have seemed, one man knocked out is one man too many.'

Keeping the dropping zone clear was not to be as easy as we had planned, for almost as soon as the Colonel had turned for the farm with Marienne the sounds of first one then many aircraft shattered the brief peace.

'Two more coming – no, three more,' someone shouted.

'There's another one over there,' another voice called in the darkness.

'And another two,' added the first voice.

Within a minute, ten four-engined aircraft were circling La Baleine. I yelled to the men running across the strip ready to meet anything on the end of a parachute, 'Keep off the dropping zone! Some packages are without chutes.'

As I shouted, the aircraft began their run-in one behind the other at about two hundred feet, leaving the packages to thump sharply into the ground with a sound like distant, heavy machine-gun fire. When at last the final aircraft had roared into the darkness, men hurried frantically across the scrub to drag the packages clear, so that the next pass, if it included men, would have a flat dropping zone.

Then, as suddenly as they had first arrived, the converted bombers – now much higher, and in groups of twos and threes – separated and, with less than ten seconds between them, thundered towards Monsieur Pondard's humpbacked field again. Containers and men mingled together like confetti caught in a gust of wind. It was not what we were expecting, and I called Jim to ask if he had another hundred men to help clear the area.

'They're dropping them too high,' I shouted across the chaos. 'They're drifting way off target. See if you can get your men into the woods.' The aircraft circled back and began another run-in, but this time at under five hundred feet. Fearing yet more free-fall parachutes I yelled again for the area to be cleared, but the planes roared overhead with their engines at full power as they rose, in salute, up into the night sky and away.

'Magnificent,' I muttered, 'but every damned German between here and Berlin must have heard them.'

Some parachutes had failed to open, and we worried that we might find a new arrival unconscious on the field. Any hope of identifying the container full of francs was lost – indeed, in the excitement and confusion I had forgotten all about it. Between Jim, Marienne and myself we organized a search of both the field and the neighbouring woods, while the Colonel, who had reappeared by the flarepath, was not amused – although glad that, so far, there were no reports of any more casualties.

'Up to now,' I said at the hastily convened debriefing, 'we've had eleven aircraft, which means four more – and we haven't had the jeeps yet.'

But somewhere we must have missed out on a message – either that or plans had changed even after Colonel Bourgoin had climbed into his first aircraft – for, over the next two hours, we received five more waves of aircraft, the first of eight and the second and third of five each. The first of these waves was again too high, forcing Jim to order a second search party into the woods. The jeeps came in the second, even higher, wave, their arrival heralded by a ripple of sharp cracks as the multiple parachutes above each one burst open.

Men landing off the zone were one thing, but jeeps were quite another matter. 'They're about to land on the roof,' shouted Jim. And he was nearly right, for one landed two yards in front of the farm's door, enveloping the roof completely in silk. Another hit the edge of an unused barn's roof before sliding rather elegantly to the ground, where it rested with all four wheels still firmly parked on their wooden pallet.

A fourth wave of aircraft came in perfectly to drop its loads along the centre line of the flarepath. No running about was necessary, but, even so, this drop was to produce the greatest surprise – and loss – of all.

Only one parachute failed to open, and as its container hit the ground there was an ominous explosion that was only partly masked by the departing aircraft's engines before flames began to illuminate the surrounding field. As we watched this unexpected and certainly unusual display, Colonel Bourgoin began running towards it, gathering helpers as he went. Marienne and I, now only partially engrossed in our tasks of removing men and equipment, half watched until we saw the Colonel on his knees trying to grab at something then jumping back into the night only to repeat the process. As his shadow and silhouette danced and flickered across the grass, he appeared for all the world to be conducting some strange pagan ritual.

'Come on,' Marienne called, 'we'd better see what the problem is.'

A sinking feeling swept over me as I followed behind. We hadn't yet seen the money container, and not much else would have had the Colonel reacting so quickly.

A maquisard rushed past us shouting, 'I'm going to get some buckets. The money's on fire!'

'Throw earth on it,' I shouted, but it was too late to save much, if anything. In desperation we scooped up handfuls of dry earth, but without spades it was a forlorn gesture. The time pencils – to prevent the money falling into the wrong hands if not recovered quickly – had been triggered by the impact, setting fire to sticks of plastic explosive.

We were forced to abandon our paltry efforts by the arrival of yet another wave of aircraft. Was there to be no end to this unheralded largesse, I thought? Then I reflected, rather ungraciously, that the drop might have been better conducted by the pilots. Of course they were risking their lives, but so were we on the ground, while German night-time opposition along the approaches was minimal if not non-existent.

However, one man unconscious, a few containers bent by unintended free fall and some francs lost was a small price to pay for the largest resupply we had yet received and, in all probability, were ever likely to receive.

'That's got to be it,' I said. The Colonel nodded, and I added, 'I hope it's not ungrateful to say so, but a damned good thing too!'

We headed for the farm.

The lorries were running their practised shuttle service between La Baleine and the farmyard, and every so often we ducked under containers swinging from parachutes caught in the trees. The path was crowded and littered with the detritus that followed a large drop, and it took us ten minutes to reach the farm, where groups of men stood surrounded by containers and soft mounds of silk. Everyone was animated and talking hurriedly.

Smiling and joking, we made our way to the sanctity of the Pondards' kitchen. Marienne, Jim and I were tall men, but the three of us were dwarfed by the six feet three inches and fourteen stone of the one-armed Colonel Bourgoin. Thickly built, broad-shouldered and with a cold, hard face, he kept his good, left, hand in his pocket. Monsieur Pondard waved to the table, and we pulled back chairs while the girls poured coffee and Calvados.

After toasts to France, to the success of the landings and to the Pondards, Colonel Bourgoin began the serious business. 'I've got a message for you, Bob. From your boss. Here it is.'

I took the crumpled envelope, slit it open with my thumb, and read the enclosure. 'Tomorrow night French Major Hauteur will bring ten million francs, two suitcases, special stores, ten containers with medical stores plus twenty containers of weapons. Getting your messages alright. Best of luck. Hope to see you in two months.'

'We'll need the money,' muttered the Colonel grimly.

We were missing a Lieutenant Herang, along with one or two others. Jim had noticed one aircraft dropping off the line, and it was in the woods near by that he eventually found the young

French officer. Back at the farm and delirious – he had landed head first, but was convinced he had been hit on the head by the Germans – he was soon placated with the doctor's morphine.

All in all the tally for the drop included 150 men and four jeeps – each designed to be fitted with twin Vickers machine guns in the front and a single machine gun in the rear. But, on the negative side, the containers holding the Vickers had all suffered parachute malfunctions, presenting us with bent and twisted weapons. As well as the Colonel's personal one-man landing zone, other injuries included two broken ankles, one broken arm and a broken collar-bone – work that for once kept the doctor happy and withdrawing his threat to take a holiday unless patients could be found for him.

7. Trouble with the Neighbours

Too exhilarated to sleep, we sat – in silence to begin with – drinking hot drinks heavily laced with brandy until it was decided that the night should continue with an early breakfast. We ate this knowing that it was probably the last peaceful moment we would enjoy. If the Germans were not to bring the war to us as a result of the night's activities, which they could not possibly have missed, we were about to take the war to them. Then, with our cups refilled and our pipes and cigarettes lit, I gave the Colonel a summary of the situation as I saw it. I had been rehearsing this moment for some days.

'First, although we have men spread across the area and we have men out on operations, as well as those who are working from home until we can arm them or have work for them, there are too many here. You'll want to run this Maquis – and the other one at Samwest – your way, but I'll be retaining responsibility for drops, intelligence and special operations. If we're kicked out of here, I'll be the chap who'll have to run round reorganizing ourselves. I'm also responsible for wireless communications, local contacts and a variety of other things, and in my opinion it's crazy to have all these people based on this one headquarters.'

Nothing I was saying was news to him – all of it had been agreed in England – but now it needed updating to match what I had found and what had evolved since my arrival.

'You and your staff, with fifty of your men, should be in a quiet place, out of the way of the Boche. Somewhere where you can plan, and from where operations can be conducted in security.'

As he made no comment I continued, 'The Maquis should be split into groups of 225 men each, with each group responsible for its own tactical area of operations, operating out of its own secure area. That way we and the other Maquis should cover both Samwest and Dingson without men having many kilometres of dangerous ground to cross each time they mount an operation. We need bags of sabotage, masses of ambushes, demolitions, control of key roads; and, in general, we need to tie Jerry up here and prevent him from reaching Normandy.

'Secondly, it's even more crazy to have so many aircraft dropping on to one zone in the same night. I want at least four dropping zones and thus more internal safety. And thirdly, Colonel, supplies. We must have dozens of dumps spread across the countryside.' I stopped, thought for a moment, then said, 'And I think that's about it.'

'Thank you, Bob. At least you know what you want.' He turned to Marienne. 'What about you, Captain?'

'I agree with what Bob has said. We've worked out that we could have a complete network across the whole of our territory, and that way the Boche would have no area in which they would be safe and no large groups to target.'

'Thank you.' He turned to Jim: 'And you?'

'I'm not sure we have time to reorganize. We should start operations immediately. If we stay here and send, say, a thousand or even two thousand out on operations, would not that simplify our situation? If we are attacked here, or anywhere else for that matter, we can always withdraw.'

'That's too simple,' Marienne said. 'We don't have our supplies spread across the countryside. If we have to withdraw we might not be able to fight for long.'

'I know, but moving the way Bob wants may be even more complicated.'

'What do you say, Bob?' the Colonel asked.

'I've lived in these parts of Brittany. It's an easy matter to move men around. We don't know how long it will be before the Allies reach us – maybe a month, or even two. The northern Maquis is in a jam. If we stay here we'll suffer in the same way, as I don't expect the Boche to sit back and simply stare at us. They must know what we're here to do, and if I was them I'd start carrying out some pre-emptive strikes. We've got to be ready to hit back, but that will be possible only if we're split up into more easily managed groups yet under central control. We've a whole day of clearing canisters ahead, and it'll take only one enemy aircraft to overfly us – photograph us – and we really will be in the stew.'

The Colonel agitated his armless right shoulder and sucked at his cooling coffee before speaking. 'Thank you all,' he said. 'We can think it over for a day and make a decision tomorrow.'

I didn't think this was good. We needed action, which was one of the reasons I had persuaded everyone that there had not been time to turn in.

However, for the moment there was nothing either Marienne or I could do: we had aired our views, and must wait to hear the result. Yet another cup of coffee appeared, which we drank while the Colonel summoned the officers with whom he had jumped the previous evening, some of whom I had met during my SOE training, while others – there were eight in all – were newcomers to the battalion. After introductions and a brief moment to catch up on news of old friends, we set off on a tour of the Maquis and the ground over which we might have to fight. La Baleine was the first of many stops where lorries continued to labour across the zone collecting containers and parachutes, some of which still hung limply from surrounding trees.

It had been impossible to clear the dropping zone of equipment before daylight, and, though obviously we were grateful for the supplies – 240 containers that night alone – it would have been an easy matter for any German aircraft flying overhead to have spotted precisely what was going on. Again I pointed this out to Bourgoin, to add emphasis to my earlier statement, but he only nodded.

We carried on round the tracks and wooded paths that criss-crossed the Maquis, so that all could see just how much stronger our defences were already becoming – emphasized, back at the farm, by the four jeeps armed with Bren guns (not the damaged Vickers) mounted across their bonnets, their engines running as though anxious to be off that very moment.

Alexis Babin – heading the intelligence-gathering section, and thus himself high on the Germans' wanted list – was also waiting.

'My men', he started breathlessly while at the same time trying to gulp a deep draught of cider, 'spent two nights in the towns in the Maquis area. The first drop went off without the Germans, or any civilian that we could find, suspecting anything, but the one last night was a different matter, and no sooner had they got wind of it than they were on the town-hall's roofs and those of the school with their powerful night field glasses. Early this morning they put an observation post in Saint-Marcel's church spire, and they've now done the same with Plumelec's water tower.' Marienne and I had a passing acquaintance with this tower, for, thanks to faulty navigation, it was close to where we had landed just a few days earlier.

'In the towns and villages the curfew now runs from eleven p.m. to six a.m., while during the day there are ten-man patrols cycling round the country. This morning the lieutenant-colonel commanding the Malestroit troops was summoned to the Coëtquidan military camp to see the general, so heaven knows what will come as a result of that – except that, right now, every civilian is being checked at home and again on the roads.'

It was probably prejudicial to his safety for Alexis Babin – a civilian – to continue running the intelligence section, so, with the Colonel's concurrence, a new arrival, Lieutenant Fleuriot, the battalion intelligence officer to whom I had spoken by S-phone during an earlier drop, was appointed in his place. Alexis would continue to be the mainstay, but he was now freed from the administration and thus, we hoped, less likely to be compromised when he emerged from his temporary hiding place.

This sudden reappointment must have spurred the Colonel, for he now decided to make others. And so, in that almost haphazard manner, the future of the Maquis in its more belligerent role began. Bourgoin's orders were, he reminded us, to raise a full-scale revolt in Brittany, and for that to happen my circuit of Hillbilly with all its contacts, plus eighteen three-man SAS rail-cutting teams – code-named Cooney – who had dropped on the night of 7/8 June and the Samwest Maquis, were now all under his operational control.

We had been receiving reports that the railway was already being seriously disrupted: the main line between Paris and Quimper had been cut in two places in Brittany. The result was that the enemy's movement of the 3rd Parachute Division out of our area between

11 and 14 June had to be conducted by road, requiring a great deal of precious petrol.

Colonel Bourgoin's 4th Parachute Battalion was at last up to strength so, while the Germans puzzled how they could beat us across our own countryside, his four hundred personnel were split into teams of eight or ten, with a number of teams attached to each Maquis battalion. Detailed study of the map – when added to my and Jim's knowledge of the area, plus recent reconnaissance sorties by bicycle – now suggested areas where the subunits should be stationed in the very near future.

Of greater significance – and importance, as it was to turn out – a meeting place was chosen and agreed should the Maquis have to disperse before that. In fact we achieved no more than a general agreement, as the discussion was brought to a premature halt by the appearance of Monsieur Pondard telling us that, as we were now so many, he had 'taken the liberty' of preparing a permanent dining room for us. This previously unused room would double as our ante-room and allow his wife and daughters more space in their kitchen to cook food for the officers and prepare snacks and drinks for those others who were billeted within the farm's immediate surroundings: the signallers, orderlies and messengers.

'My daughters will continue to look after you,' he concluded, 'and will run it like an officers' mess. I hope that is in order.'[1]

It could not have been more in order, and although we had never asked the Pondards for anything – everything had just quietly happened without any conscious decision on anyone's part – it was helpful to know that we really were not going to have to bother about where the next meal was coming from.

No sooner had we received this offer than we were disturbed by less welcome information as the duty runner knocked and entered.

'All but one of the teams – Lieutenant Déplante's – that Jim sent to the northern Maquis are back. Would you like to see them?'

'Yes,' replied the Colonel, anxious for news from Samwest. 'Send in the patrol leaders.'

They stood by the fire, clutching mugs of well-laced coffee.

'A few kilometres before we reached the northern Maquis we came across German roadblocks, and at every one our papers were checked even though the Boche soldiers knew they had just been looked at. Anyway, we managed to make some progress, and as we got closer we could hear long bursts of machine-gun fire, rifles, heavier guns – you know: just about everything.

'About two kilometres from the Maquis HQ we met a friend of ours – a maquisard. Apparently what happened was that a couple of nights ago they had a drop of five aircraft, which the Germans saw. The result was that a platoon was sent to investigate. That was not strong enough and our chaps saw them off, so they then sent a regiment and eventually a full infantry brigade made up of Germans and Russians. The fight continued until last night, when Captain Leblond gave orders to withdraw into the woods and countryside. They had previously practised for such a thing, and all knew where to go and how to get there.'

'Good for them,' someone said.

'Not really,' the reply was laconic. 'The Boche were already there, so the whole of the Samwest Maquis was then ordered to join the southern Maquis – us here at Dingson.'

We looked at each other. There were already far too many of us centred round the Pondards' farm, and a whole new Maquis, perhaps of another two thousand men, would make further mockery of our security – and logistics. They might also be followed by the enemy to our location.

We listened to a few more details, dismissed the patrol leaders – who were thankful to get back to a glass or two with their fellows – and began a replanning conference.

A small party made its way to the church, to see if the Germans had begun any form of action, but the most significant decision was to stay as a full Maquis for one more week in order that the training programme could continue. It was not much time to complete what we had to do, but it was too long to stay still. Anyway, that was the Colonel's decision, and it was against my advice.

None of us was happy, and it was with a gloomy frame of mind that we sat at dinner, listening to the BBC's evening's messages. Confirmation of the night's drop came through at 2330 hours, and when all was over I was 'richer' by 1 million francs rather than the expected 10 million, as the shortfall had apparently not arrived at the airfield by take-off time.

Round the table again, after the last aircraft had left, I handed 500,000 francs to Jim so that he could pay the more urgent of his bills, and after last cups of coffee we headed for our beds. The drop had been comparatively quiet, with no signs of German activity reported.[2]

The next morning it was time to take stock before what I was certain was about to be our own *déluge* – to follow that of Samwest. Our Maquis was now fully armed, a rough tally indicating that there was sufficient surplus to arm another four hundred men and enough clothing for three more battalions. Everyone now held four days' emergency rations, and there were five hundred extra rations should they need to be distributed. We held eight hundred pounds of explosives, several miles of detonating cord, a few hundred yards of fuse, a thousand grenades, and enough ammunition to satisfy the most enthusiastic gunner. We had enough medical supplies to open two large field hospitals plus, vitally, cigarettes and tobacco to keep morale up for weeks. Wireless sets were now plentiful, as were anti-tank mines and tyre-bursters. The only obvious item that was lacking was heavy guns for the jeeps after the disaster a few nights earlier.

As though in recognition of our satisfactory logistic situation, a signaller announced that there would be no drop that evening. More parochially, this meant all night in for those not on guard duty – an almost unheard-of luxury since any of us had arrived – and peace for the Germans in their watchtowers and church belfries. It also gave us time to discuss the imperative move into the countryside.

All that next day stragglers from the northern Maquis, and from the Colonel's 4th Battalion of the French SAS that had been attached to Samwest, drifted in under escort of our teams who were scouring the likely approaches from the Guingamp area. They were tired and hungry, with many suffering from minor gunshot wounds – which pleased the doctor, if no one else.

Captain Leblond himself made it to the farm, enabling us to piece together what had happened. In fact he had not much to tell, for the northern Maquis had been totally outnumbered. Some maquisards had 'run away', several were killed – including their doctor, Monsieur Sasonne – and others were captured, which was, we all agreed, probably the worst fate of all. For the next two days men were to continue drifting in, in various stages of shock and exhaustion.

But Samwest was not alone in its tally of deaths. Lieutenant Herang, fully recovered from his landing, was dispatched shortly after midnight, and by three in the morning he had set up an observation position so that he and his small team could observe the comings and goings of the German patrol based on Saint-Marcel's church. For some reason that we were never to know, he then moved his men to the local café, from where it is believed he thought he could get a better view; but at five a.m. it was decided to return to 'the field'. However, as they left the café, where they themselves had obviously been under observation, he and his men were the target of a long burst of machine-gun fire. Lieutenant Herang was the only casualty, dying instantly. The Germans did not follow up their assault, but disappeared into the dawn light.

Herang had had a bad time: a few days earlier he had landed on his head, and now we were burying him among the flowers of the Pondards' garden. The padre from Malestroit conducted the service, which was attended by all the officers and a number of men from the Maquis and the SAS. Afterwards we placed a simple wooden cross at the head of the grave, bearing the inscription '*Lieut Herang, 4th Battalion Special Air Service. Mort pour la France. Au champ d'honneur. Un bel exemple de courage.*' His young wife and little daughter in England would not see him again.

His was the first death since D-Day within the confines of the Maquis de Saint-Marcel, and it affected us all. But life had to continue if we were to meet our operational-readiness date of 16 June. I cancelled all air drops until we could distribute those supplies that we already had, and we kept our movement out of the camp to a minimum. Intelligence reports came in from which we discovered that there was now a price on the heads of Babin, Jim, Marienne and myself, although how they came by our names was not known. The Germans rounded up a number of Saint-

Marcel villagers for questioning; the police lieutenant of Malestroit sent regular information on German movements. Colonel Bourgoin's officers and men were hard at work training the maquisards. The weather broke, and so parachutes were issued to improve the tenting arrangements in the woods while our carpenters were busy building more secure accommodation. The two female prisoners remained repairing our clothes. Our transport was now up to standard and in good working order, ready for anything. The defences and strongpoints were improved. The medical section was running smoothly, and there was good news about our wounded, all but the most serious of whom, we were assured, would be back to fighting form within three weeks. And, finally, the men from the northern Maquis had established a new Maquis under Leblond about fifteen miles away.

We could now boast that our own Maquis was four thousand strong, while it was estimated that across Brittany there were upwards of twenty thousand maquisards waiting for the order to strike.

Our drops resumed on the night of 13/14 June, but those and others on the 14th/15th and 17th/18th were to be the last, for the Germans had by now set up searchlights with which they began to illuminate the aircraft. On the first occasion the planes had taken fright and dropped containers over, among other places, the town of Malestroit, allowing the Germans to show off their English cigarettes, arms and uniforms to the local French as signs of British incompetence.[3] After 18 June 1944 La Baleine would never receive another drop.

8. A Grand Battle

Within minutes of our final air drop during the night of 17/18 June
– when each aircraft had been lit up as it approached, forcing it to
veer away and make dummy runs over fields some miles away – I
was asleep and expecting to stay that way until at least seven in the
morning: a Sunday. It had been a long day, which had produced
186 containers and four more jeeps, and I had, on purpose, beaten
Marienne into our double-tent arrangement and was asleep before
his snoring could prevent any chance of rest – as it usually did.

But our night of peace was not to be: a burst of gunfire shattered
my dreams, although by the time I was fully awake it had stopped.
I lay back cursing what I assumed had been Marienne's snoring,
and prayed for some escape from his infernal, nocturnal noises. But
his bed – viewed through the hitched-back flap – was empty.
Puzzled, I turned over until another harsh burst startled me into
life – and this time there was no mistake. A Bren gun's staccato
rattling, close indeed, was masked by a violent explosion.

I leaped to the ground and, not knowing what to expect, dressed
quickly and grabbed my carbine, Colt pistol and cash before heading
through the cool early light for the Pondards' farmhouse. It was
nearly five o'clock, and dawn was well under way.

Colonel Bourgoin, Jim and a few maquisard officers were already
there. 'What's going on?' I asked rather lamely.

'Marienne will be back in a few minutes. He took a jeep down
to the defence positions – where the firing came from.' I nodded;
there was nothing to say. Concern showed on all our faces.

Tyres scrunched on the rough track to the farm buildings and,
cocking our weapons as we dashed for the door, we ran, thank
God, into Marienne's jeep.

It was clear that the situation was serious, for he looked worried
– and that, with Marienne, was rare and ominous. 'Just before five
this morning,' he began his report to the Colonel from the driver's

seat as we others crowded round, 'the guard heard two cars coming up the lane towards the Maquis HQ and took up their fire positions. Just as well, because they were German – two cars with about ten *Feldgendarmen*. Our men were spotted when the cars were about a hundred metres away. The driver of the first tried to turn in the narrow lane, which offered too good an opportunity, so the guard commander ordered the closest position to open fire. Which they did with a PIAT. The car exploded, killing everyone inside. Bursts of machine-gun fire were put into the second car, but missed the driver.'

Someone groaned. 'Wait,' said Marienne. 'A PIAT bomb was then fired. It hit the ground short, so a second was quickly put through the engine and overturned the vehicle.'

Now we smiled. 'One German got out and ran into the bushes followed by rifle fire, but he escaped. My guess is that he'll be back in Malestroit by now debriefing the German HQ. Men have gone after him, but I doubt they'll have any luck. In the second car we found three unconscious and one badly wounded. The doctor is already looking after that one, while the others will be brought up here as soon as they recover.'

'Anything else?' asked the Colonel.

'No. That's all at the moment. It's not too good, I'm afraid, as the Germans will have heard the noise – even if their man doesn't make it back. The explosions will have carried the three kilometres into Saint-Marcel, and probably to Malestroit.'

There would be retaliation; of that we were certain. Colonel Bourgoin took charge immediately. He – we – didn't have much time.

'Marienne,' he ordered, 'you get back to the front line. Jim, you go with him.' Turning to the other officers, he said, 'I want Commandant Caro's battalion to cover our rear from the northern limit along the Sérent road round to the west as far as L'Abbaye.[1] Commandant Gouvello's battalion is to defend the open north-eastern sector, while Commandant Garrec's battalion is to be responsible from L'Abbaye to the Bois Joli farm – and facing Saint-Marcel. The three companies of No. 4 Battalion are to patrol either side of the Maquis and between the two roads, in case they try to outflank us. That area is thick bush, and I doubt that the Germans will want to come that way – but, because they may think we think that, we'll have it covered. Sort out your own boundaries as you've been practising. The SAS will remain mobile and under my direct command along the eastern flanks.' The officers nodded acceptance of their tasks. 'The other battalions – minus their men on sentry duties – are to stand by in reserve.'[2]

The Colonel turned to one of his officers, Captain Puech-Samson. 'You'll take command of the central area if we're engaged there.' Then he turned to an officer I barely knew: 'And you, Jean-Paul, will command the northern area.' Now it was my turn – his unofficial second in command: 'Bob, I want you to send a sitrep explaining what's happened and what we're doing to counter the expected reaction. I know it's early, but we may not have another chance.' We smiled ruefully, for we knew we had stuck a stick into a wasps' nest. The Colonel continued with my own instructions: 'Tell London we want no drops tonight. Then come and join me. I'll be needing you.'

He looked at us all in turn. 'OK?'

'Yes,' we answered together, before leaving for our duties. The Colonel needed to say no more, for we all knew the area and had rehearsed for this very operation. It took me a few minutes to type up my report and brief the wireless operator; when I rejoined the Colonel, the doctor was walking into the farm ahead of three stretchers. One contained the wounded German soldier; the other bore the two dead.

'What news?' the Colonel demanded.

'The wounded man'll be dead in a couple of hours – his guts are falling out. There's nothing I can do except give him some morphine to ease the pain. The others have returned from their dreams and will be brought up here shortly.'

'Thank you, doctor. You're going to be busy today.'

'I'm always ready,' he replied cheerfully, striding off to check his makeshift operating room.

The three pale-faced prisoners were brought in to the farmyard, escorted by a band of maquisards – triumphant, unlike their charges, who were in their twenties and scared, as well they might have

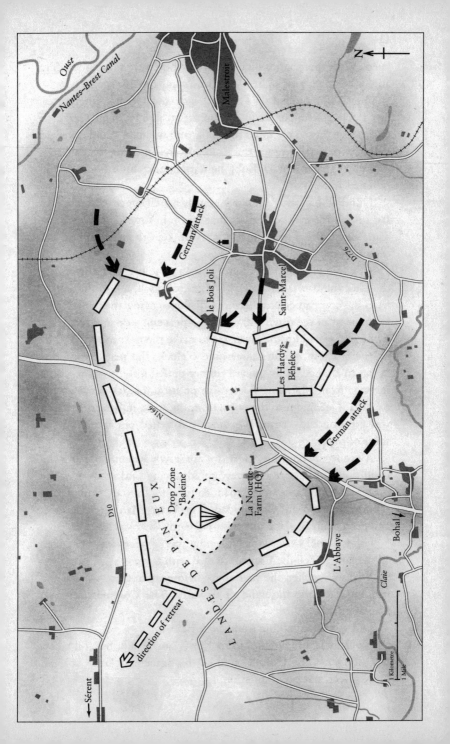

been. With their hands high in the air they were unprepossessing and rather a pathetic sight. We felt no sympathy for them.

The Colonel called for Captain Faith, our German interpreter, but I felt a stronger need for breakfast and went in search of Geneviève, kissed her good morning, and wished I could have had longer with her; however, the Colonel joined me after five minutes.

'I don't like this at all, Bob,' he started, once his mouth was full of bread and butter.

'Nor do I, Colonel,' I replied, equally handicapped. 'After breakfast I'll tell Fleuriot to contact his section in town – there may be some news direct from there if they've kept their eyes open and their mouths shut.'

So, while Fleuriot sent discreet messages to his men patronizing the cafés and bars in the town of Malestroit itself, reports filtered in from the companies and battalions deployed across the countryside to the west of the town. All remained peaceful – or so it seemed – while we waited for the Germans to make the next move.

Then, a few minutes after nine o'clock, the negative reports began to change. A maquisard runner puffed into the farm with a message from Marienne's defensive position that lay between the two roads leading into the town from the west, in between which was the Pondards' farm. We quickly flattened out the crumpled sheet of paper.

'A group of about fifty Germans are slowly heading towards the main position. At present they are advancing under cover of the bushes on either side of the road. Apparently they are bringing up reinforcements from Coëtquidan, from Guer, Mauron, Malestroit and even from Baule and Roche-Bernard – by bicycle!'

The Colonel's order for Marienne was unnecessary, but given all the same: 'Tell the Captain to deal with them.'

'Yes, sir,' replied the messenger before unslinging his rifle and running back the thousand or so yards. The Colonel turned to Captain Faith.

'Did you get anything from those Boche?'

'Not much, I'm afraid. I think they want to talk, but it'll take a little longer.' The Colonel nodded his agreement for a second, more direct, session of questioning.

'What I do know,' the interrogator continued, 'is that they were sent by the commanding officer of the Malestroit barracks to the Pondards' farm to investigate reports of parachute drops. They weren't expecting any armed opposition.'

'Well, that's good news of sorts – except they now know we are here and armed.'

The Colonel dismissed Captain Faith back to his prisoners, leaving us to chat in the sun as we waited for the Germans. It was difficult to believe that we were under imminent threat of attack – and death – in that glorious French countryside.

After twenty minutes our conversation was abruptly halted by the sound of rifle shots in the east, followed by bursts of Bren-gun fire, the noise carrying easily across the fields in the still air of a summer's day. Then a PIAT opened up with its familiar and distinctive explosion. 'So far so good,' we nodded at each other.

The Colonel, with his right shoulder twitching anxiously, was keen to take command, or at least to move closer to the operation to better judge how things were going, but, much to his credit, he kept faith in his junior officers and stayed in the farmyard. Nevertheless, his pacing to and fro, although calm, was becoming more measured, more deliberate, while for more than half an hour the battle surged on: bursts of machine-gun fire, rifle shots, mortar shells exploding, and light automatic fire – all making up the 'music of battle' – were punctuated by the occasional silence.

It was during one of the longer lulls that Marienne raced up in his jeep and, spraying us with dust, braked violently. The immediate news was good, but the prognosis was not so cheery. 'OK, Colonel,' he started, trying to contain his excitement from battle. 'We killed about thirty of them. Unfortunately the other twenty escaped.'[3]

The Colonel smiled. 'Now they know we can fight.'

'Yes – and we'll have to go on fighting. Even harder.'

'Why?'

'Reinforcements have begun to arrive, and we can hear armoured cars manoeuvring, out of sight, along the roads. This time I think we'll be for it!'

'Get back to your men, stay down there, and send a runner when you've more news.'

Snippets of information drifted into the farm, as did wounded German soldiers on stretchers. The doctor was sorting out his priorities, with enemy casualties kept separate, out of sight and under guard. So far we had lost two dead and four wounded when the Germans had taken the Bois Joli farm, only to be repulsed by a spirited counter-attack.

During another quiet period an intelligence officer reported that a German battalion was moving out of Malestroit, but, with no idea how it would deploy, there was little we could do to pre-empt it.

Then, at some time before eleven o'clock, the main counter-attack began. It had taken them thirty minutes to get into their assault positions, while all the time our men watched and reported. We were ready for them, but we knew that the next hours were not going to be easy.

Now every weapon that the enemy possessed was brought to bear on our front line in a cacophony of shots and explosions which could not drown an even more sinister noise: the occasional crack of a single bullet. A man within feet of me slumped to the ground with blood spurting two feet into the air from the side of his neck. I started towards him, but spun round as another crack sharpened my senses further. Stone splinters flew from a nearby wall.

We had anticipated an infantry assault – possibly backed up with light armour – but snipers, a threat we had not met before, were difficult to counter. Within minutes of the first casualty another seven of our men lay dying within the farm complex: all had been shot from long range. Alarmingly, most were shot in the neck, and as blood flowed freely across the grass and summer-dried scrub the doctor dashed from one killing field to the next with dressings and drips. But, so devastating was the accuracy of this 'hidden' danger, there was little he could do except drag bodies on to the packed earth outside the 'hospital'.

Marienne sent news: 'The enemy are parachutists. There are no further casualties in my sector' – a fact confirmed by Puech-Samson when he called in to collect a jeep, although he had been less fortunate with one dead and three wounded among his men. News from the northern sector indicated that they had had only a few shots in their area: the attack seemed to be coming through the middle and was not a flanking one – probably due to the thick bushes the Colonel had mentioned. These bushes were too thick for movement, but provided excellent cover for snipers.[4]

Before Puech-Samson left in his jeep, Colonel Bourgoin issued new orders: 'I want No. 5 Battalion to join you. Then, when ready, you're to launch an attack on the Germans' weakest sector – they must be spread out quite thinly to our front. Understood?'

'*Oui, Colonel. Parfaitement.*'

And, precisely as ordered, Puech-Samson launched his own counter-attack, forcing the Boche to retreat to the outskirts of Saint-Marcel, all the while being harried and sniped at – for two can play at that game, and I had ordered a number of 'HQ men' whom I knew to be good shots to move forward.

As the morning's set-piece attacks dragged into an early afternoon of heavy skirmishing we were steadily advancing, beating the enemy into retreat through heavy losses until by one o'clock the air was suddenly clear and silent. The smoke and noise of battle faded to the still of the fields, leaving us to lick our wounds – which were considerably fewer than the enemy's – and to take stock.

But we knew that this was just another lull while the Germans called up more reinforcements – which we could not. On the other hand, we were engaged in an area we knew intimately and the enemy were not fighting in Normandy.

While mayhem had raged around them, the Pondard daughters had been quietly preparing lunch for the headquarters officers and men as though it was another ordinary day in rural France. The meal, when it was delivered individually to the various defence positions around the buildings, offered no concessions to the dramas being played out across the fields and woods surrounding their home, and we relished its civilizing impact on our morale and physical state.

We had 'got away with it' – indeed we had got the better of it – twice in one morning. But we knew that events would not be allowed to rest at that. Worse was probably to come, and it was best to make the appropriate preparations on a full stomach.

Colonel Bourgoin looked round the small table at which a handful of his colleagues and the Pondard family were tackling hot soup, cold meats, cheeses and wine. 'The peace is over. The Germans know what we are up to and why. We must therefore alter our arrangements.'

Monsieur Pondard knew what was coming, for it had happened – was happening – to other farms across our sector and, for all that we could tell, elsewhere throughout the whole of France. The Germans would show no mercy to the French who helped the Allies. Even so, the doughty farmer held up a hand to interrupt – but the Colonel was adamant.

'I'm making our lorries available so that you can remove all your furniture and valuables.' Monsieur Pondard slowly nodded his head. 'Before that, though,' the Colonel continued, 'all the women will be driven to a safe farm of your choosing.' Monsieur Pondard nodded, then once more held up his hand.

'I would like to stay,' he said without emotion.

'I understand,' countered the Colonel, and Monsieur Pondard smiled gratefully. 'But while there seems to be a lull – and that is all it will be – I suggest you start driving the cattle to the west.'

With a slow shrug Monsieur Pondard stood and left the room to begin the evacuation of his home and the abandonment of his livelihood. It cannot have been easy, but his loyalty to us – and of course to France – had never wavered, and for that he would have been punished when we were overrun. We all felt considerable relief as we heard him issuing his own evacuation orders outside.

Monsieur Legrand, our newly recruited civilian intelligence-gatherer, arrived – rather surprisingly, I thought, considering the military confusions of the area in between – direct from Malestroit, to say – equally surprisingly – that free passage was still allowed for those whose papers were in order and who were apparently above suspicion.

'The Boche are moving three battalions, each about eight-hundred-men strong, into a holding position prior to attacking you in the area of Les Hardys-Béhélec,' he reported quickly, no doubt anxious to deliver his news and rush back to his mill. 'But,' he gushed, 'two lorries have passed back through Malestroit filled with dead, on their way to the crematorium at Coëtquidan.'

Legrand left as hastily as he had arrived, leaving the Colonel to ponder this escalation in the threat. Warnings were issued to the companies and battalions, and ammunition was passed forward, but otherwise there was little we could do except continue to wait.

Everything that had already occurred that day was clearly the prelude to the main attack, which began at 1345 – precisely – with an immense barrage of rifle, automatic and small-calibre mortar fire. The noise was deafening and unlike anything we had suffered earlier, but the greatest difference between this afternoon's engagement and those of the morning was a large increase in the number of snipers.

These assassins had infiltrated our lines and began almost immediately to make inroads into our numbers, one by one, until by two o'clock we had lost eleven more maquisards shot through the head or chest.

We had been able – and still seemed able – to deal with the conventional tactics of the German infantry, but against these individual men hiding among the bushes and trees that surrounded much of the Maquis we were powerless. We became adept at a bizarre form of Indian dance as we pretended to avoid the high-powered rounds cracking, whistling and whining around the farm buildings. We knew that in reality by the time we had ducked it would have been too late if a bullet was aimed at us. But we could not hide and had to be seen about the closer positions assessing the varying circumstances and redeploying as necessary. Staying behind cover or indoors was not an option.

At 1415 a message detailing further German reinforcements reached the farm. The Boche were moving up another two battalions, to make the total number against us in the region of four thousand. But – and it was a vital 'but' – we were still holding our ground and putting up a tremendous resistance. But – another 'but' – we were also losing men, though this time not to enemy bullets but to their own families. Many of the maquisards had never been in battle before, and if they had been it was always on the winning side, with small selected ambushes and the laying of explosives. This battle was something for which they had had no real training and of which they had even less conception. Some had witnessed small skirmishes or had heard, in all the ghastly detail, of the effects that a high-velocity round has on human flesh, but none had been involved in anything approaching the scale of the battle for the Maquis de Saint-Marcel.

The battalion commanders reported that upwards of two hundred men had now 'packed their bags', dumped their weapons and gone home – somehow escaping through the German lines. There was not time to deal with them, but we would have to address that serious position later – if there was to be a 'later'. One thing was becoming certain, though: we would at some stage have to move out – not to retreat, but to conduct a tactical withdrawal in order that we could regroup and continue the fight elsewhere and on our own, better, terms.

To add to these self-imposed losses we had thirty men reported dead and a further forty wounded, all of which was steadily reducing our total on the ground.

'I'm ready for a ringside view,' the Colonel suddenly announced in a rare lull from the afternoon's 'music of battle'. 'You take the southern sectors and I'll take the northern – we must make our own assessments. I'll see you back here in half an hour.'

I had wanted to influence – or at the very least assess for myself – the individual battles that we could hear on three sides, but had felt that my place should be with the commanding officer. Now I was off in an instant, running through the paths and tracks towards the southern sector where the Garrec Battalion was engaged. To begin with it was not easy to find, and I had to rely on my ears rather than my eyes, for the men were moving tactically through the spinneys and hedges, manoeuvring and skirmishing all the while to outwit and outflank the enemy, who seemed intent more on a static battle than on one of 'fire and movement'.

This was to our advantage, and as I lay alongside each subunit commander in his fire position he pointed out the course of his individual battles so far and explained plans for the immediate future in his area.

The dead lay where they fell, the smell from freshly exposed intestines and the groans from those still conscious accentuating the grimness of it all. Death is part of the infantryman's work, and, while not wishing to belittle the young section and platoon commanders' efforts – nor, indeed, those of the more experienced company and battalion commanders – I tried to take their minds away from their losses and concentrate them on killing the enemy. Too much attention to those now 'out of the battle' reduced our fighting strength, and that we could not afford.

'Tough!' I said many times. 'Compassion comes at the end.' Little did they know that I too was witnessing such scenes for the first time.

At 1515 I made it back to the farm and the Colonel.

In those few minutes I knew that, determined though they were, the men needed more than a flying visit from a British SOE officer. They needed a real morale-booster, and there was one weapon in our armoury that we had yet to deploy: a weapon that probably had greater priorities further north and east but was nevertheless badly needed by us too – air support.

'Sir,' I said after catching my breath. 'If I send an emergency message to London requesting air support we might be able to get it by six o'clock. It may not be effective, but it would certainly boost the men's morale.'

The Colonel thought for a moment. 'Bob, it's now nearly 1530. The Germans are bringing in more men. We've held our ground so far, and in one place have actually advanced nearly three kilometres.'

I thought it was time to act on my own initiative. 'If you don't mind, sir, I'd still like to give it a try.'

The Colonel said nothing, which I took as a yes.

My signaller in the pigsty was quickly through to London. I felt it was worth a go, and urgently scribbled my request.[5]

For over an hour the fighting continued: back and forth, the lines of our men advancing and retreating like the ebb and flow of an estuary's tide. Here we won a hundred yards and there we lost fifty; then, just as quickly, the gains would be lost and the lost ground regained.

However, by five o'clock we had lost all the ground fought for earlier, plus half a mile more. The fighting was grim, mostly skirmishing between the woods and hedges, and all the while the enemy snipers kept up their attrition from positions well within the farm's boundaries.

'Those bloody snipers,' cried the Colonel as a bullet smashed into a wall beyond his head. 'Bob,' he then shouted from beyond a corner, 'send any reserves we have left to deal with them.'

'Yes, sir.' To have done so earlier would have put maquisard lives at risk, but now the distances between us and our tormentors were manageable. I slipped away to pass on the orders, and on my return found the Colonel anxiously studying his watch.

'It's now 1730, and still no messages from London – nor, more importantly, any aircraft. We'll have to withdraw under cover of darkness tonight and regroup – even if the aircraft do arrive, that's what we'll do.' It was the first time I noted a hint of desperation in his voice.

I nodded: 'We've started to lose ground that we can't take back.' The latest reports suggested that our losses were now in the ascendant. 'The men are becoming demoralized and tired.'

The Germans were increasing their strength in all sectors – emphasized by our mounting casualty figures.

The majority of the younger men had never been in battle, and seeing their friends' brains and guts oozing on to the grass and mud made them sick in head and stomach. Just as terrifying to the young Frenchmen was the sight of those who were wounded and yet had to lie without help. I was not surprised that so many had had enough. I was perhaps astonished that the number of defectors was so low.

Colonel Bourgoin's own SAS soldiers were magnificent. They were everywhere in the thickest of the battles, moving constantly from one beleaguered spot to another and, when that was quiet, moving on again to where they were needed most. When one sector was safe for the time being, they would leave it for where the Germans were then concentrating their efforts. Their professionalism and cheerfulness kept our maquisards together.

But the odds were without doubt against us, and at 1830 that evening our diminishing numbers were facing approximately 4,500 men – and those mostly equipped with heavy weapons, armoured cars and a seemingly limitless amount of ammunition. Yet we all knew – and it was the message I had taken to the sectors that I had visited – that unless we could hold out until sunset it would be our last day of freedom and possibly our last day on this earth.

We had no idea what our casualties were. The doctor and his staff were working frantically: outside the small 'hospital' there were already eighteen bodies lined up neatly – the best we could do for their dignity – and that was in our HQ area alone. It was a grim sight in the evening sun.

There were, however, bright images from the day – if that is possible in war. Puech-Samson, wounded in the leg, insisted on remaining in his sector to continue inspiring his men, while Marienne's quiet voice gave constant and clear orders that roused enthusiasm across the whole of his front.

Towards evening the Germans suddenly threw everything they could at us, deducing, as they must have done, that they had to beat us before dark or we would be gone.[6] The noise was terrifying; but then, quieter than a PIAT explosion and infinitely more welcome, came the steady, unmistakable drone of high-performance engines that even the noise of an infantry battle could not hide.

'Here they are,' someone shouted – 'fighters!'

We looked up, oblivious of the snipers. Two squadrons of Thunderbolts – a staggering forty-eight aircraft – were approaching high from the north-east and beginning to lose height as they closed on our position. 'Thank God,' I shouted at the Colonel – 'I'd almost forgotten them.'

'Better late than never,' he mocked, looking at his watch. It was seven o'clock as I dashed for my wireless set to establish contact and issue instructions.

While I spoke hurriedly to the formation commander, the aircraft circled over the Maquis just out of small-arms range; then, one by one, they played follow-my-leader, diving on to those German positions I could positively identify and for half an hour wreaking havoc among the enemy positions.

The Germans were now pushed back a mile from the Maquis perimeter, leaving behind them a broad band of no man's land which would help us to make a clean break as soon as the aircraft left and the sun had set. Finally, in a long shallow dive, the planes finished off their remaining ammunition before climbing sharply and disappearing in the direction from which they had come.

There was a sudden silence.

Colonel Bourgoin called for his headquarters officers and the officers in command of the three Maquis sectors for our last conference, or orders group, in the Pondards' farmhouse.

Marienne and myself with the SAS troops would cover the withdrawal of those members of the Maquis still with us: they would leave the area independently by battalions, and make for the woods of Trédion, seven miles to the west. An SAS officer was given the task of preparing demolition charges to avoid our stores falling into enemy hands; another was charged with supervising the burial of the dead as best he could, while the doctor was to begin the evacuation of the wounded to a variety of pre-chosen farms to the west. Every man was to carry his weapon plus sufficient ammunition and food for two days.

Luckily the Germans had only managed to surround us on three sides, so we still had our avenue of escape. And the even better news that filtered in spoke of no fewer than seven three-ton lorries passing through Malestroit carrying some of the estimated three hundred German dead and four hundred wounded.

All the while the Pondard family, heedless of their own immense problems, kept producing sandwiches and cider and, while we ate, drank and planned, the Germans began moving tanks into positions of support for their infantry.

'They won't be able to use them until dawn tomorrow, and by then they'll find an empty Maquis,' someone said.

The snipers were now taking up positions closer to the farm, and with them and the certainty of a tank attack our position was once again becoming untenable. The enemy had also slipped a few heavy machine guns on to the eastern hills, with their fire adding to the snipers' efforts.

Our minds were made up – or at least the Colonel's mind was, and we agreed with him – and in this we were helped at nine o'clock that evening by Monsieur Legrand from Malestroit, who had managed once more, and even more bravely this time, to reach our position.

'The Germans', he reported, 'are now over four thousand strong, but they won't attempt to approach via the north and east as they're suspicious of what they might find in the woods. Nor do they have any real idea of your strength. The German command in Coëtquidan has ordered more reinforcements – an infantry battalion each from Rennes, Vannes and Lorient – and there's even talk of bringing in more men from Brest and Quimper.'

We thanked him for his unwelcome news before he slipped back into the dark towards Malestroit.

I sent a final sitrep reporting the battle and our immediate plans, and the moment that was dispatched I ordered the operators to pack up their pigsty and set off for the rendezvous.

The section in Saint-Marcel village abandoned their covert observation post, having supplied superior intelligence throughout the long day, and they too now made for the Trédion woods – just in time, for a growing red glow beyond the trees indicated the burning of the village, including the church, leaving us to guess at the fate of so many of our friends.

With later reflection it was interesting to note that this battle was over before the Germans could bring in heavy weapons and vehicles. They had initially been outnumbered, and were certainly surprised by the strength of our Maquis, for outside Normandy they had not expected to find such opposition – and one that was obviously (thanks to the timely arrival of aircraft) in good communications with the Allies. Thus they were to fear the Maquis – a fear made even more intense because the Germans could not gauge the FFI's full strength, since this was purposely never brought to battle again; instead, from this day on, the FFI and the French SAS were to rely on guerrilla warfare of the most morale-sapping kind. There were to be losses on both sides, but, as the Maquis never again operated from large bases, the initiative very much lay in the hands of the French and their 'advisers'.

Exploding mortar shells now added to the snipers, machine guns and general discomfort, but we were determined not to be hurried: the exodus had to be orderly and 'as planned'. At ten that evening there was a marked lessening in the harassment being directed towards us, and, as the rumble of heavy engines and the squeaking of tank tracks suggested the ominous reason why, we took the opportunity to order the Maquis battalions (or what remained of them) to leave at intervals. This they did, until by midnight there were only some SAS men, Marienne, the Colonel and myself left. To our relief, the Pondards had long since made their escape.

The surrounding country – or at least that towards Saint-Marcel – was being illuminated more and more brightly as farms, barns and haystacks were set alight. Bolstering the general drama of that and the increasing incoming fire, Marienne organized a company of SAS troops to man every weapon they could lay their hands on and fire in the general direction of the enemy. They made – as they were supposed to do – a stupendous noise, and it sounded – as it was supposed to do – as though we were manning a brigade's defensive position. While this kept the Germans at bay, another SAS officer was quietly stacking all the remaining weapons, ammunition and explosives into a pile away from the farm buildings. Then, when all was ready, the signal was given for the time pencils to be armed and placed, and with that procedure completed we began our own withdrawal.

Marienne, leaning on his carbine, ignoring the snipers, and with a muddy and blood-stained bandage twisted roughly round his head, looked proudly at his men as they withdrew, tactically, through the farmyard. I thought of what had happened at Bir Hakeim, where the French had fought so valiantly, and how Marienne and his men were worthy successors to their colleagues in that bloody, defensive battle of which even I had already heard so much.

There was one final act to be undertaken, and it was one which I had purposely left until the very last moment: the liberation of the prisoners we had taken that day. We certainly did not want to take them with us, nor could we execute them – although that option probably crossed a number of minds – so in the end we simply put them in charge of their own wounded (this, in theory, would slow their return) and, with the threat of their being shot as escapers, we removed their blindfolds and pointed them in the 'right' direction. The two girl 'collaborators' were offered three choices: come with us, stay with the Germans, or simply run away. They chose to stay with us, which was probably the safest course for them to take.

It was now time to go, and so, without the luxury of a backward glance at the place with which I had been intimately involved since my days as a clerk at Guer railway station, we slipped into the night, leaving the Germans to continue firing into an empty Maquis.

Behind us the sky glowed red as more buildings were put to the torch, but we had little inclination to stop and stare, for the Trédion woods lay some seven miles to the west and, it being high summer, dawn would shorten the night before we could make the security of the trees. In fact Marienne and I decided that, with the limited time left and the weight of our loads, it was best to aim first for the woods to the north of Callac before, if the way was clear, making for the larger and more secure Trédion woods a couple of miles on and to the south-south-west.

It began to rain, which, although uncomfortable, aided our progress as the noise of raindrops on the leaves masked that of our boots in the puddles. The route had been secured by two reduced Maquis battalions in the form of rolling pickets, and while the various units leapfrogged westward the eastern sky was punctuated by explosions from the Pondards' farm – a cacophony that ended with one massive flash and a blast of 'thunder' that echoed across and through the fields and woods. I felt for all those hundreds of hours that many brave and hard-working people had spent on both sides of the Channel in the preparation, delivery and receipt of the munitions that were now smouldering among the outhouses and fields of the Ferme de la Nouette.

We had timed our journey well, for, as dawn broke on a new and, we prayed, less dramatic day, we were able to prepare defensive positions in a secluded corner of the woods that surround two sides of the Château de Callac, owned then by the de Lignières family, and long chosen as suitable for an emergency rendezvous. The extensive barns on the south-western end of the main courtyards made perfect resting places, and were to be used off and on for the next weeks.

By eight o'clock that morning the SAS battalion had regrouped and had already dispatched runners to guide in any Maquis stragglers it could find. All day we waited expecting no one to appear, and then, within a short time of sunset, challenges and passwords were being exchanged regularly as men drifted in from their various individual hiding places.

That night we made our break again until, after skirting the village of Callac, we came to a section of the Trédion woods that forms part of the vast complex of high ground known as the Landes de Lanvaux. An advance party had already prepared defence positions and laid out a camp suitable for living in and defending.

The two girl prisoners were sent under escort to a nearby chateau. They were soon back with pails of hot coffee and an invitation for the men to go in groups to where more coffee would be waiting at 'the big house'. This was good news, and welcome for the implied local friendship, but later in the day the girls disappeared and were not seen again. We felt that, outside Malestroit, it was unlikely that their earlier 'employment' as tarts for the Germans would have been known, and guessed that they were probably safe. I was not sorry to see them go, even though they knew of our temporary location. We later learned that they had both taken jobs as nurses in a local hospital run by nuns.

Men continued to arrive – wet, cold and nearing exhaustion – but our war had to continue and, apart from small acts of sabotage, we had yet to achieve the aims given to us in London.

After a scanty breakfast that day, 20 June 1944, the Colonel called a meeting of all the SAS and Maquis officers that had made it to the wood. Jim was invited to open the proceedings. 'I've sent men out to contact Monsieur Legrand for whatever news he might have,' he said. 'I suggest we wait until they return before we make any new plans.'

We nodded politely as the commanding officer took over. 'We have time, I think, and can afford to wait here until at least tonight, by when we should have some better idea of what the Germans are up to. However,' he continued, 'some jeeps have left in pairs for two safe farms a few kilometres away. The battalions are now spread, I believe, across seven woods, awaiting orders, so', he looked at Jim, 'you will send messages for all those who can do so to return to their homes – after dumping their weapons in one cache under your command. Those who cannot go home are to stay in the area, and we'll arrange for them to be fed in local farms.

We'll have to wait until we start receiving reports, but we must accept that it will probably not be difficult for the Germans to find us here – which is why I want as many to go home as possible.'

The first news arrived at eleven o'clock that morning, and came from the Maquis itself. Apparently the Germans had continued firing into our camp until one o'clock in the morning, too frightened to enter for fear of booby traps. Receiving no answering fire, they eventually risked an approach at two a.m., only to suffer heavy casualties when our explosives went off a little later. They retired and reoccupied the Maquis at daybreak. Now the area was strongly guarded while the Gestapo and *Milice* made extensive local enquiries.

An hour later, at midday, the well-travelled Monsieur Legrand arrived to tell us much of what we had just heard – adding that the tanks had returned to their base at Coëtquidan. The reinforcements had also returned to their camps, leaving about three thousand Germans still in the Malestroit area. The curfew had been renewed from eight in the evening until six in the morning, and everyone was having their papers checked regardless of how well known their innocence might be; the town had been searched, and a number of the younger men had been rounded up. The Pondard family was reported to be safe, as were our wounded. The German doctors were visiting all the hospitals in the area to seek out patients with gunshot wounds, but so far they had been unsuccessful. Dozens of mobile patrols were on the roads, searching farms, woods and fields.

'The last piece of news, gentlemen,' Monsieur Legrand said gravely, 'is that the Boche are now actively looking for Colonel Bourgoin, the one-armed SAS officer, for his second in command, Captain Marienne, for Jim, and for a British agent named as Bob – or Captain Bob. And I can also confirm that you had two spies in your midst at Saint-Marcel.' We smiled thinly, although this was hardly unexpected.

In the thoughtful silence that followed Legrand's departure I looked at the Colonel – quiet, thinking and twitching his shoulder. He now spoke. 'I still think we have time – at least until midnight – and by then we will have a much better idea where the Germans are and what their intentions are. If they find no evidence of our survival as a fighting organization they may slacken, in the hope that if we still exist at all we will become overconfident. In the meantime I suggest we try and get some rest.'

Two of the men sent by Jim returned early that afternoon with mixed news. One battalion had reached its pre-arranged area in good order, but had been traced by the Germans and had that morning been attacked. By chance the men's two jeeps arrived in the middle of this battle, but, although nearly caught, their drivers managed to escape intact with the vehicles. Another battalion had dispersed into disorganized groups which were being chased by the Germans, all the while taking casualties. One battalion had split into small groups of four or five men which, despite being harried, were heading for our area. Various maquisards had been captured with their weapons, and we could only guess – accurately as it was to turn out – at their fate.

The report from the second team was worse. 'Two jeeps eventually caught up with one of the battalions and stayed to protect the three hundred or so men still with it. However, as they approached a crossroads in tactical formation with trees on their left and a field on their right with, at the far end, a slope covered with small bushes, they were fired upon by a large concentration of Germans in the wood. This split the battalion into two, and while the jeeps gave covering fire the men ran towards the bushes, only to be shot in the back. It was like killing rabbits.

'The jeeps faced the enemy and did a good job, but just as they were about to disengage and make their own escape a German jumped from the cover and at point-blank range shot Lieutenant de la Grandière in the head, killing him instantly. In retaliation, the German was himself killed before the jeeps made their getaway. Had it not been for the jeeps' crews the casualty list would have been considerably higher. The Germans must have known the battalion was coming, for it had been too much of a coincidence. Now that battalion is split into groups of threes and fours and being chased all round the countryside. Some of the wounded have been taken to Plumelec school, which is now a prison. And you should know that there were some Gestapo and *Milice* mixed up with the German infantry.

'Later, the same jeeps took their revenge when they caught up with the rear of a German convoy. Sounding their horns as they approached, they forced the enemy vehicles to the side of the road and as they flashed past showered burst after burst into them. The Boche realized what was happening only when it was too late, and as the leading vehicle had blown up there was no room for any of the others, so no one could overtake and catch your men up. It was brilliant.'

The Colonel thanked the team for their comprehensive and useful report before dismissing them to get some rest.

We were left alone with our thoughts – but not for long, for at three o'clock Monsieur Legrand returned again. 'The good news is that the Germans estimate their dead at 600. Your casualties', he continued, 'are believed to be 120 dead and 70 wounded, but this doesn't include this morning's fighting.'

The wider news was, in many regards, worse: civilian men were being indiscriminately rounded up and tortured, several farms had been razed to the ground, and a number of nurses who had helped earlier were now in a German prison in Vannes. The local people were now quite simply too terrified to help us. On the other hand, though there was a price on our heads, they were probably not likely to run cap in hand to the Germans for their reward. We decided to split into much smaller groups and then to lie low until the hubbub died down. Monsieur Legrand promised that his car would return in an hour's time, 'to take some of you away to wherever you want to go'.

We all agreed that Colonel Bourgoin not only was too important to stay but, with his one arm, was instantly recognizable: he should go into deep hiding for four or five days, taking his wireless set with him. He suggested I join him, but I declined: there might have been a price on my head, but I was happier where I was – and that included being with Marienne and a hard core of SAS men with whom, we decided, we could not afford to lose touch and who would anyway be needed as the basic training team for any new Maquis.

As promised, the car and Monsieur Legrand returned within the hour, and shortly afterwards Colonel Bourgoin, Jim and a signaller were speeding on their way to safety, sleep and food.

Marienne and I looked at each other, 'Well, my old friend,' I started, grasping his shoulder, 'here we go again!'

'Yes,' he replied. 'Now, I suggest we get the rest of the men on their way, tidy up the security, then regroup with what we have left.'

It did not take long to choose forty-eight men, including our three signallers, to stay with us and to organize the others into seven groups and see them off. After that we withdrew a few more yards into the bush. It was still raining heavily.

Settled into our new positions, we took stock. That we had been badly mauled was certain, although our known casualties were light compared with those reportedly suffered by the Germans. The 4th Battalion was largely intact, with three hundred men now dispersing across the countryside. Of our Maquis battalions we had little idea.

'We might as well stay here until dark, then move much deeper into the forest. Alexis Babin is due to brief us here at six o'clock this evening, and we can't afford to miss him. At least we can watch the track and move after he arrives.' I didn't know Marienne had made this arrangement with Babin, and wondered when he had done so – but his mind was on other things.

'I've got some cold meat. I'm starving,' he said.

We hadn't eaten properly for over forty-eight hours, during which we had fought a running battle, travelled heavily laden, and navigated across rough country through two nights of freezing rain. The tinned horse was welcome.

Leaving a man to keep an eye on the track for Babin, Marienne and I wandered round the new camp chatting to the men. Their own cold-meat meal was equally welcome to them, but more heartening was the sight of spotlessly clean weapons and a strongly expressed desire to reorganize the Maquis just as soon as it was safe to do so. It never would be safe, of course, but we knew what they meant.

True to his word, Babin approached cautiously up the track at the agreed time. A sentry challenged him before leading him quickly to Marienne and myself in a spot we had been trying to keep dry with brushwood, branches and leaves.

After the required Gallic greetings had been completed, he

announced, 'This forest is twenty-three kilometres long. In the middle it passes a few hundred metres south of Plumelec. Although it's quite thick, if we start after dark tonight we could be at what I hope will be the final rendezvous by tomorrow morning.' Not knowing what he was coming to, we both nodded for him to continue. 'I know two farms we could stay in for a few days – in fact we could leave most of your men there – and in small groups we could then move to within a few kilometres of Plumelec, where the forest is thicker.

'We can only move and work at night at the moment, and I think the place I'm suggesting is better for that. We could send out runners when we're ready, and start re-forming our battalions from there. What do you think?'

Babin knew the country west of our temporary camp better than we did, so we would have to take his word on these matters. But it was me – the one whom Marienne always said was never depressed – that wasn't so sure. 'Although I agree,' I answered, 'I'm bloody tired. I could go eight kilometres, but no further.'

'That's fixed, then,' said Marienne: 'We'll go as far as we can.' And without another word he stood and walked quickly towards his men who, in silence, began packing their few possessions before shuffling into line.

Five minutes later all would have been ready but for the sudden sound of firing from along our track of the previous night. We stopped before we had started. The battle, for that was what it sounded like, was an ominous warning that there might not be too many hiding places for us.

'The quicker we get out of here the better,' I said with a sudden enthusiasm.

It was only one night and it was probably only ten miles, but it was quite simply one of the worst marches of my army career. I have since marched hundreds of miles through the monsoons, jungles, swamps and mountains of Burma, Thailand and Indo-China, but not one of those compared with the few miles of that night on a march which gradually drained me of my usually robust humour. We plodded on slowly and not always surely through the thickest woods and densest bushes imaginable.

We were no longer cold – far from it, as our bodies melted with sweat, which ran in streams down our faces, under our arms, from our crotches and down our backs into our trouser waistbands. Our clothes were matted, stiff and abrasive on the outside from rain and mud, while the inside of our trousers rubbed ribbons of blisters across our stomachs, the smalls of our backs and the insides of our upper thighs.

We fell, cursing, over trees invisible in the night; our eyes strained desperately to penetrate the heavy rain which the sodden canopy above could no longer absorb; our ears were pushed to their limits as they sifted and identified every nocturnal sound a forest can deliver in case any came from an enemy lying in wait; our hands and feet burned with pain and became slippery with blood; our bodies – limp with utter exhaustion – groaned, while our tortured minds could fix on only one goal: food, a hot drink and sleep.

First light on 21 June found us on the edge of the forest, with two farms beginning their own summer's day just a hundred yards away from us. The morning was bright, the rain vanishing with the sun that now raised steam from our clothes and caked hair. Unshaven and with bloodshot eyes, we were not an impressive military sight, but we had covered the ground we had set ourselves. Babin stopped just inside the treeline and motioned to us to lie quietly.

Cautiously, yet trying not to look suspicious, he made his way across the small field to the nearest of the occupied buildings. There was a pause of five or so minutes while he disappeared, then he meandered to the second building, this time accompanied by a farmer.

About twenty-five minutes later Babin reappeared and melted into the trees a few yards from us. Moments later he was whispering into our ears, 'These two farms can each take twenty-five men. Wait for half an hour, then start getting the men into the two barns you can see.' He pointed through a low branch: 'The hedges should offer some screening from the road. In each barn you'll find a ladder to the loft. By then we'll have hay and food ready. Tonight you can wash at the well – I'll show you where it is later – and I'll bring you hot water for shaving.'

He stopped and looked at us and the men behind. 'OK?' he asked. The murmur of appreciation was led by the two officers.

After the agreed time our two groups made their way in threes and fours to the allotted buildings and climbed the ladders, the last men pulling them up behind them. The floor of our attic – and the other – had been covered with a thick layer of dry straw, while in each loft trays of bread, butter, cider and fresh cold meats had been placed on wooden planks. Too tired to eat, we drew lots for sentry duty before turning in – still wearing our wet clothes.

We slept soundly throughout the day, and woke only when the farmer called for the ladder to be lowered so that he could carry up a huge pot of coffee. We ate the meal that was still waiting for us, and by the time we had lit cigarettes and pipes we agreed that life was not so bad after all.

In the barn beneath, the farmer – helped by two casual labourers employed for the harvest – had brought several buckets of hot water. In small groups we descended from our eyrie for a shave; then, with nothing to do until we could make a better assessment of German activity in our new area, we returned to the hay and more sleep.

The next morning, as we brushed clean our uniforms, Babin wandered into Plumelec to gather what news he could. He was back at noon to say that the Germans were continuing to search farms and villages, but with a decreasing amount of success – although they were constantly asking if anyone knew the where-abouts of a Lieutenant Marienne, for it was him they held respon-sible for the 'Battle of Saint-Marcel'. Babin had also persuaded a young girl to go to Malestroit to collect a suitcase of civilian clothing that I had lodged in a safe house. She was to keep it with her until we asked for it, and until then my clothes were to be mixed up with those of her brother in his room. Of the Maquis battalions there was no news.

Our stay did not last long, though. At ten o'clock that evening both lofts were roused by their respective farmers to be told that a workman had disappeared after telling his mate that he 'knew how to make a lot of money'. It was chillingly obvious that we should waste no time in arguing over the likely source of his new wealth, and even less time on making the decision to return to the woods.

This was a blow, but once back in comparative safety I turned to Marienne. 'We should have guessed that some would be scared and others would want to capitalize on our misfortune.' I was referring to our own deserters as well as to this more recent example of treachery.

'I don't blame them, I suppose,' he answered. 'We've created one hell of a mess for them. It's no fun to be searched, have your wife beaten up and taken away to prison, and then get yourself shot. There's only one answer, and that's to get ourselves out of here as quickly as possible.'

'I agree,' Babin chipped in. 'I know a place some considerable distance from here through the forest – a large farm and nothing within two and a half kilometres of it, out of the way in an area covered with bushes, shrubs and a few trees. If we can make it, I suggest we give it a go. But I also think you should leave all your men here, Marienne, with food and supplies.'

'I'm against the men living in the wood. Surely we can split them into even smaller groups around the local farms.'

'It could be done, if that's what you prefer, but we must wait until the man I sent to speak to Monsieur Legrand is back.' It was midnight by the time he returned and found us in our new hiding place. By now we had had twenty-four hours without rain, but that was the only bright spot in a continuing tale of misfortune and disloyalty.

Legrand's message was simple: two of the maquisards had been captured by the Gestapo and had given away the whole story of the formation of the Maquis: my arrival, the drops, Marienne's arrival – everything. The Gestapo had good descriptions of me and Marienne, and were 'very anxious to make our acquaintance'.

This news confirmed the earlier decision that we still needed to put as much distance as we could between us and Saint-Marcel. As the 4th Battalion's instructions had been to move west anyway, we were at least heading in the right direction. We knew, too, that there were many thousands of maquisards in north-west Brittany waiting to be organized, and they needed our involvement.

'We should get cracking right now,' I said. Nobody disagreed, and for the next two hours we marched until Babin suggested a halt while he moved ahead. We were glad of the rest, but it was a long and anxious wait. When he did return, the news was good and would at least allow us to keep some control over the men while we established a new Maquis: eight farms had each agreed to take up to five men.

'That's fine,' said Marienne on hearing this. 'The two officers, Babin, three wireless operators and four SAS men will form the basis of a new group in the isolated farm we're heading for, while the others are billeted out here for the time being.'

Arrangements were made, and by seven o'clock Babin was back again, having led small parties to the different farms. We slept until eleven that night, when we made the next, and we hoped final, move towards our destination, which we reached early in the morning of 24 June.

Babin, as usual, had gone ahead to check that the earlier promises were still open, and shortly after that we were in a large communal kitchen with white bread, butter, coffee and omelettes.

Rum and cigarettes followed with our instructions. 'Two hundred metres from here', the farmer explained, 'there's a small field of corn with trees and bushes bordering it, and along one side a large and dry ditch. I'll put some hay in it, and you can stay there during the day – or be out and about as you wish, but not in the farm – then you come up to the farm at night-time. That way, if the Germans come here they won't see you, and if you spot them you'll have a good start to get away. If they take us . . .' he paused to drag on his Gauloise before blowing smoke slowly towards the ceiling, 'well, they'll have to come and get us.' And with that he glanced towards a corner of the room and a brace of shotguns.

'We certainly hope it won't come to that,' I said. 'But we really are grateful for what you're offering. Thank you.'

'Don't thank me,' murmured the farmer. 'I fought in the last war against the bloody Germans, and in this one both of my sons have already been killed by the bastards. In 1939.'

I rose, put an arm around his wife, and kissed her on her forehead.

9. Suspicions

We slept in the ditch until six that evening – when the dogs came barking – the sun having dried our clothes. The dogs might not have been a good thing had the enemy been about, but, as Babin had said, there was clear ground in all directions and, anyway, their arrival preceded the farmer clutching several bottles of cider and an invitation to join him and his wife for dinner. 'I'll have food sent down for your men – that way we'll try to keep the movement down to a minimum. It'll be their turn tomorrow.'

Babin left for the village, as I was anxious to get a message to Monsieur Legrand stating our new position; in return, we badly needed news. Marienne wanted to dispatch men to brief the remainder of the 4th Battalion, and we were both keen to start contacting our own Maquis battalions as a prelude to reorganizing ourselves. Although we had been quiet for a few days, we knew we were still tying up German troops who might otherwise have been facing the Allies in Normandy.

Before he left, the farmer had pointed out a small stream where we could wash. 'Marienne,' I called, 'you've been wallowing all day in mud. I think you should go first.'

'Thanks for the compliment,' he replied, 'but I wouldn't give much for your chances with the girls either!'

The next two hours were spent cleaning ourselves, our clothes and our weapons, so that by eight o'clock we were reasonably respectable – or so we thought. But Madame took a long and disapproving look at us as we walked into her domain, before announcing that Monsieur would be ordered to prepare hot water in the barn and while we were having our second wash of the day she would sponge and press our battledress. 'Now, you do as I tell you,' she ended.

'*Oui, madame,*' we replied meekly as she led us out of the room. Properly clean and smart at last, we sat in the kitchen discussing the situation across France until a new-suited and equally smart Babin banged on the door and entered. Cider was poured, but that was the last bright moment before he delivered his report, speaking from rough notes. In one sense the situation was little more than we expected, but it was made no better for that.

'The Germans are widening their searches. They surround random villages at four in the morning, then search them thoroughly. They've found a few maquisards and made them prisoners.' He turned to Marienne: 'They've also rounded up a number of SAS men, killing some and taking the others away for torture. The farms and houses where they've found men, arms and uniforms have been burned to the ground or blown up, and the owners put against walls and shot. Their families are forced to watch, and they're repeating these atrocities across the countryside. Understandably, the locals are terrified. A few girls have been arrested, and the inhabitants of Malestroit, Vannes and Plumelec talk of screams coming from the prisons at all times of the day and night.

'Three of your wounded men who were put into the Malestroit hospital – you know, the ones with broken legs and ankles from the drops – were removed and shot. The mother superior of the nuns' hospital has been beaten up and taken to prison as well. There seems no level too low for these bastards to stoop.

'Two hundred *miliciens* with their Gestapo friends have dressed in your uniforms and are now knocking on the doors of isolated farms saying they're English and French. If they're offered help, the men are instantly shot, the women beaten, and the houses burned.

'They've also got a complete brigade of Cossacks combing the woods and fields – rumours say there are as many as three thousand of them. Roadblocks have been intensified.

'No one is allowed on the streets between eight at night and seven in the morning. If they spot anyone, they shoot to kill. In some villages they've been parading every man between the ages of eighteen and fifty in the central square, and walk the spies up and down the ranks. Any maquisard they identify is shot instantly. This has happened a number of times.'

I had heard enough and wanted Babin to stop, but Marienne shut me up: 'No, Bob, let us hear everything.'

'On top of all this they are concentrating on anyone who has only one arm. So far they've picked up two one-armed men: one was forty and had lost his arm in a car crash, and the other was an elderly retired general and commander of the Légion d'honneur, who was most indignant. They are taking no chances.'

Now at last he stopped, but as neither of us said a word he ended with 'I've sent a few men to seek out the Maquis battalions in their various hiding places, and have arranged for them to brief me on the locations at a safe place about three kilometres from here.'

Babin turned to the farmer: 'I've a pass to use a bicycle but no bicycle! May I borrow yours?' The farmer nodded. 'Thanks. I'll stick to the paths across the fields and woods – luckily I know them as well as anyone – so it'll take me about forty minutes each way, with the meeting in between. I hope to be back by four in the morning.' And with that and no further ceremony he made for the back door.

'Thanks for all you're doing,' we called after him. 'And good luck.'

The four of us talked for an hour or so before sitting in silence, each with a cigarette or pipe and deep in thought. The circumstances leading up to our present position were hardly unexpected, which is why we had, well in advance, chosen lying-up places for just such a response from the Germans.

'Perhaps', I thought ruefully, 'if we hadn't been so successful in our defence of the Maquis de Saint-Marcel and caused so many casualties we wouldn't be being hounded quite so assiduously.'

And so we sat until Babin's nearly always cheerful face once again pushed its way round the kitchen door: he was half an hour early. The news was still not good, although there were glimmers of improvement. 'Grog, the name for the Samwest replacement that you sent in with Lieutenant Déplante, has already begun operations and has just been joined by Nos. 3 and 4 Battalions, which have already carried out sabotage tasks to the south of Malestroit. They've been supplied by 429 containers over the last three nights.

'Nos. 1 and 2 Battalions are still dispersed and being chased around the countryside, while the remaining battalions have reorganized and are each about 250 men strong. Of Colonel Bourgoin and Jim there is no news. Two more of your men have been killed by the Russians, who have reached our previous hiding place in the Trédion woods and are continuing to head in this direction. Monsieur Legrand has no news except that the Boche are not slackening their search for us.'

Marienne thought through two Gauloises, then he looked at me and said slowly, 'What do you think of this as a plan?'

'Tell me,' I replied, for I too was hatching a plot.

'We stay here until tomorrow night, then we return to the Trédion woods. The Cossacks will have patrolled the area and won't expect us back there.'

'They could double-bluff us,' I suggested.

'I don't think they think like that!'

'Go on, then.'

Marienne continued: 'Once we've established a new base in the woods, we split the SAS among a number of small individual Maquis units. We contact Bourgoin and find out what his intentions are, and then we join up with Grog. We can continue to use this farm as an emergency base and rendezvous position should that be necessary again.'

His ideas mirrored mine, and I nodded my assent. With that and a final early-morning cup of coffee we returned to our home on the edge of the field, where we slept until noon.

The farmer's wife woke us in our ditch with a cold lunch and cider, and with that inside us we began packing our meagre belongings and checking that nothing was left that could possibly have implicated our hosts. Luckily it was not until we had finished the 'tidying-up' process that the sentry suddenly broke the silence with the muffled cry 'Cossacks! Coming this way!'

'Get under cover! Everyone!' Marienne shouted. 'Don't shoot unless I give the order!'

Through the bushes we watched this most feared of enemies search the farm buildings before galloping through the neighbouring field and then our own. Thank God they had no dogs, for we would then not have stood a chance, but as it was they never halted in their rushing to and fro – and yet missed us completely.

As they made their way back to the main roads via the long farm tracks, we breathed again: it had been a long hour and a half, during which I had been convinced that the game was finally up. We might have killed a few of them, but the end result would never have been in doubt: capture – and capture meant death.

And so we made our way back where we had come from during those difficult days before – but this time the ground was dry, the night warm and the journey swift. As we approached the edge of the woods opposite a farm believed to be used by some of our men, Babin left us to move forward. That farm revealed five men, and the next the same, but the third farmer had had to send 'his' men to another farm half a mile or so away. Two hours into the dawn we had our fifty-odd men together again, only to be dispatched on a reconnaissance of the woods for a new base. However, the weather now turned bad – so bad in fact that we returned all the men to their farms while we moved further north in search of a better place.[1]

Our luck remained on the ebb, for at one turn in a path we came face to face with a single mounted Cossack, who, as surprised as us, fired randomly as he hurriedly turned his horse away. We, equally astonished, did the same, managing to hit him in the arm – or at least it fell limp by his side as he cantered off, no doubt to collect his compatriots.

Slipping and sliding through the mud and puddles, we managed to put some distance between the ambush position and ourselves. But we had been discovered in what we had hoped would have been one of the safer places: now that hope, too, was dashed.

Circling for miles through the woods we reached an isolated farm where, trusting that our bad luck could not last for ever, Babin went forward to work his charm. Luckily – though he did not know this in advance – he had met the farmer and his wife before the war, and so we had soon taken off most of our clothing to dry while, of greater importance, I managed to separate the francs that I had left and spread them out on the hearth.

Two hours after arriving cold, wet and tired we were warm, dry and settling down to a day of rest in the hay of an attic above the main farm building. However, our sleep was not to last, for an hour later the farmer's head appeared at the top of the steps that led to our dormitory. Holding a steady finger to his lips, he pointed towards the small dormer window. We tiptoed towards it. Outside, a party of dismounted Cossacks was inspecting a battledress blouse that they seemed to have just found; but it was clear, even from a distance, that it was not one of ours. Nevertheless it spelt disaster, and while they were momentarily preoccupied with this piece of clothing we hurriedly and silently donned our own uniforms and prepared to fight. Yet a residue of luck lingered with us, for the Russians suddenly mounted their chargers and rode away in the opposite direction to the one we were planning to take. We made quickly for the woods, where a small rise along the edge allowed us a grandstand view of the country we had just left. With plenty of open ground for an enemy to cross, we would have enough time to make a run for it should we be approached.

Although we were anxious to get reorganized, the Cossacks clearly had not yet finished with the vast Landes de Lanvaux, and until they had done so we would be thwarted at every move. For two hours we watched them return to comb the immediate area of the farm and the outbuildings, then at noon two rifle shots echoed across the fields between us, and shortly afterwards a plume of smoke began to curl upwards, growing quickly into a dense cloud of white and light blue as hay and wood caught fire. More shots followed, and a farm not quite out of sight off to the west was similarly treated. Eventually all three farms in front of us had been torched: heaven knows what fate had befallen their inhabitants.[2]

'This area is too hot,' Marienne growled with a menace I had not heard before. 'I know what we'll do, and I don't give a damn if you approve or not.' I nodded my agreement in advance. 'I'm going back to get my men from the farms. I'm going to get the maquisards back come hell or high water, and I'm going to start my own war. I'll make them pay for this if it's the last thing I do on this earth. Are you with me, Bob?' It was my duty to be with him.

'When do we start?' I said, already knowing the answer.

'I knew you wouldn't let me down.'

'Babin,' I said, turning to him lying alongside me in the grass, 'round up everyone you can find. We'll meet at the last hiding place. And', I emphasized, 'I mean *everyone*.'

At four that afternoon we met again. 'All your men left their farms this morning,' Babin reported – 'and just in the nick of time, for the Cossacks made a series of coordinated attacks against every location they suspected of harbouring them. They found no one, of course, except the owners, their families and our own wounded. They shot the wounded in their beds, shot the civilians in the farmyards, and then burned the buildings.'

We leaned back against a tree. Our men were being killed in cold blood as they lay wounded and unable to defend themselves. Women were being raped then shot in front of their husbands, fathers and children; and if it was not that way round then fathers were shot in front of their women, but only after the women had been publicly raped.

With rather less caution – thanks to Marienne's anger – we collected and reorganized until at last we felt ready to return eastward and back to the farm in which we felt safest – despite having had to leave it rather quickly a few days before.

The farmer met us. 'I see you're back,' he said, 'but I'm not surprised, as there can be no better place than this in Brittany. Nothing around us for kilometres. I knew you'd return, so I've sent my wife to one farm and all my valuables – such as they are – to another. Now if the Germans come and find nothing – then burn my farm – so be it. I'll rebuild after the war, and that's something that I've always wanted to do anyway. You know, more comforts and labour-saving devices and everything will be fine. The Boche might even do me a favour!'

His sangfroid – although commendable – was chilling. 'All I need now,' he added, 'is four of your men to help with the harvest.'

Marienne offered eight men: 'You've done a great deal for us, so it's the least we can do. Some were farmers before the war, but they'll need to borrow appropriate clothing.'

'Thank you, Captain, and if you want to send eight more of your men to my sister's farm I'm sure that will be appreciated. She's a widow living three kilometres from here.'

Not all farmers were to be cowed by the Nazis' murderous antics.

Marienne turned to Babin. 'See if you can get false papers for them from the mayor of Malestroit – we'll need twenty sets, and I'll suggest names later. They should be made out for towns destroyed or occupied by the Allies on the Normandy front. But first go to Plumelec and ask that girl to bring Bob's suitcase to the farm. Then find a reliable man in Plaudren – just south of here. I'll need his help.'

'I know a suitable person!' he said, mounting the farmer's bicycle.

After being harried and chased from one end of a six-mile stretch of the Landes des Lanvaux woods between Trédion and Saint-Jean-Brévelay known as the Bois de Saint-Bily, we felt that now at last we might be about to sort ourselves out.

With Babin on his travels, Marienne and I returned to the cornfield clutching two lengths of bread, a selection of cold meats and a bottle of cider. The only thing we lacked – badly now – were cigarettes, so it was much to our surprise that, later that evening and back in the farmhouse, Monsieur suddenly produced a full packet of twenty Player's!

'Surprised?' he said. We nodded as he explained: 'Do you remember that day that one of your aircraft made its drop over Malestroit? Well, I was in town very early that morning. In one of the cafés the Germans were so pleased with their finds that they offered me a packet, and I took it thinking that one day it might be useful. Today seems to be the day! Help yourselves.' He roared with laughter.

At one in the morning Babin's familiar laugh sounded outside the back door, followed by his pre-arranged knock.

He had done well: the girl would be producing my suitcase at breakfast time, Malestroit's mayor would have all the false papers ready within two days, and he had recruited the 'suitable person' from Plaudren, who was willing to help. 'He's not young, but he is good.'

'Go on,' I said.

'There's a small bar in the village whose owner is an old *résistant*. One of the first to join the Maquis, he's not bothered by the Germans. He left the organization to take over our intelligence-gathering in this area. If you see him you'll not be making a mistake.' Babin thought for a moment: 'On the other hand, it might be easier if I get him to visit us here.'

Cheered by Babin's better news, we eventually made for our field, where at three in the morning the first of our Maquis teams began to arrive as instructed. By dawn all had been redistributed as agreed with the farmer.

Such a success was this new move that we arranged to bring the rest of the 4th Battalion together as well, and, that having been decided, I suggested to Marienne that I should set off to round them up – plus the Colonel and Jim if they could be found, and also the two eldest of *les demoiselles Pondard*.

'It's not what you think,' I blushed, 'but if one of them accompanies me and the other goes with Babin on his excursions there'll be much less chance of a young couple being picked up by the Boche than a man by himself or even two together. We have papers excusing us from work in the north. It strikes me that it would be as good a cover as we can manage at the moment.'

Hitting me playfully on the shoulder, Marienne replied, 'You sly devil! But I guess you're right.'

Babin returned – which was just as well, for a little later a stranger approached our hide, walking close behind the farmer. We could take no chances, for the farmer might have had a gun in his back, and as the sentry slipped the safety catch off his rifle he looked back at us for orders.

'Hold your fire,' whispered Babin loudly. 'It's *le patron* from Plaudren – Monsieur Lecœur.'

The purchase of bicycles was arranged, the billeting-out of the SAS men was fixed – although it would take about two days for the selected farmers to be contacted, checked and cleared – and in the middle of all this my suitcase arrived balanced across the handlebars of a bicycle pushed by a young girl from Plumelec. We were beginning to feel a growing sense of purpose.

The best news of all was that the young lady knew the Pondard sisters and, even better, knew where they were and that they were well.

'So you must be Captain Bob,' she exclaimed as it suddenly dawned on her.

'You've heard of me?' I wasn't too sure that I wanted my precise identity known – even to the prettiest girl I had seen since the Saint-Marcel Maquis.

'Oh yes!' she said. 'Geneviève often talks of you.'

'Are you sure she's not muddling him up with me?' Marienne chipped in.

She looked closely into his face. 'Certainly!' she replied, kissing Marienne on his cheek but turning back to me with a grin.

'I would very much like to see the girls this evening,' I said, bringing the subject back to the present. 'For pleasure, of course, but also for some serious business. You had better warn them of that, in case they have second thoughts.'

'They're keen to help,' she answered, and with another kiss for Marienne she followed the farmer and Monsieur Lecœur back down the track.

When she had gone, we unanimously decided that only the farmer and his wife, Monsieur Lecœur, the girl from Plumelec and, shortly, the elder Pondard sisters should know of our new location. 'From now on,' I said, 'all our meetings must be on neutral ground, and I suggest Lecœur's café.'

Monsieur was back at eight that evening, wheeling a brand-new bicycle. 'I'm afraid I had to pay twelve thousand francs for this one,' he apologized. 'If I'd been able to use coupons it would only have been four thousand.' I counted out the money, then asked him to wait to see if the Pondard sisters would turn up, as I was keen to start planning the next phase of our work.

The girls arrived at nine o'clock that evening, and once the kissing and hugging had stopped and they had confirmed that their parents were fit and safe it was time for dinner. Afterwards, and with everything but the Calvados glasses cleared away, we all – myself, Marienne, Babin, the farmer and his wife, Monsieur Lecœur and the Pondard sisters – drew chairs into a wide semicircle around the big open fire.

'Our last Maquis was too large,' I began – 'too large and too important to be ignored by the Germans. Since then the whole area has suffered badly through the mistakes we made. Now we can only look forward,' I emphasized, 'so Marienne and I have decided to rebuild our forces in this area, and a signal will be sent to that effect. We'll split the Maquis and the SAS into small groups, permanently at one hour's notice for operations. At the moment no one has the vaguest idea where we are. The Cossacks have searched the area and found little – although that, of course, won't stop them arriving again unannounced. But with the lie of the land here we do have the advantage of a good alert time. I want nobody else to know that this is our headquarters, that this place exists at all – including all the maquisards and the SAS soldiers. Just the present fifty men, including ourselves, will be based here, although even that number is reduced by having eight men with Monsieur's sister and a further eight men working this farm. Papers for all those people will be with us shortly – thanks to the mayor of Malestroit. Anyone calling at this farm – and that includes our own men – will be met with blank expressions and will be told that no one has ever heard of us. This applies even to our friends and people we know. We can take no chances, and none of us wants a repeat performance – especially as there's no guarantee that we've been purged of traitors.

'The SAS troops will be split into groups of eight and will form up in various sections of the woods near by and, if we can find some more, in farms.'

I paused to look at Monsieur Lecœur. 'We'll need some more locations' – he nodded – 'and I'd like you, with Marienne, to find a good, easily defended emergency rendezvous area within three kilometres of here.

'So, to begin with, Babin and Anna Pondard and myself and Geneviève will call on the groups at their present locations – if we can find them – then direct them to the new rendezvous position. Marienne will conduct all the initial briefings, and Monsieur Lecœur will direct the groups one at a time to their new bases.'

'Henriette,' I looked at the third-eldest Pondard girl, who up till then had not been fully involved, and poured a small measure of apple brandy into her glass, 'I'd like you to stay with Marienne for liaison work between the groups and this headquarters. The girl from Plumelec will be asked to help out if this becomes excessive. I'll arrange to meet Geneviève every evening in the café or, if

necessary, in Callac. And we'll have to chose a suitable place there
as soon as we can.

'Before the SAS men get here, Marienne will continue to prepare
his plans, and once things start to happen I will reopen contact with
London. In the meantime I'll try and find a suitable field where
drops of not more than one aircraft per night might be made. One
of the mistakes at the other place was the vast aerial armadas each
night.'

I looked up, taking a long gulp of the fiery spirit before finishing,
'That's the plan. Any questions? Good! Babin and Anna can start
out at eight o'clock tomorrow morning, and Geneviève and I will
leave half an hour later. We'll cover the Trédion area, and you two
can sort out Malestroit and the not so obvious places around our
old Maquis.'

It was too late for the girls to return home, so arrangements were
made to stay at the farm, although Monsieur Lecœur felt it was safe
for him to leave.

The next day was going to be a long and probably dangerous
one, and as a treat – for myself – I began it by taking fresh coffee to
the girls. Returning to Marienne, I shook him warmly by the hand,
wished him luck, and was back in the farm for a seven o'clock
breakfast. Babin and Anna were the first away, and after giving
them a fifteen-minute start Geneviève turned to me.

'Bob,' she said, 'first I suggest we go to Callac, a few kilometres
away, to stop my mother worrying. She's staying for a few days
with a Madame Gambert, who runs a small village shop there.'

Although nothing had ever been said between us, it was not
entirely unplanned that we should work together. Our eyes had
often met, and every time I saw her I was sure my heart sped a
little. At her father's farm life had been too hectic and I was too
new in the area to have given any serious thought to anything other
than the war. Now the opportunity to work with her had been
presented I jumped at the chance – certainly before Marienne had
been able to make any alternative suggestions in his favour!

We bicycled away from the farm in a north-easterly direction,
and within the hour were leaning our bicycles against the wall of
Madame Gambert's remarkable emporium.[3] Geneviève had been

right when describing her mother's new home, but, though the shop may have been small, it appeared to sell everything from ashtrays to women's clothing and from men's clothing to farm machinery. It might be very useful.

No sooner had we made our introductions and satisfied ourselves that all was as well as possible, given the dramas of the time, than an inner door was flung open by the Maquis doctor – whose reputation for making himself comfortable was well established.

'Good morning, Captain,' he began. 'How are you?'

'I'm fine,' I replied, 'but the situation is pretty rotten.' It turned out that he, like us, was sleeping in the fields, but tending to his widely scattered patients by day. Like us as well, he knew nothing of Jim and Colonel Bourgoin's position or situation, although something that Geneviève said made me raise an eyebrow – other than that I kept quiet.

Once we had been briefed on the whereabouts of those whom he did know about it was time for Geneviève and I to get on the move. After a mile or so I selected a field off the quiet lane down which we had been pedalling. Through a gate and hidden from view, I turned and faced her.

'Where are Jim and the Colonel?' I was almost brutal with the suddenness and directness of the question – implying, as I meant it to, that I knew she knew the answer.

'I don't know,' she replied too quickly.

I turned and grabbed both her elbows; holding them firmly, I spoke as clearly as I could, only just managing to keep my voice level and even.

'Geneviève,' I looked directly into her eyes from a few inches away, 'you've been with the Maquis all the time, and I'm quite sure that you know where its leaders are. You must realize that Jim should not be with Colonel Bourgoin. The Colonel may have his own reasons for hiding, but he – Jim – is responsible for the Maquis. He's its leader. It's his duty to supervise its reorganization, to give his men the benefit of his knowledge and experience. His own safety should come last in his list of priorities. Just think of his men being slaughtered daily, the women being arrested, the girls being raped, the farms being burned, the farmers being shot. They worked for him once, and were loyal to him when he was in place. Now they're in a desperate situation they need his leadership and loyalty in return.

'And there's another thing. I must see the Colonel quickly if we're not to let resistance in this area of France fizzle out. With all the possible German reinforcements along the Atlantic coast ports, we could lose the war – and I'm not exaggerating.'

I let go of her arms and took a pace backwards. There were tears in her eyes, but whether of fear or of pain I could not tell.

'Now, Geneviève, I'll ask you again.'

She nodded, and looked down at the grass.

'Do you know where they are?'

'Yes.'

'Where?' I said harshly.

'They're living in a farm about twenty kilometres from here, by a small village surrounded by fields, ten kilometres north-west of the old Maquis.'

'Why didn't you tell me this before?'

'Sit down and I'll explain,' she said.

I sat, grudgingly, leaning back against the hedge.

'I went there three days ago and received a terrible welcome from Jim. He told me to get out and never come back again. I didn't see the Colonel, although I was certain he was somewhere close and probably listening. Jim was insulting, and made me promise to keep quiet about his hide. He seemed worried – frightened really – that I'd discovered him. I felt hurt after all we'd suffered for him and his men at the farm. Now, because of what you've said, I've no inclination at all to keep my promise.'

She was clutching her knees in both arms and shaking. I put a hand on her shoulder. 'Thank you, Geneviève,' I said, softly. 'I'll take Marienne and pay them a visit, but I won't let them know who told me. If they ask, I'll say we knew all along and leave it at that.'

She smiled as we stood to push our bicycles back into the lane. By noon, with some difficulty and not a little subterfuge, we had contacted four groups of five men each. All were 4th Battalion troopers, and all were without money, news or orders. At each place I explained how to contact Marienne, paid for their keep, gave the leaders a sum of money for their immediate future, and explained that under no circumstances were they to travel by day.

The afternoon's efforts were not so successful, for we only managed to track down one group of three men, to whom I also gave francs.

Leaving the bicycles and Geneviève in Plumelec, I walked the last three miles to our new headquarters, where, over dinner, Marienne and I agreed that the sooner we paid a visit to the two absent commanding officers the better.

10. The First Kiss

The following morning Marienne and I joined the farmer for breakfast, to find Babin already enjoying fresh coffee and bread. He had little to add to his previous reports and, like us, had had only a modicum of success in rounding up stragglers. The teams he had located all called for tobacco and cigarettes, but apart from that were raring to get going. He reminded me, which I had nearly forgotten, that today was the day for collecting the papers from Malestroit. Unlike those issued in England, these were of course not forged, although they would be made out in fictitious names.

I thanked him, and after confirming that he was available to descend upon Jim and the Colonel that evening we parted company. We would need to tell our respective *demoiselles* not to expect to see us for a couple of days.

I reached Callac in good time to find Geneviève waiting for me at the back of the shop, dressed in a light summer dress that the warm breeze was blowing around her slim legs.

'You look stunning!'

She smiled and stepped towards me. 'I wondered if you'd ever notice!'

I kissed her lightly on the lips. She blushed. 'I'm no saint,' I said in reply, 'so I've been trying not to!' We laughed and turned to our work. 'Malestroit is our first stop today.' I was serious again. 'We must collect the papers and, if we can find a friendly shop, enough tobacco and cigarettes to keep the men happy.'

'That shouldn't be difficult,' she said.

She had not been idle in my absence and, at the doctor's earlier request, had arranged for me to call on those patients who were still in his care and not that of the Germans.

The 'hospital' visits took two hours and covered a number of outlying farms, the journey being made easier by the absence of German patrols. By noon we had also contacted another team of soldiers, and we ended our morning of hard bicycling at a small café by the river Claie. Over a bottle of white wine, ham, bread and Camembert I looked closely at my companion. A number of odd events during the morning had puzzled me, and now, with time to reflect, I wanted to see if she felt the same. But I needed a little more evidence before taking her into my confidence.

In silence we mounted our bicycles and headed towards Plumelec and its neighbouring farms. Everywhere we were met with a surly welcome – indeed, they were hardly welcoming at all.

'Let's get out of here – and quickly,' I ordered. 'Something's wrong, and I can't figure out what.' She must have deduced the same, for without a second thought we were speeding south towards the Trédion woods, where we had earlier built two temporary camps. It was Geneviève's idea to visit them, to see if they had been reoccupied. 'We might find a clue to all this suspicion,' she had said before pedalling on ahead.

We found the tracks into the woods, and soon entered the nearest hiding place. It had been lived in until recently, yet neither the SAS soldiers nor the maquisards would have left such obvious signs. An eerie feeling persisted which almost matched that which we had experienced in the village. Precisely that same feeling must have overwhelmed Geneviève, for we said, almost together, 'Let's try the other place.' Twenty minutes later we were standing deeper in the woods and feeling even more uneasy with what we had found.

Laying the bicycles on the ground, we sat down on the grass of a small glade with a bright-blue gap in the canopy through which the afternoon sunlight slanted towards the east along leaf-interrupted shafts. I tugged out a packet of French cigarettes, lit two, and gave one to Geneviève.

We needed something to take our minds away from the puzzle – a puzzle that, I knew, had dangerous undertones I could not yet identify.

'I like you,' I said, partly because I could think of nothing else to say and partly because, as a fact, it was long overdue. 'In fact I think you're wonderful.' She wasn't to know that I was trying to refer to her work with us, but before she could reply we were startled by a crashing in the bushes in front and someone shouting loudly in bad English.

'Put your hands up! Stay where you are!'

'*Pardon?*' I replied in French. '*Je ne comprends pas!*'

The man repeated the order – this time in his native language – while four companions came out from the undergrowth to stand either side of him. All wore British battledress, with the maroon berets and shoulder flashes of airborne forces, and were armed with Sten guns.

'Can I throw away my cigarette first?'

'Don't move. We're maquisards attached to the 4th Battalion of *parachutistes* under the command of Colonel Bourgoin, and we're looking for Marienne and Bob. We dropped with them some days back, and are now lost. We've visited the farms in the Plumelec area, but no one's been able to help. Do you know their whereabouts?'

'Know what? Tell you what?' I feigned.

'Where our officers are. Where our battalion's headquarters and the new Maquis are. We got split up after a battle near Saint-Marcel, and are desperate to catch up with them so we can continue the fight.'

'Marienne? Bob? Maquis? Battalion? Are you crazy? I haven't the slightest idea what you're talking about.' As there was no response I went on, 'I heard that the Germans had destroyed a Maquis and taken a lot of prisoners, but that's all.'

It wasn't good enough. 'Tell us all you know!' two of them shouted almost at once.

'Damn it! Tell you what? You bloody maquisards have caused enough trouble around here. I've never had anything to do with these people of yours, and I don't want to start now,' I shouted back.

There was a pause before the apparent leader said less aggressively, 'What are you doing here anyway?' They looked at both of us in turn. 'Yes, in this place – this Maquis.'

'I had no idea it was a Maquis. We stumbled on it and decided it was a peaceful place for a cigarette.'

'Oh yes!' he snarled.

'Yes!' I snarled equally unpleasantly. 'Wouldn't you do the same thing with your girlfriend on a day off?'

'Probably,' one smirked.

The leader turned to him. 'Shut up!' he said, then faced us again. 'Kiss her! Go on. Kiss her!'

'I can't!' I replied as coolly as my rising anger would allow. The first kiss I had been planning did not include an audience.

'If she's your girlfriend, why can't you kiss her?'

'Have you ever tried to kiss a girl with your hands reaching for the stars?'

'Put them down and get on with it.'

I looked towards Geneviève, who was frightened and puzzled.

As I turned away from the soldiers and hid her face from them with mine, she whispered, 'Do something – I've been waiting a long time for this!'

Her lips were warm and responsive, and I wished we could have stayed together, but I was determined – even if she was not – to offer our intruders the minimum of gratification. We parted, slowly, but with our eyes searching each other's face for some understanding.

'Get out of here, the pair of you. Don't ever come back. And if you tell the Germans of us . . . well . . . we'll find you.'

'Come on,' I said to Geneviève, but hissed over my shoulder as I stooped for my bicycle, 'One day you'll pay for this. I'll not forget your faces, and I hope the Germans win this bloody war.'

We rode away as quickly as possible, lurching and skidding down the rough woodland track until eventually we broke clear at the edge of a field and, panting but still astride our bicycles, rested against the fence.

'Bob, who were they? Did you know them? What were they doing?' Her questions, pent up for twenty long minutes, came tumbling out.

'You know that we couldn't get any information out of the Plumelec farms?'

'Yes.'

'Well, I now know why everyone's so frightened and suspicious.'

'Go on,' she prompted impatiently.

'Those chaps are the reason why.'

'I don't understand,' she persisted.

'Geneviève, they're *miliciens*.'

23. The road from Saint-Marcel to L'Abbaye. It was along this road in the early hours of 18 June that two German cars were ambushed, precipitating the Battle of Saint-Marcel.

24. Defending La Nouette later that day.

25. A medical team at the farm before the battle.

26. La Nouette after the battle.

27. An aerial view of Saint-Marcel.

28. Members of the Maquis de Saint-Marcel re-equipped after the battle.

29. The Château de Callac, where many of the parachutists and Resistance fighters who had survived the battle immediately regrouped.

30. Monsieur and Madame Gambert's house in Callac today (*left*, behind the cars). It is largely unchanged since André used the attic bedroom. The building to the right was the shop.

31. The balcony of Malestroit town hall where André and the mayor smoked while Geneviève padded her underclothes with false papers.

32. A recent photograph of the barn where André and Geneviève had a lucky escape after watching the Germans enter Trédion.

33. American troops being greeted on the liberation of Malestroit.

34. Raising the colours at Saint-Marcel after the Germans had left. The village was destroyed as part of a series of reprisals after the battle at La Nouette.

35. The impressive monument to the Resistance stands close to the main Vannes–Ploërmel motorway, and very close to La Nouette farm itself.

36. The inscription at the base of the monument proclaims that Resistance forces and Free French parachutists battled against the Germans for 24 hours, killing 560 enemy troops and suffering the loss of 42 men.

37. André (*right,* in the uniform of the 9th Parachute Battalion) with his half-brother, Jean, after the war.

38. André (*below*) returned many times to Brittany after the war. Here he is seen at Saint-Marcel's Musée de la Résistance, fifty years after his exploits there, pointing to the exhibit of his fake identity card.

She gulped a short breath. 'Oh my God!'

'Two French traitors disguised as parachutists. You notice that the others didn't speak? Germans. Almost certainly Gestapo.'

She spoke softly and with tears in her eyes. 'That was a narrow escape. When they said they were looking for you and Marienne I nearly gave the whole game away. At the last moment something made me suspicious of the way they wore their uniforms.'

'Thank God for that,' I exclaimed, 'or we would both be on our way to a cell or, worse, to a wall!'

But more personal emotions still coursed through my blood, and, if I had nothing else to thank them for, the enemy had at least forced me to kiss the girl who was now occupying a major part of my life. They had forced me to do something that I had been too shy to do myself – as it were. I needed to continue the momentum! 'And, by the way . . .' I took a deep breath in case her earlier and apparent enthusiasm had been only for the benefit of the Gestapo. 'I apologize for that kiss. I had no choice.'

'What are you apologizing for?'

'The kiss, Geneviève – the kiss. I'm sorry.'

'You think you could do better?'

'Yes,' I said, my heart leaping.

'Then get off your bicycle!'

It must have been a good five minutes before we surfaced as I pushed her away gently and looked in her eyes, 'Geneviève,' I murmured reluctantly, 'it's four o'clock. We must push on. It's a long way back to Callac, and we haven't been to Malestroit yet.'

Suddenly she became businesslike again. 'It would be better to go first to Sérent and ask there what conditions are like in Malestroit – and at least we've been forewarned about the reception we're likely to receive. From there it'll be eight more kilometres.'

We pedalled for an hour to the outskirts of Sérent, where we learned that nothing out of the ordinary was reported to be happening at our destination, so it was with some surprise that, on turning right on to the Malestroit road, we were confronted by a gendarme surrounded by civilians. Before we reached them and as we slowed to a stop, Geneviève whispered that she knew the policeman and his companions.

'*Bonjour, Mademoiselle Pondard*.' He lowered his hand. 'What a surprise.'

She smiled at him as I caught up alongside her.

There was no need for introductions, and I certainly offered none.

'Unless your papers are in good order,' he said, 'I wouldn't advise visiting Malestroit today. The town is surrounded by Germans. All men between the ages of eighteen and fifty have been rounded up and are being paraded in the main square for identification.'

'Thank you,' she replied. 'We'll take your advice.' And with that and a number of cheery waves we reversed our course and headed back into Sérent. We had had one too many close shaves for the day without deliberately giving ourselves another.

Reaching the village centre safely, we called on the only *tabac*, where I surprised the elderly proprietress with a request for a hundred packets each of cigarettes and tobacco.

'The ration is one packet per week – surely you know that!'

I explained – with some initial trepidation – that the men I represented could not visit her themselves and, even if they could, they had left their ration cards in England.

She indicated that she understood with a sly nod, but added, 'How can I trust you?'

'How can I trust you, madame?' I countered.

'I'll get my gendarme friend,' suggested Geneviève, and once he had been summoned I explained that I was Captain Bob and that the morale of my men depended on the success of our mission.

She refused money, saying that she would give me a letter stating that the 'goods' were being redistributed to smaller shops. If I was stopped, it would be my problem to explain how they came to be in my possession in the first place, and I was prepared to cross that bridge when – and if . . .

Half an hour later we were back in Callac, and after leaving Geneviève and some tobacco for the wounded I set off as quickly as sense dictated to join Marienne, where we distributed the remainder of the bounty. That having been done, I debriefed him on our day – without mentioning our enforced kiss.

'I don't like it, Marienne,' I concluded. 'I only got away because they said they'd dropped with you and me and I knew that they hadn't.'

'Well, at least we know the name of the game now – and luckily before anyone's been taken in by them. But I agree: it'll probably be only a matter of time before someone slips up.'

Marienne had also had an eventful day. He had rounded up a number of SAS teams, including one officer who had escaped naked when ambushed during an early-morning wash: his uniform was now one more in the hands of the enemy.

'Frankly, an extra battledress is not going to make much difference,' I said.

'Quite – but what with that and your news I'll warn the girls, and they'll get the message around all the farms and as many of the locals as they think should know.' He looked up as the farm door opened to reveal Babin's usual grin.

'Good day?' I began.

'Yes and no. We weren't stopped – the roads were clear – but I only contacted one team.'

'You were lucky,' Marienne interrupted while pouring Babin a glass of Calvados. 'Listen to Bob's story.'

When I had finished, Babin cried softly, '*Miliciens!* Gestapo! I thought there was something odd. I saw a team of three sniffing round various farms and didn't like the look of them, so I didn't go anywhere near – even after they'd left. It's going to make it bloody difficult for the locals to know who's who, and frankly I'll hardly blame them if they're not too careful with what they say – they have more to lose than us. Their farms will be burned, their women will be raped, and then they'll all be shot. Our chaps will just be shot!'

And with those thoughts we turned, gloomily, to supper and a last cigarette.

At eleven that night and with blackened faces we slipped into a clear, warm countryside across which we were able to make good time without having to take too many precautions. We were on our way to find Jim and Colonel Bourgoin.

We had fifteen miles to cover to the north-east, and by four o'clock had covered about nine of them. A convenient barn loomed ahead in the beginning of the dawn light, and we rested there with cigarettes and cooling coffee from a flask. With six miles to go, and with me and Babin in civilian clothes and Marienne in uniform, we washed off our 'night make-up'. If we were lucky the rest of the journey could be conducted under cover of trees and thick scrubland. Marienne would have little chance of bluffing his way out of a German roadblock, but Babin and I would have a better chance if we were no longer camouflaged.

As the clock crept towards seven we approached a low, bush-covered crest line from the top of which we had a panoramic view of the French country. A lone farm nestled in a copse of trees about half a mile away.

'That's it,' said Babin. 'That's where they're hiding.'

Although we were certain there were no enemy watching, we made a tactical approach. We had no idea how we would be treated, but if Geneviève's account was only half correct it was not likely to be favourably.

Two hundred yards out from the farm several maquisards seemed to be acting as sentries – half-asleep after what had probably been a long and boring night. We surprised them – but not enough to have them jumping for their weapons. It did not bode well. Although I realized the initial need for Bourgoin to rush into hiding, I reckoned there was a limit and that at the end of that time risks had to be taken if we were to carry out our mission.

'Who are you? What do you want?' the maquisards shouted. They should have recognized us, but, just to make sure, I stepped forward.

'I'm Captain Bob, and this officer', I said pointing to Marienne in his SAS uniform, 'is Captain Marienne. We're here to see Colonel Bourgoin.'

The maquisard who appeared to be in charge must have accepted our identities – but replied quickly, 'My orders are that no one is to visit here, and that comes from the Colonel himself and is confirmed by Jim.'

He turned to Marienne: 'Can I see your papers, please, sir.'

This was close to the last straw for Marienne, who clearly had been recognized and who had been instrumental not only in the maquisard's training but probably, through his leadership on 18 June, in saving his life.

'No, blast you,' he said deliberately in a voice colder than any I had heard from him as he drew his pistol. 'You'll go right now and tell the Colonel that we're here.'

The man hesitated. Marienne continued, 'Or I'll blast your bloody brains out.' That was enough, and the maquisard sped off down the heavily rutted track while we moved to a patch of grass and sat smoking – out of earshot of the sentries.

Marienne broke the silence: 'I'm beginning to boil, and if I don't get an answer in a few minutes I shall force my way into the farm.'

I looked up without speaking, for I had not seen Marienne in such a mood and did not want to anger him further. 'Here's the sentry coming back now.' I squinted down the track and into the rising sun. 'And I think he's got Jim's brother with him.'

Marienne stood, but I put a hand on his shoulder and said, 'If you don't mind I think I'll have a word first. Just wait here a moment.' I felt rather than saw Marienne nod.

Stepping in front of the two Frenchmen, I said, 'Good morning.' Then, with a laugh, added, 'I must say you were not that easy to find.' I wanted to reduce the apparent tension, for we were all in this together.

But Jim's brother brought an unwelcome response: 'The Colonel and Jim can't see you now.' At least he came straight to the point.

I watched Marienne's face grow red with anger, then Babin's, while I too fought to control my temper. We had not come all this way from England to hear such unprofessional, almost craven, rubbish.

Trusting my temper marginally more than Marienne's, I decided to continue speaking for the three of us. 'Then you can go straight back and tell the two of them this. First, I do not take orders from either of them. Second, if they do not come to their senses in ten minutes Jim can consider himself under arrest. The liberating forces will know how to deal with someone who has refused to support them. And, third, you will tell the Colonel that I intend to re-establish contact with his headquarters this evening, and will have no hesitation in sending an adverse situation report.'

Jim's brother looked at me with a vacant expression. His mouth slowly opened to reply, but he must have thought better of it for it shut again.

'Now get going,' I barked, to prevent any further discussion.

Glad to be temporarily rid of our company, he was soon back with an invitation to follow. We were led past a young woman playing with two small children – they didn't look like farm people – to the back of the main building, where, sitting on the ground with their backs resting against a haystack, were Colonel Bourgoin in civilian clothes, Jim and an officer I did not know.

As soon as we appeared Jim stood and, squaring up to us, said without an ounce of friendliness in either his voice or his words, 'Look, Bob, you can't do this sort of thing – butting into our hideout and getting us spotted by the Gestapo –'

I didn't let him finish. 'Shut up, Jim. Just shut up,' I repeated as my blood pressure rose another notch. I looked down at the three of them without attempting to disguise the contempt I felt.

'The three of you,' I growled, 'just listen to me.' They shifted awkwardly against the hay, but I was in no mood to give any quarter. 'Since the Maquis was disbanded we've done our best, yet when we finally catch up with you skulking like terrified rabbits you try to turn away. What have you done here? Nothing but hide I'll bet. Did you bother about the safety of your men? No! Did you try to reorganize them? No! So, what have you done? Not a damn thing except look after your own backsides! And now what do you intend doing? Nothing!'

Beside me, on either side, Marienne and Babin nodded.

There was a long silence, but if the three officers expected me to use the pause to cool down and apologize they mistook our mood. I continued to stand over them, my hands on my hips and my eyes glaring.

It was probably thirty seconds before the Colonel spoke. 'Well, Bob,' he said, 'we must all keep quiet until the hunt for us is over – or has at least calmed down a bit more. It's impossible to reorganize under the present circumstances, and in the meantime the men will be fine in all the various farms. There are a few teams in this area – they're safe for the time being – and we've been trying to contact the others. Jim has begun plans for a new Maquis, so we've not been totally idle.'

Marienne could take no more. 'None of that is good enough. Now let me tell you what *we* have done, and what *all of us* are going to do.' Marienne seemed oblivious to the fact that his audience included his commanding officer, but I agreed with him and was prepared to jump to his support should that become necessary. He continued, covering all our marches, the good and bad luck, the farmers killed, the farms that were razed, our supply of new papers waiting for us in Malestroit, the way we had begun to reform the teams, the positive actions of the Grog teams, the manner in which we were looking after them all, and – he emphasized this last point – 'Our good fortune at finding you at long last.'

He had spoken for an hour, without any need to play up the dangers we had faced and overcome, and in doing so he had repeated that we had yet to lose a man despite the three of us having a price on our heads. But, he admitted, we didn't have the disadvantage, from the identity point of view, of having one of our number with only one arm. It was the only concession he made in a full-frontal attack which hit home hard.

Another, longer, silence followed, and as no one seemed keen to break it I followed on with my own plans, aiming my comments directly at Jim.

'I've already begun setting up a new Maquis, and I expect you to take it over under the supervision and control of Marienne . . .' I began. And so for another hour we discussed the plans that Marienne and I had already put into action. We asked neither Jim nor the Colonel for their opinions, making it quite clear that what we had already begun we would all continue.

With the Colonel still anxious to keep a low profile, or even no profile at all, there was no argument that Marienne should assume command of the whole Maquis of maquisards and SAS soldiers, with full powers to make any operational decision. The Colonel would take over only when he himself felt that it was safe to do so; in the meantime, Marienne was to assume responsibility for the three *départements* of Morbihan, Côtes-du-Nord and Ille-et-Vilaine. I would be jointly responsible, with him, for the reorganization of the whole thing, and at the same time carry out my original job as adviser to him – in lieu of the Colonel – for special operations, drops, security and the main link with London.

We broke up at 10.30 with our plans aired and discussed. There had been no serious counter-arguments, as Marienne and I held all the key cards and the Colonel acknowledged that – although it was not until lunch and a cup of coffee that we received the nearest we would get to an apology.

At last there was no more to say, and by ten o'clock that evening we had slipped back into 'our' field without, as far as we had been able to detect, being spotted.

With a report that all was well up at the farm, we were received with a magnificent ham omelette, cheese and cider, followed by coffee and Calvados.

The next morning I caught Geneviève in the middle of her breakfast, and after a rather chaste good-morning kiss she asked, 'What's the programme for today?'

I told her, and we were soon pedalling towards the river near which we had lunched a few days back and where, as had been arranged by Marienne, we met Puech-Samson. I quickly explained 'the story so far'.

Encouragingly, he had with him four SAS soldiers and five maquisards, while his leg wound had healed sufficiently for him to move about without too much discomfort. With this team of ten fully briefed and already gathering together their meagre belongings, Geneviève and I pushed on towards Malestroit and the waiting papers.

After only one cursory look at our current papers at the permanent roadblock stationed at the entrance to the town, we were soon sitting in the mayor's office. He looked sternly across his desk. 'Captain, I have the twenty sets of identity papers ready, but the problem will be getting them out of the town. It's quite easy to enter, as you have just seen, but everyone is searched much more thoroughly when leaving.'

'We must get them out today,' I replied unhelpfully.

The mayor shrugged. After all, he had done his bit and stood to be accused if we were caught with 'his' papers.

Geneviève came to the rescue. 'Are they very bulky?' she asked. 'Because, if not, then I think I can help.'

I shook my head slowly as the mayor answered, 'They are – quite. Twenty identity cards, twenty refugee cards, twenty ration cards, plus various birth certificates, army-exemption cards, bicycling permits and other odd ration cards.'

'Can you hide all that and get away with it?' I asked. You're only wearing a light summer dress.'

'Yes, I think so.'

'Where and how?'

'Never you mind,' she laughed, and turned back to the mayor. 'Give them to me, and if you'll leave me alone for a few minutes I'll see what I can do. Go and smoke a cigarette on the balcony or something. But lock the door first.'

I pulled out a packet of Gauloises and offered one to the mayor as we stepped into the first-floor balcony's sunshine. We talked for ten minutes: his news was not good, and I had not expected it to be. The enemy were still searching the fields, woods, farms and outlying villages. The *Milice*, disguised as French and British para-troopers, were active everywhere: farms were still being burned and farmers murdered on the flimsiest of excuses – and sometimes, he said, with no excuse at all. Stray maquisards continued to be rounded up; the prisons in Vannes and Rennes were grossly overcrowded; screams could still be heard from behind the walls; and there were rumours that large prizes were being offered for information that led to even more detentions. A doctor, three nuns and two girls had been arrested in Malestroit; the town's police lieutenant was under suspicion for helping us; and his own local gendarmerie was run by a German officer.

I offered a little news in exchange, without divulging our plans, and in return he said that he would try to persuade the local police to arrest those men who were masquerading as British soldiers – a forlorn hope.

He agreed to see Geneviève every three days to pass on the latest information, and at that moment a shout from inside the room told us that she was ready for inspection. The same lovely Geneviève stood grinning at me, and for a moment I noticed no difference –

until my eyes moved slowly down over her breasts, waist and hips. She was definitely plumper, but not obviously so to anyone who did not know her. In fact she seemed rather buxom and alluring – an image, I thought mischievously, that perfectly fitted her farming background.

The mayor wished us luck – as much for his own preservation, I imagined, as ours. Sensibly, he didn't come out into the street to wave us goodbye, and soon we were on the main road that heads north-west along the banks of the river Oust, where the expected roadblock barred our passage. A chill ran through my stomach and down my back. Up to now we had had genuine papers – even if mine were in a false name, they were at least the real thing and not forged in London. This time, though, we also carried incriminating evidence that, if discovered, would destroy any righteous indignation.

We came to a stop with our legs splayed either side of our bicycles. A German soldier, rifle hung across his front, stepped forward. '*Papiers, s'il vous plaît.*'

We dismounted properly and walked towards him. Three or four of his colleagues leered at Geneviève from the edge of the ditch, while another pair aimed a tripod-mounted machine gun towards my midriff.

The soldier studied my papers carefully and handed them back without a smile.[1] He stepped closer and ran his hands over my pockets, down my legs and under my armpits.

'*Ça va. Partez,*' he growled with a rough accent before pushing me away and turning towards Geneviève.

I dared not look, but made a play of slowly mounting my bicycle in the middle of the road. Out of the corner of my eye I could just see him running his hand, too slowly, over Geneviève's ample form.

With immense relief I heard the words '*Vous aussi. Ça va.*'

I turned and jerked my head towards the open countryside. 'Come on, we'll be late for lunch,' I said as calmly as I could, and with a smile for the Germans we pedalled strongly away.

Once clear I crept up alongside my partner. 'Lucky again,' I said.

'Yes, but I was terrified. I thought his hands would notice my shaking if not the papers themselves. The beast took his time, and it had nothing to do with searching.'

'Can you keep them till we reach Callac?'

'Oh yes,' she said, and an hour later we dismounted at her mother's temporary home and spread the papers before us.

'How did you hide them?'

'I'd have thought that was pretty obvious, but if not you'll just have to work it out for yourself: I must keep some secrets.' She roared with laughter.

As, according to Geneviève, the day was still young, she suggested a picnic by the river. 'The Claie is so beautiful at this time of the year. I'll get some bread and cider.'

We sat on the bank and at the edge of the ripening corn, where no one could have seen us. My arm was round her shoulder as we smoked and drank before tearing off lengths of fresh bread and filling them with slices of ham. Our moment of peace passed too quickly before it was time to return to the tragic reality of our lives – but not before we kissed at length and passionately. Then, in silence, we cycled back to the pile of papers in the Gamberts' kitchen.

Not having 'undergarments' behind which my secrets could be hidden, I had no choice but to take a risk and stuff the papers into my pockets for the final leg of their journey.

Back in 'our' farmhouse, Marienne, Babin and I exchanged reports on our day's activities. Babin had seen a couple of *miliciens* in Allied uniforms asking questions at an isolated farm, but no more than that. Monsieur Lecœur had spent much of his day collating local intelligence. Particularly good news was the discovery of two more of our teams, which Henriette had led to their new hiding place.

Marienne's day had been mercifully free of dramas: only once had he noticed a couple of *Milice* traitors disguised as Allied soldiers fussing around a remote farm. He hadn't followed their visit for fear of confusing the frightened inhabitants further.

Marienne finished our collective debriefings. 'One of the teams told me that a couple of miles from Plumelec and above the hamlet of Cadoudal there is a hollow between ridges which have excellent views across the country. In this dip lie three farms – the main one being Kérihuel. They are well hidden, surrounded by good cover and with concealed approaches, good defence positions and plenty of hiding places in the nearby woods.

'The Germans themselves seem to be scaling back their searches outside the towns as they don't seem to be getting too many results. I'm thinking that the farms will be worth a recce, and if suitable we could move our HQ there and leave the other teams this area.'

'Take Babin with you tomorrow night – he'll know the best route,' I said. And with Babin nodding his approval we settled down to a welcome dinner, at the end of which I called for a toast to Geneviève.

Afterwards Marienne and I lay back, each on a hay palliasse at the edge of the field, neither of us feeling like sleep. A good moon gazed down at us through a cloudless night sky.

'Bob,' Marienne drew on a cigarette and breathed out slowly, the smoke hanging above his face, 'planes will be coming over. Men will be dropping all across Europe.' He paused, dragging in another cloud of nicotine-laden smoke. Then, 'Shall we get a drop this moon, I wonder? Tomorrow I'll open up our link with London.'

'I wonder if the moon realizes the important role she's playing in this war?' I offered.

'If she did she'd blush with pride!'

I wriggled deeper into my straw, and spoke of my last few days with Geneviève and of my admiration for her courage and desire to help. 'She even refers to the Maquis as "her" Maquis.'

Marienne's silence was longer than usual, and when he did speak it was softly. 'Are you in love with her?'

I suppose I had been expecting this sometime, though it was a question I had not dared to ask myself. 'I don't know. I like her immensely, and admire her even more than that.'

'Does she love you?'

'I don't know that either, Marienne, and in a way I hope not.' I changed the subject. 'I overheard some of your men talking the other day. They mentioned adventures in North Africa and a lucky escape. What was all that about?'

'Little to tell actually, Bob.' He lit an English cigarette, which we kept for the evenings: not to be taken 'on the road'. 'I was there under the Vichy government – a lieutenant in the French Army. But I left to join de Gaulle, then got caught before reaching the Free French forces. I was court-martialled, sentenced to death, and due to be shot the next morning, but during that night the Allies landed and liberated me. I immediately joined de Gaulle and, well, that's about it and here I am lying in the moonlight with only you as company!'

'It's a rough life!'

11. Regrouping

Marienne fell asleep almost immediately, and I tried hard to follow his lead, but the incidents of the last few days were too vividly imprinted on my mind.

Geneviève was young, vivacious, intelligent and certainly brave, so, now that the question had been asked, could I answer it to myself if not to Marienne? Life was too much of a turmoil and I did not know her well – the next few days would tell. And the next few days had to tell considerably more than that, for, since arriving in France, we had caused more trouble to our own side than we had to the Germans, and it could not be long before our leaders in England came to that same conclusion. The sooner we could get the new, dispersed, Maquis operational under the command of Colonel Bourgoin and Jim the better, and if that could be achieved soon I promised myself a weekend break in Callac with Geneviève and, frankly, 'damn the war'!

And with that I must have fallen asleep.

The strong dawn light woke me, and I made my way to the farm, filled a bucket with cold water, and poured it over my head. Babin was waiting, but one look at his face suggested that I didn't need to ask if the news he had brought was bad. I asked anyway.

'One of our arms dumps has been raided,' he reported – 'a captured maquisard was tortured until forced to give its location away. And, if that's not bad enough, you should know that it's the Callac dump that's gone.'

Too close to home.

'Once they'd confirmed all they'd been told, the poor lad was made to dig his own grave then stand in it while they shot him.'

I thought for a few moments while Marienne savagely denounced the Germans as 'bastards and scum'.

'It's partly our fault.'

Marienne looked at me. 'Yes, I think that's true.'

Anna and Geneviève chose that moment to arrive for the day's work.

'You've heard the news?' they asked.

'Has it affected you?' I replied.

'They searched a number of houses – including ours – but found nothing. Trédion, though, was not so lucky. They acquired a number of Sten guns in various houses to add to their haul from the dump. They've burned one farm and intensified their searches. One of the teams heading for this place was nearly caught by some *Milice*, but they managed to withdraw and get the bastards off the scent. The Germans have killed one man, but, as far as I know, nobody has been captured alive to give anything away about the new Maquis – or even that we're planning to re-establish one.'

We had to get on. 'Babin and Anna,' I ordered, 'continue with the work you're doing. Talk to the battalion commanders about the weapons situation. Tonight I want you to take Marienne to the possible new HQ.' I turned to Marienne: 'You know what to do. Geneviève and I will go to the Trédion woods and see if we can find the two teams on the run there and point them towards a safer place.' And with those simplest of orders we pedalled off at intervals on our various missions.

I reached the edge of the woods at about ten o'clock that morning and stopped with Geneviève alongside me.

Without pointing, she told me to look across the adjoining fields, 'See that small copse – off to the right – this side of the main wood?'

'Yes. By a patch of disturbed earth.'

'That's the old dump.'

I nodded.

'And now it's a grave.' There were tears in her eyes.

We had been passed by a German patrol, but received only suggestive signs from them, aimed at Geneviève. German lewdness was a fair price to remain unmolested. Monsieur Gambert greeted us in the Callac shop, where the sound of gunfire could be heard from the woods to the south. We decided to investigate.

After pedalling as nonchalantly as possible through Trédion and then for a further two and a half miles, we sat in the same place as our previous day's picnic. But there was no time to repeat that precious moment: more shots rattled across the fields almost as soon as we had laid down our bicycles. The firing came from somewhere between Callac and Trédion.

'Stay here,' I said quickly, 'on this side of the river. I'm going to cross over. As soon as I've disappeared, follow down the river for a kilometre and wait for me there. Don't hide or do anything suspicious. You're just enjoying a summer day.'

She nodded gravely as I went on, 'The moment you see me leading the teams back, try and cover our tracks. Sit there for a few minutes, then get back to Callac. If you get stopped, try and detain the Germans for as long as possible – and I know enough about you to know that you'll find some deliciously effective way to do that.'

She smiled.

'If anything goes wrong, let Marienne know as soon as possible.'

'And I think I know enough about you to know that nothing *will* go wrong.'

Geneviève stood and kissed me gently on the lips. I held her waist tightly, smiled into her eyes, then turned for the river's edge.

I was quickly on the other side – the river only coming up to my knees – from where I waved to the slight figure in a cotton dress.

There was no time to think about tactics, so I set off at a half run and half gallop towards where I had last heard the gunfire, and after a good half-hour I felt I was getting close. Self-preservation then took over, and I began a belly-crawl into thick scrub. Creeping forward, I was able to watch my 'lost' men crouching in similar scrub about a hundred yards away and firing at an enemy I couldn't see. A line of thick bushes linked our two positions, allowing me to creep closer until the enemy came into view. I watched them steadily encircling my soldiers, and wanted to shout a warning, but as neither side had seen me I held my tongue and continued my stealthy progress.

Shortly, I recognized an officer I knew from the Saint-Marcel Maquis, Lieutenant Taylor, and at that moment there was suddenly no time left, as the Germans had worked their way on to our own ground.

I shouted softly, 'Taylor!'

He turned. Surprised. The enemy, also surprised, opened fire. They missed, then stopped long enough for me to cross the last few yards at a run. More firing followed me, but I remained unscathed.

It was not the time for pleasantries. 'Have you anything important in your kit?'

'No, sir. Only clothing, food and ammunition.'

'OK. All of you,' I swept a glance around Taylor's teams, 'leave everything here. Dump anything that might delay you. You're going to follow me. The wood is twenty-three kilometres long, but we'll get down to the river then follow it until we reach Geneviève, who'll be on the opposite bank. There are no Germans there – or at least there weren't when I left her. If there's a problem, she'll try to divert them. If not, cross over and she'll lead you away. If we remain here they'll bring in reinforcements. I'm surprised they haven't done so already.'

I'd talked enough. The firing started again, and this time it was too close.

'Right,' I shouted, 'give them everything you've got.' They needed no encouragement, while we escaped under cover of a roar of assorted weapons as each man covered another in a series of dashes towards the river's bank.

The Germans were so taken aback that they held their fire just long enough for us to gain new cover. It then took us some twenty minutes to reach the bank, from where I could see Geneviève standing at the entrance to a path into the woods on the far side. With the two teams following close behind me, we splashed to the opposite bank where, without stopping, I grabbed my bicycle, kissed her, shouted what she had to do, and continued my mad dash through the trees and bushes, leaving her to her fate.

We ran for over fifteen minutes, then stopped for a moment or two to catch our breath and to ensure that we were all safe before setting off for another fifteen minutes. Finally I stopped the headlong rush and, while we sat in a clearing, smoking, I issued Taylor with his new orders. He was to lead his men westward, to the main Plumelec–Vannes road, and then find the Kilometre 47 roadside marker stone. Geneviève would be waiting there, and would lead them to Marienne. Provided, of course, she had not had to act as a decoy. I had arranged to meet her in the meantime in Callac, where I would tell her what she had to do.

It took me eighty minutes to reach Callac: eighty long minutes not knowing if Geneviève would be there. She was – although she had perhaps had a close call.

I burst into the shop. 'What happened?' I asked, unable to hide my relief at her safety.

'About ten minutes after you left with the two teams, the Germans arrived panting and puffing – I don't think they're as fit as us. As I'd heard them coming from some way off, I felt that I should be doing something, so I splashed water over my face and patted my cheeks a few times. They were on the opposite bank and didn't seem to want to get their feet wet.' I smiled at her – and her bravery. 'They shouted across, and one of them, actually a *milicien*, asked if I'd seen a group of men running away. I said, "Yes", and pointed to the bank they were on. I shouted that they'd all run back into the woods once they – you – had seen the river and the open meadows.'

'Well done,' I murmured inadequately.

'I told them that you said you'd shoot me if I told them the direction you'd gone in. It was a sort of bluff, but I don't think they quite understood as they turned quickly and ran back along the false trail.'

'You are wonderful,' I said, 'as I may have mentioned before.'

She smiled and took my hand. 'I'm not only doing it for France. You know that, don't you?'

I looked at the floor between us. 'Yes,' I murmured before looking into her eyes. There was yet one more task I had for her. 'Could you add the finishing touch to the day?'

She nodded.

'I want you to go on your bicycle to the Kilometre 47 marker on the Plumelec-to-Vannes road and wait there for the two teams. They must be got across the road and on to Marienne. He'll be waiting for you some distance from the farm, so we don't give away its position to anyone except the Lieutenant. Do you think you can do that?'

'Of course. It'll take them three hours to get there and me only one, so I don't have to go quite yet. Nor do I want to be hanging around on the edge of the woods for too long. Anything might happen.'

I washed in the outhouse while Geneviève left a pile of clothes from the shop outside the door. Clean and fresh, I was soon munching sandwiches, drinking cool cider out of a stone flagon, and thanking God that Geneviève was on our side. Sitting opposite me, she looked so lovely in her light dress that I suddenly knew how to answer Marienne's question.

Several German cars passed through the village, but I had to get on the road myself and so with papers in good order and carrying nothing more incriminating than packets of cigarettes – and the authorization to be distributing them to other *tabacs* – I slowly pedalled my way towards Marienne. The relief to find him, Geneviève and Lieutenant Taylor peacefully drinking cider in the farm's kitchen was immense.

'As agreed,' Marienne said after we had recounted our different experiences of the day, 'I'll get to the proposed new Maquis by dawn, make a full daylight reconnaissance tomorrow, and return here after dark. I'll take a few men with me, and if I like the place I'll leave them there to start preparing the defences and routes in and out.' He turned to me. 'Will you take over in my absence?'

'Better if another officer – Lieutenant Tisgne, say – did that. I've still got a lot of cycling to do, and I'm hoping to meet you at the new Maquis anyway. One of the first priorities is to find a suitable dropping zone.'

Unfamiliar footsteps sounded across the cobbled courtyard.

'Who the hell is this?' I asked no one in particular as we all stood. Marienne reached for his pistol, in case the sentries had been bypassed or killed.

Beyond the window a well-built man in his mid-forties was talking to the farmer, who seemed to be replying with exaggerated gesticulations. Geneviève slipped out of the door, saying she would investigate but not reveal our presence until satisfied. Apart from our immediate circle, no one was aware of our existence at the farm, although clearly our uninvited visitor knew something – and I didn't like it. I too drew the pistol I had collected from among my small pile of possessions at the edge of the field.

Through the window we watched Geneviève look in our direction and mouth the words '*C'est bon*?'

Unseen by our visitor, I raised my thumb in acknowledgement, but still slipped the safety catch off as the man was led towards the door. Inside, he seemed surprised to see us, having received no hint that we were there.

Facing the three of us – all armed – he blurted first, 'I am Lieutenant-Colonel de Magny, commanding a Maquis in the Côtes-du-Nord *département*, near Mur-de-Bretagne.'

Not having heard of him, I nodded suspiciously and said, 'Go on.'

'I met some of your men a few days ago; in fact eleven of them are now in my Maquis. They suggested I search for you in the Trédion area, and this I began to do – starting in Callac, where a doctor I used to know well said he had been in the Maquis near Malestroit before it was destroyed.

'He said he felt safe confiding in me, but didn't actually know precisely where you were and pointed me in this general direction. So for the past hour I've been wandering around until I came across this farm. It struck me that if I was restarting a Maquis this is the sort of place I would choose. I called in on the off chance that I was right.'

We were taken aback, and looked at each other without saying a word.

I broke the silence. 'Oh Lord!' I exclaimed – 'another example of Maquis security. May I see your papers, please, Colonel?'

'Of course.'

'It's not that I don't trust you, but you shouldn't be here at all. The doctor should not have given you any information – indeed, he should have denied our existence.'

The Colonel nodded.

'Thankfully, as you say, the doctor himself does not know our precise location, but that won't prevent me from giving him a piece of my mind tomorrow.'

As I holstered my weapon I turned to Marienne. 'What did I tell you this morning? Even our own bloody officers can't follow the rules of the game – sometimes they're worse than the men.'

The Colonel interrupted: 'Don't blame the doctor. He knew I was in charge of a Maquis.'

Holding out my hand for his papers, I stared at him without emotion.

'Here,' he said, 'plus a letter from Lieutenant Varnier of your battalion, who, with his ten men, is with us.'

I knew Varnier's writing, and his letter seemed genuine. It also confirmed what the Colonel had just told me. The Lieutenant explained that they had been picked up by the Colonel's Maquis and were being cared for until able to make contact with us again. He asked for new orders, and that we should thank the Colonel for his kindness.

'I apologize for being so rude,' I said, folding Varnier's letter into my pocket and handing back the identification papers. 'We've come up against so much negligence since our arrival – not to say treachery – as well as *miliciens* masquerading as maquisards. We're a bit sensitive to strangers – and especially ones who know a great deal about us.'

The ice having been broken at last, I introduced my few companions and their duties before agreeing that Varnier and his men should stay put for the moment. The Colonel's Maquis had chosen a dropping zone which, he said, had Varnier's approval, and now all he wanted was aircraft. Could we fix them?

'We can manage the drops,' Marienne offered. 'In fact we've quite a backlog of equipment due, and our next radio schedule is tonight anyway. I'll need the coordinates, and with any luck that'll be fixed.'

The Colonel obliged, and added his pre-arranged BBC coded message.

'You came well prepared,' I said.

'In the meantime,' Marienne suggested, 'you should split your Maquis into fighting groups of no more than a hundred each and start ambushing German lines of communication – bridges, railway lines and so on. I'd hope that you can liaise with our own forces, who are now spread over a large area. We communicate by courier, but it's a tenuous business.'

'I'll fix all that. In fact we've carried out various reconnaissance tasks for just such action.'

After agreeing that nobody was to come to the farm again, de Magny left us feeling nervous. Once again the right man had managed to find us, but if it had been a *milicien* who had walked in with a similar story who knows what the doctor would have done?

Nevertheless, Marienne and I drafted a long situation report in which we asked for a drop for the Maquis at Mur-de-Bretagne about nine miles north of Pontivy. Then, full of food and drowsy from the previous night's fitful sleep and a full day on the road, I eventually slipped outside to lie down with my head and shoulders supported by hay.

'May I join you?'

I didn't look up, but patted the ground to my left. Geneviève knelt alongside me, clutching two cups of fresh coffee and a bottle of Calvados.

'Do you think I need all that to make me take an interest in you?' I teased.

She made no reply, but slid her legs forwards along the hay and snuggled alongside me. Neither of us said anything for a long time. 'Thank you for this morning,' I said eventually. 'You were a marvel.'

'I was paralysed with fear.' Her voice was soft in my ear.

'It didn't show.'

'That's because I was frightened for you – and I couldn't let you see that.'

'Why?' I wanted to hear the words I was too scared to say myself.

'Stop asking me questions, Bob. You're worse than the *Milice*!'

I swivelled on to my left hip and kissed her, and as she responded with enthusiasm I kissed her again.

The next thing I was aware of was a pillow under my head and two blankets across my back, and I knew then that I was a lucky man and that it was even more imperative to get the war won and behind us.

The next morning I found Geneviève in the kitchen making breakfast.

'Thank you for those blankets,' I said, kissing her gently on the cheek.

'What else was I supposed to do when you dropped off as I was talking to you? The moon was so bright I hoped you might have paid more attention.' She kissed me back, and soon we were on our way to Malestroit, praying like mad that my permit for riding around the countryside was good. It seemed to be, for we were eventually waved through the now permanent roadblock with no more than the usual obscenities.

The mayor had little news. The police lieutenant was still under suspicion but going about his normal duties, and the 'dump' we had seen on the edge of the woods had been excavated and the maquisard's body properly buried in the town cemetery. We thanked him for that and moved on to Monsieur Legrand, who also had little to report except that Geneviève's family farm – or what was left of it – was no longer under guard. It would, he suggested, be safe if we felt the urge to look around.

The defensive positions that had guarded the main approach were destroyed, as was the farm itself. The Pondards' house was now gutted and roofless, as were the pigsties and barns, with their bare walls reaching towards the cloudless July sky. The blast of our explosion had destroyed much, and what had been left had then been vandalized by the advancing enemy. The ground was littered with broken glass, smashed furniture and charred lengths of timber. It was a scene of utter destruction, and unrecognizable as a laughter-filled home.

For thirty minutes we sifted aimlessly through the rubble. Twisted weapons lay scattered among the crushed remains of hundreds of containers. Everywhere, loose ammunition rolled beneath our feet.

There was not a single thing worth keeping.

Geneviève took my hand. 'Bob, let's go,' she said, and quickly and without a glance backwards we were on the road for Plumelec.

Well clear of the Saint-Marcel Maquis, we stopped to lean our bicycles against a hedge and regain our breath.

'It took my father twenty years of hard work to develop that bit of land. He built much of the farm himself – with his own hands and those of the owner. Then he and my mother struggled all their lives to improve on it. And what's left today? Nothing but wasted fields, and all we received for them were a few non-committal grunts from the Colonel.' Her cheeks were etched with channels of moisture through the dust. 'If this area is liberated by August we might be able to save some of the crops, but this coming winter will be hard – very hard.'

'Come on,' I said, 'let's have lunch – a proper lunch in a restaurant.'

Over coffee, I laid my hands across hers. 'Do you need any clothes?' I had had an idea.

She looked down at our entwined fingers. 'I do,' she whispered.

No one could begrudge government money being spent on an agent who not only had lost everything she possessed but who continued to risk what little she had left – including her life.

At Callac I left a number of exciting-looking parcels to await our return. The brief shopping expedition had been a success, but it was vital that we call on Marienne in the new Maquis as soon as we could. If he liked it and I approved, then we were finally on our way towards a resumption of sabotage and disruption.

As we left Plumelec we passed the observation tower, where Geneviève braked and pointed. 'From the top of the tower,' she panted, 'and without field glasses, you can see the sea. They say it's one of the highest spots in Brittany.' Alongside its base an army hut was guarded by bored soldiers.[1]

From there onwards the narrow country road falls and twists to the south, giving us a wonderful stretch of downhill freewheeling, with the wind blowing Geneviève's dress. 'In nearly two kilo-metres', she shouted over her shoulder, her long hair streaming across her cheeks, 'there are eight bends – so watch out.'

At the bottom we laughed with exhilaration, and I leaned across to kiss her flushed cheek. I had never felt happier – nor, even, more at peace.

A small stream runs through the hamlet in the valley, and I suggested a drink in a café by the bridge, but she vetoed the idea. 'We must walk from here, which will take some time. The track is rough, and if we have to escape into the undergrowth we can't take the bikes with us, so we'll lose them. They'll be safe here.' With the proprietor's permission, we left them round the back of the café.

She was right, of course, and the track was too pitted and rutted for cycling anyway. Despite the numerous forks along our route, Geneviève always knew which turning to take, and I wondered how she knew this place so well. But I kept my silence. She would tell me when she thought I needed to know.[2]

As we crested the hill and dropped again back into woods and scrub, the roofs of Kérihuel farm could just be seen through the leaves; other farms lay beyond and further down the valley. An elderly woman was hanging washing over a line supported by a long, forked stick.

'*Bonjour, madame.*' We had decided that Geneviève should do all the talking. 'Have you had any visitors today?'

'No,' came the abrupt reply. 'Who are you?'

Taking a risk, Geneviève replied, 'Geneviève and Bob.'

'Captain Bob?'

'*Oui, madame.*'

'Wait here,' she said, turning away. Five minutes later Marienne was shaking my hand and kissing Geneviève.

'We're about six and a half kilometres from Plumelec, but before I show you the emplacements that I've chosen let me explain the situation.'

I told him to go on.

'The way you came is the difficult route, but as we are now about fifteen metres below the ridge line you'll appreciate that it's almost impossible for us to be seen. Everyone here is willing and ready to help, so we should have no trouble on that score.

'The Germans have never been here, but whether that's a good thing or not I don't know. We may be due for a visit, or they may not know this place exists. In some ways I wish they had checked it out – but there we are. Now, if you follow me I'll show you round.'

Marienne had chosen well, and in many respects it was much better than Saint-Marcel. We walked for four hundred yards down a slope and across two fields, both of which were well screened from prying eyes. The hedges and banks were high – in places, as high as ten feet – and we stopped to allow Marienne to wave a hand in a full circle.

'We're a good distance from the collection of farms, well protected from all sides, with high ground that we can also dominate. On this side', he pointed to the south-west, 'there's the edge of the Trédion wood a few hundred metres away, with excellent cover between us and it should we need to escape again.'

With our initial tour complete, and agreeing that the site was ideal, Geneviève and I retraced our steps.

Back in Callac she excitedly unpacked her parcels, eyes shining as she spread new clothes across the dining-room table and proudly showed them to Madame Gambert.

'Go and try some on,' I implored. 'I want to see you in them.'

She bundled a collection over an arm and tripped upstairs like a young girl with a new present – 'Which', I thought, 'is what she is.'

Monsieur turned to me as soon as he had shut the door behind Geneviève. 'Stay and have supper, Captain,' he smiled. 'We can put you up for the night as well, should you wish.'

'That's very kind,' I replied. 'May I take you up some other time, as the others are expecting me and will be worried if I don't appear? And', I said hesitantly, anxious not to be rude but to give my host no more information than he needed, 'we have so much to do now that we have a new base.'

Monsieur looked at me with a widening smile. 'I thought you'd say that.'

'Say what?'

'That the others would be anxious if you didn't appear. So I sent Anna there earlier today to tell your officers that I would be asking you to stay the night!'

I had been ambushed, and I liked it.

Madame Gambert opened the door slowly to begin with, then, with an added flourish, swung it full against the wall. Geneviève stood there – still in her old clothes.

I turned to Monsieur Gambert. 'I accept your offer with pleasure – but on one condition.'

'Yes?'

'That Geneviève puts on her new dress – otherwise I'll leave immediately!'

Five minutes later Geneviève reappeared, and my heart leaped. She was attractive in whatever she wore, but this new dress was a real delight – as was the dinner.

The Gamberts drifted off to bed at about eleven that evening, leaving me to admire Geneviève's new dress in private.

'Let's get some fresh air before I follow them,' she said, and I meekly nodded.

In silence – a silence that was broken only by those animals that begin their work as the sun goes down – we took a path that I knew led to the river. Reaching the river bank, I trampled a circle in the grass as a dog might do for his bed.

I lay down and held a hand up for Geneviève.

'Why did you smile when Monsieur Gambert told his wife that I would be staying to dinner?'

'When I was upstairs with Madame I had wondered whether or not you would stay. But she had no doubt!'

'So you knew it was not a last-minute decision?'

'Of course! I knew you wouldn't stay unless Lieutenant Tisgne knew you were safe – so I actually sent the message.'

I rolled over to kiss her.

Catching our breath, I returned to the subject. 'With that scheming brain of yours, I think you should take over the Maquis when – if ever – Jim gets it organized.' I meant it as a joke.

'And why not?' she said seriously. 'I could probably do a better job than he has so far.' She was right, and I smiled as she continued, 'But the real reason for asking you to stay for dinner – and the night – was to thank you for all your kindnesses.'

'Then you should include the others,' I volunteered.

'I will – but I wanted to start with you. You see, Bob, we've helped a great many people over the past four years, yet rarely have we met men like you and Marienne. You're about the only two who have shown any real consideration towards us and understood the problems that we face. Oh, I know that you face them too – and probably worse problems when the fighting starts again. But you're the only two who have ever said thank you, and that hurts after all that we've lost.'

'Look at me Geneviève,' I said, propping myself on an elbow and facing her. In the moonlight her eyes were misty, and she looked more beautiful than I had ever seen her.

'Is that the only reason for inviting me to dinner?' I asked. 'To say thank you, when it's we who must thank you?' I was stalling: too frightened to say what I wanted to. If she was braver than me, then so be it.

She was. 'No, Bob. There's another reason.' She squeezed my hand to hurting point. 'I love you so much, and that makes me even more frightened.' Then she rested her head on my shoulder and gently cried.

12. Hay Barns and Dawn Cordons

At nine o'clock the next morning, and with our clothes freshly pressed, we leaned our bicycles against the headquarters farm build-ing and, trying not to look sheepish, followed the smell of coffee. We needn't have bothered to hide our feelings, as neither Babin nor Marienne had returned from the new Maquis.

The morning's good news was that all the surviving teams of both maquisards and SAS soldiers had now been registered back into the fold and allocated their various new hiding places. They were spread out, but all within the range of our new communicating system using the girls on their bicycles. We had – or were about to have – teams stretching from the west coast to Guer.

There was not such good news from Monsieur Lecœur, who came with a disturbing story that earlier in the day at a neighbouring village the inhabitants had been woken by a 'paratrooper' running down the main street shouting for someone to hide him. He was, he shouted, being chased by 'the enemy'. Unfortunately someone did offer him temporary sanctuary – a move that had the village quickly surrounded by Germans, for the man was a *milicien*. The victims of this ruse were badly beaten and threatened with death should they repeat their act of apparent kindness.

The news from Normandy was more heartening, with fighting continuing 'satisfactorily', except in the Avranches and Caen areas.

Marienne strode in before lunch, well pleased with his efforts of spreading the teams far and wide and with thoughts of our impending move to the new Maquis. I had work still to complete and, despite pleas from Marienne not to go until I had told him what I had been up to the previous evening, I was anxious to be on my way.

Geneviève and I made our way back to Callac and the doctor, who must have known I would be wanting to speak to him. He opened the conversation quickly. 'Bob,' he asked, 'did you see

Colonel de Magny? I apologize for sending him on to you, but he's an old friend of mine and quite safe.'

With a diplomacy I did not know I possessed, I advised him that it had not been a good idea and that in future he should use one of the girls as a harbinger. In reply he told me that the Germans had ordered the arrest of any man found on a bicycle unless he had a certificate signed by a doctor. I wasn't sure why a doctor's note was needed to pedal round the countryside, but I kept quiet.

This might have been a blow, but, as though to atone for his earlier mistake, Doctor Mahéo had already persuaded a friend of his who held a medical position in a nearby village to send across the necessary new documents. As I was now temporarily grounded until their arrival, we spent the day visiting those wounded within walking distance. It was also a useful time to look for a local field that might serve as a dropping zone.

Waiting for me back at the Gamberts' house was the promised bicycling authority – and the doctor was back as one of my favourite resisters!

The following morning I went into Malestroit, after arranging to meet Geneviève for lunch at the restaurant by the river. In the village I sent messages through the various couriers who were now operating under the mayor and the mill-owner's control, and placed all the Maquis teams within their range on to a high-readiness state: all weapons, ammunition and explosives that remained were to be gathered together and hidden in new, more easily reached, hiding places. Then, with no progress made on finding a replacement for La Baleine, I headed for our assignation.

Geneviève was not there, so I caught up with the German-controlled newspapers and wondered whether the Allies still had a navy, army and air force: from the papers' exaggerated claims it seemed that we could not have!

My study exhausted, I ordered another pastis – and then a third as a now familiar silhouette slipped past the frosted window towards the door.

'Sorry I'm late.' She kissed me on the cheek. 'I've caught up with all the wounded, met the last of the Maquis teams, and then, luckily, met an old girlfriend of mine in Plumelec.'

'Oh. And what did she have to say?'

'Apparently, at four this morning the Germans surrounded the village and carried out a house-to-house search. They found nothing, thank God, except an old hotelier with a shrewd mind and a pretty daughter. He had a few bottles of old brandy left, which the soldiers drank without paying; but the main thing was, as they sat there getting more drunk, the girl, who speaks a bit of German, kept hearing the name "Trédion" being mentioned. At that she started to listen more carefully, under the pretence of hovering near by to refill glasses.'

'Good lass! What did she discover?'

'They plan to do the same at Trédion tomorrow morning.'

I sat up. 'On our way back we'll call in and warn everyone. I'm sorry the old man lost a few bottles – though it was worth it. I'll see if I can reimburse him.'

'No need to do that.'

'Why?'

'He's made plenty of money in his time. She's not his daughter for nothing. She has beautiful legs and a good figure. He makes her liven up the tables with her coquettish behaviour and gets the young men – it's the Germans now – to buy drink after drink in the belief that they'll receive some of her favours in return. Then, just as the rounds of drinks are slowing down, the girl's father takes over serving at table. By then he's made a good profit from the increased sales and his daughter is safe for another night.'

'A good pair!'

'They're certainly that.'

'I might call in one day and try my own luck.'

'Don't get your hopes up. The old man would start serving you from the start!'

After lunch we split up again, but by eight that evening were together on the outskirts of Trédion, whose main street was lined with houses. Neither of us had been molested once by roadblocks.

'You take one side and I'll do the other,' I said. 'Only knock on the doors of people you know. They can spread the word on.'

'See you at the other end.'

Thirty minutes later we met where the wood creeps up to the very last of the houses, and by nine o'clock we were in the Gamberts' Callac house. There, after supper, I asked Monsieur Gambert if he knew of a good vantage point from where I could watch the expected search.

'Yes,' he said. 'About a halfway between here and Trédion – the other side of the small river – there's a barn on top of a slight rise. You've probably seen it without realizing its significance, but from the attic with a good pair of field glasses you should have a fine view right down the main street.'

'That sounds perfect. Perhaps you can explain to Geneviève in more detail while I get together various bits and pieces.'

'She knows it,' he said as I turned to collect a pistol, spare ammunition, a torch, two blankets, a packet of cigarettes and a bottle of Calvados.

With Geneviève leading the way through a series of interconnecting paths that bypassed the main tracks and roads, we reached the bottom of the short climb to our night's quarters. The moon was milky behind a thin layer of high clouds, but producing enough light to watch the proceedings. I had not asked Geneviève if she wanted to come with me: somehow I just assumed that she would. And, conversely, she did not feel the need to ask. I found that comforting.

'Why do you want to watch the search?' she asked.

'They seem to be making it a habit, and sooner or later we're going to get caught out. If I can study their methods, then we'll be forewarned. Funny you didn't ask before we set out.'

'I didn't want to risk you deciding that I shouldn't come.'

'I've said it before – you are wonderful. And I love you for it.'

'At last.'

'At last what?'

'You've said you love me.'

'I said I love you for being wonderful – for helping. For being part of the team.'

'Is that all?'

'No!'

'Then say it.'

I took her by the elbows and pulled her close. 'I'm so sorry. I've always been too scared of what it might all mean.'

'The war and all that?'

'Yes, the war and all that.'

'But you know how I feel. And now I know you feel the same.' She paused and, as I hesitated too long, asked, 'You do feel the same, don't you?'

'Of course. It's just that I may not be here for ever. As soon as this part of France is liberated I may have to go somewhere else. I guess I just couldn't ask you to take on that possibility if you knew I loved you.'

'I've thought of that too.'

'You understand?'

'Yes,' she said.

The moonlight caught the excitement in her eyes, and her lips lengthened into the broad smile I had come to miss every time we were apart. I pulled her elbows even closer, and kissed her. 'I love you. I really do love you, and I suppose I have for almost as long as I've known you.'

'Oh!' She professed mock surprise. 'Not that long, then!'

'Long enough. Now we must get on with the war.'

My secret was no longer a secret, but my fear for her was intensified.

'Now, to return to your first question, I want to see if the Germans leave any escape avenues. I'm certain they won't, but I just want to make sure. I want to see how and where they place any sentries or stop-points. I'd like to know how many men they deploy and how they communicate, and I want to see if they use the *Milice*. If they do, it's better for us that we don't get caught. I can bluff the Boche, but it's not so easy with one's own countrymen. I want to know how long they take, how they arrive, and what they do with their transport. I want to see how – and from where – they're commanded, and I want to spot any flaws that we could exploit.'

'We should reach the barn in a few minutes. Although it's over this hill,' she pointed upwards, 'it'll be best to skirt round the edge and approach from the east, where there's a bit of cover. And they may be using it themselves to keep an eye on their own men and see if any of the inhabitants try to escape. I've been here before – we used to help the farmer when we were much younger.'

Ten minutes later I motioned to Geneviève to keep quiet and sink to the ground. Over the hill's crest I could just see the roof of the barn, and as I crawled slowly forward the upper floor came into view. A window in the attic opened directly towards Trédion, and below that, once I had moved forward and to my left for another few yards, four small barn doors faced me. I watched and listened in the moonlight, but not a sound came from the building: unless someone had been expecting us and was himself lying in wait, it seemed empty. I slid back until I could see Geneviève's white face against the dark of the valley beyond.

'Come on,' I whispered loudly.

A central door yielded with no effort and, more importantly, with no noise. We slipped through, and pushed it gently shut. The inside smelt of old, damp hay and was pitch black: no moonbeams could penetrate the shuttered windows.

'Don't move,' I said softly, 'in case you knock something.'

Wrapping my handkerchief round the end of my torch and pushing the switch forward, I lit up our shoes with a narrow circle of soft light. The room, the breadth of the whole building, was cluttered with light farm machinery that showed no sign of recent use – or at least the thick layer of dust on every surface had not been disturbed for some time.

Above our heads a black square hole in the attic's floor presented our next challenge.

'Don't touch anything – don't disturb any dust. When we leave, I don't want anyone to know there have been visitors.'

The only exception would have to be a ladder propped against a wall. We would have to risk it. Gingerly I carried it, upright, to beneath the opening and, while Geneviève held the torch, poked it through to rest with enough inches clear into the attic.

'Perfect,' I said. 'I'll have a look first.'

As my eyes came level with the attic floor I muttered, 'Blast!'

'What's wrong?'

'It's jam-packed solid with hay. Somehow we'll have to tunnel through. Come on up.'

She squeezed beside me on the upper rungs and lifted herself on to the ledge around the hole: there was just room.

'Now what?' she asked.

'I'll replace the ladder and climb up the blankets. Don't worry – we trained for this sort of thing!'

Luckily a beam ran along the roof above the hatch. Although the two blankets, tied corner to corner and dangling through the attic's floor, reached nowhere near the ground, I was able to grab an end. I propped the ladder precisely where I'd found it, then wiped the rungs and sides. 'Better', I thought, 'that there is no dust rather than smudged dust.'

Having climbed up to the narrow ledge opposite Geneviève – our feet dangling into space – I hauled up the blankets and untied them from the beam.

'I'm going to tunnel through the hay, and when I've found the window I'll call.'

It wasn't easy, and as far as time and distance are concerned it must have been one of the slowest journeys in my life; at the end I was hot and very sweaty.

'OK,' I whispered down the narrow alley I had forged. 'There's just room.'

I tugged the hay back from the window to make a nest wide enough for two – it was going to be very intimate! – then spread one blanket over a thin base of loose hay while the other I earmarked to tug across us in the cold. I pulled the pistol, spare ammunition and bottle from my pockets and placed them by the window just as Geneviève's feet thrust into our hide, kicking me in the ribs.

'Why are you going backwards.'

'Because', she said as though to a child, 'I've been pulling the hay back into place, trying to make it as solid-looking as it was before we arrived.'

'I still think you're wonderful,' I said as she doubled round to face me.

'What's the time?' she asked, ignoring my compliment.

'Nearly midnight. You get some sleep, and I'll wake you in time for the show.'

I looked at my watch for the hundredth time. Nearly two a.m.

I looked at my watch again: 2.10 a.m.

A movement caught my eye, and I raised the field glasses. Was that someone moving through the undergrowth, stealthily among the bushes and trees? The strain was telling, as the whole countryside seemed to be on the move. There was nothing. I lowered my gaze.[1]

I looked again: 2.11 a.m. This time there was no hallucination: a number of shadows were moving into position from the direction of the Trédion–Callac road, two hundred yards off to our right – the west. I nudged Geneviève with an elbow.

'Our friends have begun to arrive for the party.'

There was just enough light to see without the glasses, and what I saw at that range was indistinct images – but unmistakably soldiers – creeping towards the nearest of the houses. I thanked them for starting their operation from our end, for it would make my study so much easier. But, I suddenly thought, surely they could not ignore the barn – our barn – that dominated their approach. A chill ran down my back as I thought that we might have been just too clever for our own safety and realized that we could actually have been better off with less of a grandstand view but a more secure one from the edge of the woods.

I had no idea when the next phase would start, and dared not rest in case I should miss it. There followed long hours during which Geneviève dozed fitfully. I needed a cigarette – but kept the packet shut. I could have done with a coffee – but there was none, and I kept the Calvados tightly corked.

Dawn began to lighten the horizon at about 4.30, bringing the promise of another clear, beautiful summer's day. Then, even through our closed window, we could hear shouted orders and immediately men rose from their positions, cocked their weapons, and began to move towards Trédion.

The cordon was being tightened with Germanic efficiency, and was as frightening as it was impressive to watch. I twisted back from the window with my feet braced against the sill and my shoulders pressing into the hay.

'Keep back, now,' I said, 'in case any of those bastards looks back and sees a movement.'

I raised the glasses. 'They're closing in now, about ten metres apart, near to the houses. All the roads are blocked by teams of five men – each group includes a machine gun. There are various other groups, probably hidden from the village by bushes, but I can see them from behind – more cut-offs. It's impossible to say, but if it's like this all round the village – and it must be – then there are about four hundred of them. Possibly more.'

Horrified at the scale of the operation, all Geneviève could bring herself to say was, 'They must want to catch us very badly.'

'They're not doing anything now – just waiting.' I paused, eyes screwed close to the field glasses' lenses. 'Hang on! Two cars and four lorries have just entered the village from our direction. They're in the village . . .' I paused, 'now. Men are getting out quickly. Christ! This lot are all *miliciens*. For some reason they're walking towards the far end and out of sight. Dead ground, dammit. I guess they'll start there and work their way back towards us. Here, have a look.' I handed the glasses to Geneviève.

'They've started, both sides of the street at once.' She held her breath, eyes concentrating hard. 'Ah! Now there are six more lorries appearing out of the dead ground from the far end. All the men in the fields are moving in a bit. There's no way to escape.'

'Thank God we were able to warn everyone!'

For over an hour we watched in turns as the *Milice* did the Germans' dirty work – although we saw no sign of any arrests, experience suggested that untold personal abuses would be taking place behind the closed doors.

Eventually all the soldiers from the fields and roadblocks and the French traitors from the houses met up with the vehicles now lining the road, facing our direction, and, once laden, the lorries and cars set off slowly to the north, past the barn and towards Callac. They left behind about eighty soldiers, for whom there had been no room, who now marched off in the opposite direction.

My attention turned back to the convoy, which, judging by the sound, had begun to slow at the nearest point to our hiding place. My heart froze – or so it felt.

'Geneviève,' I said, trying to keep my voice low and calm, 'we may be about to receive visitors. Whatever you do, don't make a squeak. If you want to move, cough, scratch or sneeze, do it now.'

I watched, mesmerized and terrified, as five soldiers dismounted to be joined by five *miliciens* by the side of the road. Quickly, and in what must have been a pre-planned manoeuvre, they fanned out either side of the direct route to our hide and began, with rifles at the ready, to cross the intervening rough ground. The light now allowed us to watch the assault party split into two: one half aiming for the south side – our side – of the barn and the other for the north. Beneath our window they were soon in position, with one of them waving towards his out-of-sight accomplices. Not one spoken order had been given.

'Five traitors are about to enter the barn.' I took her hand. It was steady, with her face calm and unafraid.

'Why can't we pretend to be lovers? Seeking some privacy.'

'Why pretend?' I said with false bravado. 'The Germans might fall for that, but not those other bastards. They know who they're looking for, and you're with me. They'll come to all the correct conclusions. Now – shh.'

We felt, rather than heard, the door open – no squeaking hinges, but a shaking of the floor beneath our backs – then voices shouted.

'*Personne ici*?' one called.

'There's an attic,' said another. 'Look, there's the hatch.' We imagined their faces turning up in the direction of a pointing arm.

'Get that ladder,' the same voice continued. 'Take a look.'

The ladder was dragged across the cobbled floor, then we heard it scrape the entrance to our eyrie. Every ascending footstep sounded like a countdown to eternity.

'It's full of hay.'

'It might be full of those scum as well.'

'Nothing can move up here.'

'Don't be stupid. Climb over it.'

'It's up to the roof. Come and see for yourself.'

A second set of feet climbed up.

'He's right,' a voice shouted down. 'Someone get a rifle from one of the Germans.'

Geneviève's grip tightened on my hand. I returned her squeeze.

A *milicien* said, 'Here's one.'

'Good. Put the bayonet on and pass it up. I can probably reach the other side from here!'

A click rang in our ears as the blade was pushed home. My shirt was soaking with so much sweat I thought they must smell us before stabbing us. Back and forth went the sharp rustling of the hay as the *milicien* at the top of the ladder thrust and withdrew, but his borrowed bayonet never reached us – although we sensed its presence through the hay a number of times.

Geneviève's fingernails dug sharper into my hand as the *Milice* planned their next move.

'There's no one here,' one suggested. 'We're wasting our time.'

'Maybe you're right,' another said, then shouted, 'If there is anyone in the hay, this is your last chance. We're going to set fire to it. We'll burn you out.' Five mocking laughs made my skin crawl. I might not have seen their faces clearly, but I would remember those laughs.

I smiled grimly at Geneviève, who was shaking slightly – not enough to rattle the floorboards – and biting her lip.

The ladder was removed, then we felt the heavy rumbling as the large door was pushed until, with an elaborate slam, it was closed.

'That's it. Come on everyone.'

Without moving my body against the floor I craned my head until I could see outside. It was uncomfortable but vital, for we had been taught to guard against a ruse that had been the downfall of too many SOE agents who had relaxed prematurely. My guess was right, and my blood ran cold for the umpteenth time that morning for, sure enough, five German soldiers were standing outside smoking and laughing but only three *miliciens*. I awarded myself no prize for guessing where the missing two men were – about four yards beneath us, still and silent.

I shook my head very slowly at Geneviève and mouthed, 'There are two men below. Don't move.'

Through the window I watched eight men walking as quickly as the ground would allow towards the waiting convoy. They climbed in, and the vehicles continued their interrupted journey north to Callac.

Forty long minutes passed before I risked rolling my head to one side. Geneviève was still biting her lip. Paler than before, she managed a smile past her clamped teeth.

'Don't fall asleep,' I mouthed.

She shook her head.

I decided on another twenty minutes. We knew they were there, but they did not know we were. They had to move in time, and we did not. They had a threshold of boredom; with our lives at stake, we did not. Nevertheless, in another twenty minutes I would take the fight to the enemy. They would be surprised, and with their colleagues now out of earshot we might be able to best them before reinforcements could be summoned. I had studied the window carefully, and was certain that with the catch lifted it would open easily. I would tell Geneviève to make a noise, and while they pondered what to do – and while, I assumed, they stared towards the hatch and the ladder to make up their minds – I would drop from the window and shoot them in the back.

'It might work,' I thought, 'and the danger to Geneviève would be minimal to begin with, as they wouldn't be able to get at her through the hay.'

With just ten minutes in hand before my self-imposed deadline, and stealing myself for action, I heard, then saw, a staff car return from the direction of Callac and stop where, earlier, the convoy had waited.

Two blasts on the horn carried easily across the still hillside. Was this a signal in our favour or not? We waited.

'Come on,' said a French voice. 'The car's back. I felt all along there was no one up there. But orders are orders.'

'Damn them all!' said the second voice. 'Every day the same job. Yesterday Plumelec, today Trédion, and tomorrow Callac. And I don't suppose we'll be any luckier there.'

The door opened and closed. I checked that both of them had left, just in case they were even cleverer than I had been prepared to give them credit for; five minutes later I felt it was safe enough to whisper, 'I'm certain there's no one left, but we must be careful. Also, I want to leave the place as we found it, in case they return to check.'

As I thought, the window opened easily and I was soon swinging below the sill. On the ground I cocked my pistol and swung the door open. The ground floor was empty.

'I'll get the ladder.'

I heard her scrabbling through the hay, trying her hardest to fill the tunnel behind her, then a dusty, grinning face was framed by the hatch.

With the ladder back in place we didn't worry too much about marks in the dust, for they weren't ours, and after a quick look to see if all was clear we were running for the nearest trees to the east. A hundred yards in from the forest's edge we entered a small clearing with a clear view in both directions along the track. We stopped, and for the first time since leaving the Gamberts' house I felt at ease. I also lit those longed-for cigarettes.

'I really need this,' I said, striking the match and applying it simultaneously to two cigarettes wedged between my lips – 'I don't know about you.' She pulled one from my mouth and, drawing in a deep puff, lay back on the still-damp grass. Here, in the forest, the sun had yet to rise above the surrounding canopy of tall trees.

'God! That was a close shave. I thought they were going to crawl through the hay and make a real search. And I don't think they'd have taken any prisoners.'

'I was becoming properly scared when that *milicien* started ramming his bayonet. Every time I heard it being pushed in I wanted to scream – even if it didn't come anywhere near me. It was horrible.' She had spoken for the first time since we had left our nest. 'We must have been up there for hours. What's the time?'

'Only eight o'clock,' I replied. 'I know it was unpleasant, but we're safe. And, what's more, we've valuable information which we must use. I wouldn't put it past them to throw a cordon round Callac during the day so that no one can get in to warn them. They must want to know why they're not finding what they're looking for. It's vital we get to the village first.'

I opened the Calvados, and for some time we mimicked the monkeys as we picked the tell-tale straw off each other's clothes and hair. Another cigarette – and a delayed kiss – and we were off to Madame Gambert's promised breakfast and the new day. And so – with full stomachs, satisfaction over a well-spent night, and a warning passed to the inhabitants of Callac raising our morale – we left for Plumelec and the new Maquis, which we approached via the web of back lanes. Sentries were carrying out their duties with a renewed purpose, while the wireless operators had established communications and had already dispatched Marienne's first report from his newly operational unit.

Everything was as I would have expected, including a map board with the locations of our teams plus a list of their recent activities and plans for their future ones. I recounted, with Geneviève's help, the events of the previous twenty-four hours, at the end of which Marienne agreed that it was clear that Callac would not be the last of the local villages to be properly searched, and that from now on there would be no further involvement of the local population other than in the already earmarked outlying farms. We also agreed that a liaison visit to Lieutenant-Colonel de Magny and his Maquis based on Mur-de-Bretagne was due.

I ended my briefing, 'We now have all the teams in place, on immediate notice for action and grouped under your command. And that has to be good.'

I managed an hour's sleep before working with Marienne on our operational plan until lunch, when, during a visit by a farmer's wife to see what we were lacking, Marienne explained that the men were low on tobacco and cigarettes. She could not help, but I could. It was always a risky business carrying large stocks across the country, for, although the various shopkeepers were generous, plausible excuses were hard to invent; yet the morale of the men depended, in large part, on a regular supply. I considered this logistic support to be a significant part of my job, and assured him that I would continue to do my best.

After lunch, Geneviève left to warn Colonel de Magny of my impending visit, Babin went off in the hope of gleaning news from Monsieur Legrand, and I mounted my bicycle for a round of briefings. By eight that evening I had had enough. Geneviève was already in the Gamberts' house, having been spared the seventy-mile round journey to the Colonel's headquarters as she had seen him with the doctor. I was expected the following afternoon.

A number of messages of thanks filtered into the house from

various villagers, three of whom had been keeping Sten guns hidden for us. Without notice of the search they would have been quickly found. Another 'crime' was the possession of parachute silk. Many girls had collected strips of this invaluable material to make into knickers, petticoats and even wedding dresses, but to a German it meant collaboration with the Maquis, and that in turn meant death – after rape.[2]

By eleven that evening it was time to be away from Callac, so the doctor and I gathered a few comforts for the night and made our farewells. I did not think it wise that Geneviève should come with us, but she insisted and I offered no resistance – especially as she knew a field that would be well outside cordon-distance from the village. But she didn't stay, and once happy that we were happy she left us after a goodnight kiss.

'How are your medical supplies?' I asked the doctor, gazing at the stars.

'Good. Because of the lack of drops, most of the local doctors have been helpful, so there's nothing I'm short of at the moment. Mind you, with no new battle casualties, there's been no drain on my resources. I reckon we're at about two hours' notice to help you with a field dressing station wherever you want it – within reason, and Germans permitting.'

'That's exactly what I wanted to hear,' I said, warming once again to the man. 'Now I can sleep in peace. Goodnight, and thanks.' I shut my eyes.

The dawn sun woke us.

'Morning, Doc,' I started. 'I wonder how the search has gone?'

He looked past my cigarette smoke. 'Ask her yourself – here's Geneviève.'

'How awful men can look when they're unshaven, unbrushed and with eyes still sleepy!'

'If you can joke, I take it the search went off well from Callac's point of view.'

'Yes. They did exactly the same as they had done at Trédion and, as before, they found nothing.'

'Excellent,' I said.

'Of course. But the Boche are not pleased.'

'That's their problem.'

We had a long day in the saddle facing us, for it is over thirty miles to Mur-de-Bretagne, and our journey included two towns. Geneviève knew roughly where the Maquis was hidden – about five more miles out of town to the west, well camouflaged in the large Forêt de Quénécan.

The meeting was useful and encouraging, for we agreed a list of targets that should be attacked. I left happy, and at the end of our seventy-mile round bicycle journey the soreness was more than compensated for by the results of our efforts. I had also managed to convince the Colonel's signaller to verify our own identity, for, although we were sending messages, London was probably worried that we had been infiltrated and were thus not secure enough to receive messages in return.

But, back in Callac, chills were still ready to run down my spine.

'There's a tough-looking girl who wants to see a Captain Bob,' said Anna. 'I don't like the look of her, and said that we didn't know you. She refuses to leave and has been here for two hours already.'

'Tell her to go into the garden, and that someone will see her there and try to help her. Can she get out of the garden without going through the house?'

'Yes, but with difficulty. There's a wall about two metres high.'

'Fine,' I said before fetching my pistol, cocking it, and applying the safety catch.

A few minutes later Geneviève appeared. 'She's waiting outside.'

I drew a deep breath, prepared to face this latest potential threat. They were right: she was certainly tough-looking, being six foot tall, muscular, lean, sharp and rather unfeminine. Yet, undeniably, her gold-coloured hair and steady, clear eyes suggested a dangerous charm. I decided to tread carefully.

'I'm looking for Captain Bob,' she said – almost shouted – as soon as I stepped out of the house. 'I have news for him from Colonel Bourgoin and Jim. Are you Captain Bob?'

I didn't remember anyone that looked as tough as this when I had last visited the Colonel, and I would not have forgotten her if I had seen her. I was also taken aback by her confidence and direct approach, without any of the usual Gallic salutations.

'Who are you?' I asked sharply.

'Jim's liaison officer,' she replied without hesitation – 'and have been since the old Maquis was disbanded.'

I didn't think it had been disbanded – merely reorganized across different locations – but said nothing of that. Instead I insisted on identification.

'Certainly,' she said, still full of confidence. 'Here's a letter from the Colonel.'

The one side of paper confirmed what she had just said – which was hardly surprising – but I needed more than that, so I posed a number of questions. This was in itself a risk, for it gave her a clue, if not to my own identity then at least to my part in the Resistance as a whole.

Luckily she answered satisfactorily, but I wished – not for the first time – that I had been warned to expect a visit.

'The Colonel has been without any news for a week, and wants to know how things are getting along.'

I was tempted to retort that if he had bothered to come out of hiding to command his battalion then he would have known the answer, but I held my tongue – he had his reasons, and, while I did not wholly agree with them, I understood them.

'All right,' I replied. 'You'd better stay here for the night, and then you can take me to see him tomorrow.'

'That's fine. I still don't know if you are Captain Bob, but if you are you should know that I was in Malestroit this morning with the police lieutenant – the French one, not the German.'

'I am,' I answered simply, before continuing quickly, 'What news did he have? You probably know that he's under suspicion, so he may not be able to collect much.'

'We managed a few minutes together. He asked me to tell you that tomorrow morning the Germans will be searching Sérent, and that he would leave it to you to do the necessary things. He also said that, as they have been unsuccessful in their recent searches, Sérent will be subject to a particularly meticulous scrutiny.'

'I'll get Geneviève to warn the village this evening. She may just have time.'

I gave up my room to the newcomer and took a couple of

blankets to a field behind the house, where I must have dozed, for Geneviève suddenly woke me with a mug of strong coffee. I lay back against a hedge with a newly lit pipe, watching wisps of blue smoke curling into the hedge. She asked me what I was thinking.

'I was thinking for the thousandth time how immensely pretty you are, and how wonderful it would be if we could be together for the rest of time. There, now you know!'

She blushed. Although we had often spoken of what might be at the end of the war, we had never discussed it in terms of ourselves. She sat beside me, took my hand, and kissed it.

'We're well into July,' I said. 'Within a month this area should be liberated, and I often try to picture what will happen after that.' I was pretty certain what my movements would be, but did not elaborate.

We slept under the stars, and at dawn joined the others for an early breakfast before another busy day – and one that I prayed would see the restart of our own hostilities on a larger scale.

By now I had become a fit and fast cyclist, but Jim's liaison girl was more than a match for me, and it was all I could do to keep up with her for the two-hour journey to meet the Colonel, at the end of which I was given an enthusiastic welcome – in contrast to the previous occasion. Soon we were sitting round a table with maps and plans.

I brought the Colonel up to date, so that we could begin our discussion from the same starting point. 'All the SAS are grouped and teamed up again. They're in safe hiding places, and all under the control of Marienne. There's a daily liaison between us and them. The leaders of the Maquis have been ordered to stand by for operations. Only the officers know where the new headquarters is – plus, of course, the forty or so men we've always kept with us.

'The ammunition dumps are safe, and the wounded men well cared for. I have a new dropping zone, and we've reopened the wireless links with London. But, although they're receiving our messages, we're getting no orders in return – and that would appear to be our only setback.'

I told them of our own activities over the past few days – including the village searches, our night in the barn, and the Maquis de Mur-de-Bretagne's resumption of operations – and I ended with the suggestion that it was high time that he, the Colonel, started taking charge again.

Both he and Jim took this slight on their behaviour in good part, for they had begun to realize that they couldn't live in hiding for ever – especially not if we wanted our part of France liberated. In fact it seemed to galvanize them further, as the next two hours were spent planning. All SAS and Maquis officers would meet in the Colonel's present location in precisely six days, to receive his operational orders. I would have preferred this to be on the morrow, but we were very widely spread.

Our farewells were as brief and as cordial as had been the hellos, and I was quickly astride my saddle to arrange for more cigarettes and tobacco at a *tabac* on the outskirts of Malestroit, where I was stopped but allowed to pass after a careful look at my papers.

Back with the Gamberts, I translated some of the Colonel's orders into instructions for my own immediate team. 'Anna, I want you to warn Nos. 1, 2, 3 and 4 Battalion commanders that they will be needed for a conference with the Colonel in exactly six days from now, at ten a.m. sharp, and you, Henriette, please do likewise with the others. Each of you on your return come back via the *tabac* in Malestroit. He'll have everything ready for you.'

I turned to Babin: 'You'd better contact Messieurs Legrand and Lecœur and make sure that our intelligence network produces a first-rate and up-to-date summary for the Colonel's conference.' Turning to the doctor, I said, 'We're going to be needing you again.'

13. Tragedy

The next few days were busy.

My team of girls were occupied in liaising with the SAS and maquisards and, too often, arguing with the Germans over why they were seen on the road so frequently. But they behaved magnificently, and never incurred any form of suspicion.

Geneviève herself was the near-permanent contact between me, Marienne – the *de facto* commander of both the SAS and the maquisards – and the two *de jure*, but absent, commanders, Colonel Bourgoin and Jim.

All day and through most of the nights I either inspected the maquisards or bicycled through the surrounding towns, villages and fields to meet suppliers, farmers and those few men still allowed to drive *les camions* – and, more particularly, those who were prepared to supply and transport our fresh meat and vegetables. We also needed petrol and oil for our jeeps, and fuel for our cookers.

Teams of maquisards would, night after night, meet their SAS training platoons, so that hundreds of men were spread across the countryside practising and repractising their skills. The nights were short, yet by dawn every man would be back in his base, hidden from prying eyes and sleeping well.[1]

Jim's liaison girl – the tough-looking one – was now well known in the Callac and Plumelec areas. She stayed most of the time with Marienne – took her meals with him and his men – and would sleep in one of the three farms. It had not taken us long to realize that she was a great asset to us, accomplishing the various tasks given her with speed and efficiency.

Babin and Monsieur Lecœur reorganized the intelligence net, with the result that we were able to warn the inhabitants of two more villages of impending searches. Our luck held, for after their fifth abortive search in six days the Germans believed that they must have destroyed the Maquis. So confident were they of this that the night-time curfews were lifted and the Cossacks were recalled to their camps.

Meanwhile the invasion was progressing favourably, if slowly.

I still possessed 300,000 francs, and Marienne returned to me 80,000 that he did not need. Monsieur and Madame Pondard and their younger children were now living in a small house just outside Malestroit and, apart from Babin and myself, no one outside their immediate family knew where that was. Babin spent most of his time in Callac, as that was the central collecting point of his intelligence network, and, conveniently, it kept him close to Anna. We both relied on the girls' cheerful companionship during fourteen-hour days spent bicycling and talking our way out of roadblocks. Our work was incessant and dangerous, but their near-permanent smiles gave us the confidence to fight on.

Two days before the Colonel's meeting I joined Marienne in his headquarters to put the final touches to the presentation we intended giving at the conference. Then, as I was preparing to leave, Marienne asked me to stay the night, as he had some disturbing news he needed to mull over. After listening carefully, I decided not to stay: instead, I lit my pipe before wending my way back to Callac deep in thought.

He had had three maquisard troublemakers whom he had been obliged to keep under close observation throughout the previous day, until his patience had snapped and they had been dismissed from the farm – but not from the Maquis. One had returned to Monsieur Lecœur – who was asked to keep an eye on him – but the other two, with their weapons, were reported to have absconded and to be hiding in one of the Gamberts' barns. I had no men with whom I could confront them, and, as they had disobeyed enough orders already, they were unlikely to give themselves up to me. However, I offered to try the next day to get them to another farm, where they might be supervised and brought to their senses.

Geneviève opened the door to my 'special' knock. 'You look worried,' she said.

'I was perfectly happy before I saw Marienne,' I replied. 'And I will be again once we've sorted out three maquisards – two of whom are hiding here.' I explained the position. She knew of the men in the barn, but until that moment had not appreciated the significance of their presence.

'We've done such a colossal job in tying down the enemy,' I moaned, 'even if we haven't been fighting him, and it would take very little – just one defector in fact – to destroy what we've regained.'

The next day I was on the road well before six, and ten hours later I met Geneviève at Plumelec, from where we bicycled towards Marienne's Maquis. Our belief that enemy pressure in the area might have been slackening was abruptly shattered close to the turning to Cadoudal, where we were surprised by a German patrol springing from hidden positions beyond the kerbside bushes. Quickly and with unpleasant efficiency, they bundled Geneviève away from me with a terrified look on her face, while I was crushed against a wall then forcibly turned to face four sub-machine guns, inches from my head. Questions, in pidgin French – made even less fluent for being screamed directly into my ears – were muddled and mostly incoherent. Even if I had understood them and was minded to cooperate, I couldn't have given answers for they made no sense. I shrugged as innocently as I could with heavy hands restraining both shoulders, rifle butts jabbing into my ribs, and fists thudding into my cheeks. Then, as suddenly as the Germans had appeared, with their having gained no satisfactory replies to their uncoordinated interrogation, I was released and able to comfort a shaken Geneviève. We sat at the edge of the road smoking and thanking God that they had not been *Milice*.

What worried me most was the proximity of this patrol to Marienne's headquarters, although from what little I had gleaned – thinking back to the questions – I reckoned it was probably a coincidence. Nevertheless, enemy activity along the approaches to the new Maquis was serious, and the sooner we could warn Marienne the better – which we did once certain that we were not being followed.

I left them then for an hour or so to bicycle around the maze of local tracks so I could gauge whether or not our ambush had been a simple, chance encounter. I was stopped four more times, and on each arrest my hands were forced into the air as punches smashed against my unprotected stomach and face. I began to think the risk of deliberately exposing myself was too great: the pain certainly was!

My lame excuses centred around a lovers' argument and the need for fresh air and exercise to recover from my emotional setback. As one of the enemy sections knew that I had had a girlfriend and that she was now not with me, it was the best I could do. Convinced, now, that the patrols were speculative and spiteful in nature rather than based on firm intelligence, and as I had given them no military reason to be suspicious, I made my way, cautiously and again unseen, back to the Maquis. There, using maps and diagrams spread across a rickety wooden table, we confirmed what we should advise the Colonel. With that fixed, I stood to leave for Callac.

'Spend the night here – the two of you,' suggested Marienne.

'Thanks,' I said, 'but I have to brief a team of maquisards for manning each of the four entrances to the village.'

'You'd better get going, then!' He turned to Geneviève: 'See that he gets a few hours' sleep. Tomorrow's an important day.'

'He'll sleep all right!'

With a wave of hands we headed back down the path to the café by the bridge, to the long climb up to Plumelec and the easy run back to Callac – but with a cover plan firmly rehearsed should we be confronted further: my girlfriend and I had made it up, and the sooner the patrol let us through, the sooner we could re-establish our relationship. Even a bestial German trooper would see the decency in that!

This time it was Monsieur Gambert who opened the door to my knock. 'Your maquisards are in the garden.'

I went straight through, to find them in civilian clothes – as instructed – and eager. These men I knew well, and I had always found them intelligent and trustworthy.

'Good evening,' I began after offering cigarettes. 'The Trédion approaches to the village will need observing from now on. Night and day. Find yourselves places under cover, and stay there. If you see any Germans or German transport heading this way, warn us immediately.'

I turned to a second team. 'You'll be responsible for the Sérent side. Before the road actually reaches the buildings there's a farm on the right side; from the attic window you'll have an excellent view. The farmer will feed you and send messages, but you're not to leave the attic. Monsieur Gambert will send food out to the Trédion-road team. None of you will be armed, but you'll have a good supply of cigarettes, which are waiting on the kitchen table.'

With the house empty of maquisards, the Gamberts, Geneviève, Anna, Henriette and I sat for a few minutes over a last cup of coffee, then I made my way to bed and probably the last clean sheets until liberation. 'Tomorrow', I thought, 'we start again to "set Europe alight", in accordance with Mr Churchill's original instructions.'

Sharp at six I was on my bicycle, washed, shaved and balancing a bundle of clothes for Marienne. The air was cool, clear and windless, but with a promise of sunshine and warmth.

The roads were deserted: a legacy of the now-cancelled curfew and, despite the previous day's scares, the belief of the Germans that we were no longer a threat. It was grand to be out on such a lovely morning, and with the promise of action I pedalled hard but happily. The last free-wheeling miles had me singing, but at the bottom I found it was easier to balance the parcels of clothes and tobacco rather than carry them, so the bicycle was transformed into a makeshift trolley. It was good exercise up the far side, and I enjoyed it until, at a fork in the track, I rested for a few minutes to catch my breath and admire the view before it disappeared into 'dead ground'. I was about to crest the brow and begin the final descent into the valley with the three farms.

My daydream of Geneviève and a peacetime France was slowly interrupted by someone appearing to call my name. 'Not possible,' I thought. 'Only Marienne knows I'm on my way, and that's not his voice.'

'Captain Bob?' I stood upright facing the hill.

'Captain Bob?'

I looked round me. The muted voice seemed to come from the direction of thick bushes about fifty yards to my left. I let the bicycle fall gently to the grass and raised a hand in recognition, for Lieutenant Taylor was now in the open and waving his arms frantically. As he seemed rooted to the spot, I picked up the bike and pushed it towards him through the low scrub.

'What the hell's the matter with you,' I said unkindly, for we were on a section of the hill visible over some distance. As I approached, his features became clearer: his face – which never had much colour – was as white as newly milled flour; his eyes were wide open and staring; his hands shook. He hadn't answered my question.

'What's happened?' I said less sharply. The new Maquis head-quarters was the best I had seen: 'impregnable' was how we had described it. Impregnable, that is, if you don't allow for traitors . . .

'Don't go up there, sir! Don't go up there!' He pointed up the hill and, by implication, down the other side.

'Why?' I asked unnecessarily, for there was only one reason that I could think of. Treachery.

'They've all been killed,' he blurted out.

'What!' I exclaimed, then noticed the three men behind him, one holding a Bren gun across his chest.

'Marienne has been killed. All the others too. Just one – Sergeant Major Jaron – got away.'

'Are you sure? For Christ's sake . . .' I was near to shouting, but there was no reply – just a blank look.

'All right,' I said, calming down. We needed to get to the bottom of this quickly and without emotion. If it had just occurred then we were not in the best place to defend ourselves, but until I knew more facts I could make no decisions.

'How did it happen?' I asked, the pitch of my voice returning to something like normal. 'Tell me slowly, and leave nothing out – but we haven't got long. The bastards will know there are more of us out here, and that we never did disperse as they thought.'

I motioned for the five of us to lie down for fear we were being 'skylined', then looked at the Lieutenant. The three armed men faced outwards in all-round defence.

'I saw them myself,' Taylor said – 'all lying on the ground. Dead.'

'Go on.'

'What happened I'm not sure. Only Jaron knows that, and he's disappeared. Anyway, I was sent off on a job by Marienne last

night, and on my way back from the village – Plumelec – I was
stopped by someone I knew. He took me into a doorway and said
that he had just heard that a party of *miliciens* had been up at the
Maquis . . .'

'Another bloody person who knew where we were!'

'. . . and that all the men there had been killed, and that they
were inspecting the place and carrying away all our maps and notes
and what weapons they could find.'

'Oh God!' I groaned. 'Are you all that's left?'

'Yes, sir – just us and Jaron. When I heard the news I came up
here as quickly as I could, but being careful and collecting these
three men on the way.' He swung his arm round the group. 'We
got into a good position, unseen, and from where I could see
Marienne, Tisgne, the SAS men, the maquisards and the farmers –
all dead, lying out in the open. There seemed to me to be about
eighty *miliciens*, but I gave the order to open fire.'

'You wouldn't have stood a chance – but well done!'

'It would've been better if the Bren had fired more than one
shot – as it was, all that did was give away our position without
inflicting any damage.

'The *Milice* returned our fire, and we decided that the best thing
to do was to run like hell. We got over the top of the hill and
landed up here. As we weren't being chased, we thought we should
wait here and warn anyone coming. We also knew you'd be
arriving to collect Marienne for the conference.'

'Well done,' I repeated. My mind was numb from the news and
unable to comprehend the loss not only of a fine soldier and friend
but of one who had almost single-handedly kept the whole show
on the road. At Saint-Marcel our losses had been high and, I
thought selfishly, less personal, but the enemy had not then taken
our maps and plans.

Still clutching at straws I asked, 'Are you sure they weren't
just lying flat on the ground because it was easier to guard them
like that?'

'They were dead,' Taylor replied without emotion.

'I'll take your word for it,' I said. 'Any idea where Jaron could
be?'

'He stopped here to tell me that they'd all been killed, so I told him to find a hiding place and stay in it. He was in one hell of a state, and no use to me like that.'

'Right,' I said. 'Have any of the *Milice* left yet?'

'No – unless they know another track. I guess they're still searching the place.'

Any moment now the triumphant traitors would be making their way back past us. It was time for action.

'Try and work yourself into an observation position. I'll need to know their movements and direction once they leave – you may have to stalk them a bit, but that'll be up to you. Then try to find Jaron and report back to Callac – you know where, but be careful. I'm going back to issue new orders. We must get all the teams away from their present areas as soon as possible. They'll have the locations of all our other bases.' I patted him on the shoulder: 'Keep your head down,' I encouraged, and turned back towards Callac.

At the bottom of the hill I stopped at the *bar tabac*: the owner was a brother of one of the farmers who had faced the *Milice*. With the speed at which bad news was travelling, he might know more details.

Tragically, my guess was correct, and I found the middle-aged man and his wife clutching each other in the back room, both sobbing violently.

'Don't stay here,' the man managed to croak – 'they'll kill you like all the others. My brother is dead. Please go away. Immediately.' He took a deep breath and hugged his wife closer. It seemed to calm him. 'My daughter – only seventeen – was helping at one of the farms. Her uncle's farm. She came down about an hour ago, almost out of her mind.'

I had to break through the emotion. It was important to understand what had happened so, as with the village searches, we could be warned for the future. With my greatest friend and ally dead, my own emotions were close to breaking too. But I had to know.

'Please, monsieur, if you can tell me anything – anything – that will help us avoid a repeat please tell me.'

He helped his wife to a chair before pouring three large cognacs.

'Apparently at five o'clock this morning four civilians,' he spat the word, 'escorted by a maquisard sentry, walked in – calm as anything. The sentry seemed to know the men he was escorting, and told the farmers that he would show his "friends" to Marienne's camp. As soon as they had gone more civilians arrived, but these had guns and actually admitted that they were *miliciens* and said they would kill anyone who tried to warn Marienne.'

The *patron* was in full flow, telling the story in a flat, emotionless voice as he imagined the scene in his brother's house. 'To enforce these orders they lined everyone up against an outside wall, then told them to lie down with their hands behind their heads. While that was happening all the children and babies were dragged downstairs and put into a corner of the yard opposite the grown-ups, so that each could see what was happening to the others.'

'That's barbarous!' I exclaimed.

'The *miliciens* then told the parents that they would shoot the young if they moved. While all this was going on more *Milice* arrived to occupy various points around the farm, until my daughter thought there were about forty of them. Although he tried to resist, it was not long before Marienne was brought in.' The man stopped and finished his cognac.

'Go on,' I encouraged him.

'My daughter could say no more, except that she had seen Marienne – and the men with him – shot in front of everyone. And then everyone else was shot – one by one, in slow time. For some reason they let her go – maybe they knew she would spread the story and thought that would have the effect of putting the rest of us off helping you, I don't know. She collapsed at that point, so we helped her to bed.'

'May I see her?' I asked gently.

'Yes, but please then go. If they find you here we too will be killed, and there's been enough of that.'

The girl was in no state to answer questions, and particularly not the sort I wanted to ask.

I pedalled up the long hill that Geneviève and I had freewheeled down with such laughter, then sped through Plumelec without stopping, for that village already knew of the tragedy. Within forty minutes I was banging on the Gamberts' door in Callac.

Everyone was white-faced, with tears drying on their cheeks.

'You already know,' I said unnecessarily.

'Yes,' Geneviève answered. 'A farmer from the Trédion area came here a short while ago to say that he has Sergeant Major Jaron hiding in his fields. He asked that you be told as quickly as possible.'

'Anna,' I said, 'tell all the sentries on the roads that I want them here. Now.'

While we waited, I drew up new plans on the assumption that the *Milice* – and thus the Gestapo – would soon know where every single SAS soldier and maquisard was hiding and what his tasks were.

With all gathered, I said, 'The *Milice* have our plans and maps. Now each one of you must help as you have never helped before.' I knew they could do no more than they had been doing, but it had to be said. 'We've got to warn everybody, before the enemy gets there first.'

I turned to Geneviève: 'Tell that farmer to bring Jaron here. Then warn Colonel Bourgoin and anyone else in that area. Tell them what you know of the incident, and impress on them the fact that the *Milice* have all they need to know about us and our future plans. They might even know where the Colonel himself is.'

She nodded, and left the room without saying a word.

'Anna. Warn Nos. 1 and 2 Battalions. Tell them to move from their present locations. Stress that this must be done immediately and, when settled, tell them to send a runner so that we know where they are.'

She nodded and left.

'Henriette,' I continued, 'go to our last camp and warn the SAS teams still there. Get Monsieur Lecœur and the farmer to help you.'

She left on her mission, and I turned to three of the four maquisard lookouts and explained where the remaining battalions were as well as the areas of each of the Maquis for which they were responsible. The fourth lookout was to find the doctor, warn him, then stay to help move the wounded.

'Babin,' I said, 'contact Monsieur Legrand. Get him to warn the intelligence section. Move them if necessary. Even bring them here.' He too nodded. Nobody seemed in a talkative mood.

'Monsieur Gambert, will you warn all the local farmers, grocers and people who have been helping us to hide anything that might implicate them and to take all the usual precautions?'

'Madame Gambert, will you please go to Malestroit and put the mayor and the French police lieutenant in the picture, and on your way there or back do the same at Sérent?'

My final chore was to accost the two maquisards still skulking in the barn. I didn't inform them of Marienne's death, although I was pretty certain that they might have had a hand in it; instead I ordered them home without their weapons, which I dumped in the river near by. From their unwillingness to argue I suspected they knew what had happened.

Back at the house, Sergeant Major Jaron was waiting to see me. I came straight to the point: 'Tell me what happened.'

'Yesterday evening, Marienne ordered the sentries into their usual positions – one SAS and one maquisard together in pairs – in the farms and the various points that covered not only the approaches to the camp but the camp itself. When all were in their positions, those of us off duty turned in at about eleven, after clearing the messages through to London. At five this morning we were in our long tent built against the bank – you know the one.' I nodded. 'There were only two entrances if you remember. Then someone outside suddenly woke us with the call "Marienne. Marienne." Assuming it to be a sentry, Marienne replied immediately. Whoever it was then shouted, "Get out of your tent, you lousy bastard."

'Marienne, realizing what was happening, said he would fight rather than give himself up to a traitor. Then the man shouted back, "We've got all the farmers and their wives and children. One shot from you and they all die. But if you come out now you'll be made prisoners of war." Well, he knew as well as the rest of us that the *Milice* did not take prisoners of war – and especially not French SAS soldiers.

'We were wide awake and grabbed our weapons, waiting for a

sign from Marienne. Then the man shouted again that if we did not come out they would kill all the civilians anyway. They were eighty men strong, he said, and had all three tents surrounded.' Jaron stopped – not enjoying the memories.

'Marienne shouted back that he would surrender only if the safety of the civilians was guaranteed and if we would be treated as prisoners of war. That assurance was given, although Marienne probably guessed that it was not likely to be kept. We had no choice really, but he had to go through the motions I suppose. Anyway, they gave us five minutes to sort ourselves out and come out with our hands up. It was plain that Marienne was playing for time, although now it's difficult to see how extra time would have altered anything, but he was thinking, weighing up the odds.

'Marienne tried shouting, "You are French *miliciens* and we are Free French soldiers. I cannot trust the word of a traitor, but I will surrender only to save the farmers and their families – but that is the only reason." And with that he beckoned for us to follow as he walked slowly out of the tent.

'They were right: the whole camp seemed to be filled with the traitors, and I suppose the *milicien* was correct when he said there were eighty of them. They had machine guns covering us, and every man had a small German automatic weapon.

'We were marched to a farm, where we saw the liaison girl just trying to escape using our arrival as a diversion, but she was caught and beaten up. They put a gun in her back as she lay face down on the ground, saying that she would be the first to die if we tried anything funny.

'Meanwhile other *miliciens* were rushing round clutching our papers, maps and orders – everything they could lay their hands on. As we entered the main farmyard we could see the farmers and their families lying down on their backs with their heads next to one of the walls. It was then that they searched us for weapons and papers, and as they did so everyone was beaten in some way with rifle butts.

'Then all the civilians were ordered to stand in the centre of the yard while we took their places. The civilian men had been separated from the women and children and forced to the ground. It was well planned, as the *Milice* shot each one in turn with his automatic, while the wives, mothers and daughters watched. Some of the men killed were only sixteen. The wives all screamed, but the *Milice* ordered them to shut up or they'd be next.

'Anyway, they were taken off – plus the liaison girl – but I think at least one girl did escape.'

I confirmed that she was safe but terrified.

'Well,' Jaron continued, 'that was the signal for them to start on us. They used all the foulest language they could think of. They abused us, kicked us, butted us, and threatened to shoot us – which we knew they would do anyway. Part of me began to wish they would just get it over with.

'Suddenly Marienne stepped forward with a look on his face that said everything about his honour and their treachery. He was slow, deliberate and very calm – not shaking like the rest of us. This stopped all the *Milice* from doing what they were doing so they could watch. The man who seemed to be in charge – though whether or not he was I don't know, but I shall never forget his face – put his hand out to grab the small gold locket that Marienne always wore round his neck.'

I knew it well, for sometimes he would proudly show me the photograph of his young wife that it contained.

'Marienne fixed the bastard with a look that must have touched even his conscience, and said quietly but so clearly that everyone could hear, "You can leave that. I want it with me when I die." The *milicien* slowly lowered his hand, and as he did so you could have heard a pin drop across the countryside.'

There were tears in the Sergeant Major's eyes, and I could feel them welling in my own. I looked away and blinked. The death of my companion, and probably at that stage in my life the only permanent friend I had ever had, was beginning to affect me. Yet I had to hear the end. Not trusting my voice to remain uncracked, I motioned for Jaron to continue.

'After about thirty seconds the spell was broken by another *milicien*, who taunted Marienne from a cowardly distance. "You want to know how we caught you, don't you?" Marienne didn't answer. "Well I'll tell you," the man went on. "Last night", he said, "we were drinking in a village café and saw a well-known maquisard at the bar. We told him we wanted to join his Maquis, and he told us what we wanted to know. So we took him outside to sober him up and encourage him to tell us more. In the fresh air he tried to retract, so we promised him a few grams of lead if he didn't help us and hundreds of francs if he did. To start with the fool chose the lead – until we mentioned that his family would be killed and, to prove our point, we wrote down his address and his wife and children's names. That seemed to do the trick, and he brought us here. He knew the way all right, and all the sentries. So, Marienne, you thought you could evade us. Well, you were wrong!"

'Marienne, still calm, told them how disgusted he was that Frenchmen could sell themselves to the enemy by killing their own countrymen, acting as traitors, acting as cowards, but he was shouted down by someone who screamed, "If that's all you have to say then shut up", then aimed his gun at him. I shall never forget Marienne at that moment. His face was white, but he was smiling as he turned round to us. His confidence gave us immense courage as he turned back to the man with the gun. He was still smiling, and looked the *milicien* straight in the eyes.'

I could guess what was coming next, and gripped the table.

'A burst was fired. Marienne was hit in the middle of his chest from only a few metres away. Tisgne was next, then another man. The gun was aimed at me, but all that happened was a click. I couldn't believe it, but it took a moment to realize that I was still alive. As he was changing magazines, I decided to make a break for it and ran right through the middle of the *miliciens*. They were so surprised, then so worried that they might hit each other, that nobody opened fire. By the time they recovered I was dodging through the trees. Bullets cracked and whistled about my ears, but luckily none came too close. I didn't stop running until, by chance, I came across Lieutenant Taylor and . . .' he stopped, fumbling for a handkerchief – 'well, here I am.'

'What happened to the maquisard who gave everything away? Do you know him – his name and so on?'

'He must be a prisoner, as he knows who they are, but I'll catch up with him. He didn't expect any of us to escape, so I should think he's worried sick.'

I knew enough, and what I had heard only emphasized how careful we had to be. If I had my way, no maquisard would ever leave the Maquis except for operations.

'Thank you, Sergeant Major. Get some rest, and try to put it out of your mind.' I didn't think there was much chance of that.

The farmer who had brought Jaron had been hovering at a discreet distance. 'Look after him,' I said. 'When we need him again I'll send someone. Remember, his face is known to the *Milice*.'

When they had gone I walked unsteadily up to the attic. Palls of grey smoke rose from a number of farms on the horizon and, closer, shots could be heard from the Trédion woods, where I knew we had men hiding.

Downstairs again, and more composed, I received reports from Malestroit that told of the *Milice* briefing German headquarters in Coëtquidan from Marienne's papers: the Gestapo, the Cossacks and a buoyant *Milice* were roaming the country and had already rounded up a number of our teams, while reinforcement army units had been summoned from Vannes, Rennes and Brest. The only bright news was that – apparently – we were now tying up an estimated two army divisions.

Lieutenant Taylor's team had stayed in hiding until – as far as they could tell – the *Milice* had left the area, leaving three blazing farms behind them. A man was sent to summon help, but there was little anyone could do for the buildings and the dead: Marienne and his men still lay where they fell, with pigs, set free by the departing *Milice*, already snuffling round the corpses and licking at pools of congealed blood.

The local priest was arranging for the bodies to be removed. They were later buried in Plumelec cemetery.[2]

I slept, exhausted, for a couple of hours, until woken by Monsieur Gambert at five in the morning. Behind him, as he entered my room with a most welcome cup of coffee, stood the doctor. It was the end of my last night in comfort.

'Bob,' the doctor said, 'I'm sorry about Marienne. He was a

grand fellow, and meant so much to all of us. His was the true spirit of resistance and freedom. All the people I met yesterday want to express their sympathy.'

'Our loss is tremendous, but France's is greater,' I replied rather theatrically, then changed the subject. 'How are your patients?'

'I had one hell of a job moving them to safer places.' He stopped to think, but could only mutter, 'What are you going to do?'

'I'll do everything in my power to save Marienne's men, the maquisards and his work, and I'll work day and night until I've succeeded. I'll reorganize the Maquis for the third time, and if that's impossible then I'll tell everyone to form independent parties and fight the enemy as they best can in their own areas. It'll be unco-ordinated, but possibly better for that under the circumstances. I'll arrange for airdrops and the distribution of arms and ammunition. We'll ambush the Germans, we'll sabotage their lines of communi-cation, and we'll make them pay in their own blood for the vile crimes they've committed. Every man and woman in the area will have to take the risk and help. We'll need information like we've never needed it before, and I'll do everything possible to ensure that one day a battalion of maquisards will march through a liberated Malestroit.'

Monsieur Gambert and the doctor quietly left me to my coffee as I lay back against the deep pillows. Things had gone wrong – often – but there were many positive factors that I could tick off on my fingers.

We had over four hundred SAS and now four thousand maquis-ards in the Morbihan alone. The battle at the Pondards' farm had forced the Germans in Brittany to deploy two divisions, the Gestapo, a brigade of Cossacks, and the *Milice*. They had even had to request help from other units outside our area. All these troops were needed badly in the Normandy area, and that was something of which we, across our widely sundered Maquis, could feel proud. We had killed up to eight hundred of the enemy, and probably wounded rather more.

I knew that across the rest of Brittany there were other large concentrations of maquisards: two thousand in Loire-Inférieure, the same in Côtes-du-Nord; three thousand in Ille-et-Vilaine, and another two thousand in Finistère. All the Maquis of the other regions were under the command of British or French parachutists or local French commanders.

So, if we could not fight by ourselves, I would organize our men to join up with the others. We had all been through trying periods, and I knew that my Maquis was certainly not alone in this regard for we had welcomed some of the remnants of the Samwest circuit.

I fell asleep again, to be woken – again – by Monsieur Gambert. 'Drink this,' he said. 'Everyone was out on their tasks at five, but we decided to leave you be.'

By eight I was on my way, with a full breakfast in my stomach and trepidation in my heart – bound for the Colonel and Jim. I was not looking forward to the meeting, for I was strangely happy with running the show by myself now, and wanted to do so in memory of Marienne. The two officers had been out of things for so long that I resented the fact that they might alter my – and Marienne's – plans.

In fact I was met warmly, and after lengthy greetings I recounted the various eyewitness reports of Marienne's death and the sacking and razing of the farms and barns across our area.

There was a long silence before the Colonel spoke. 'Keep on doing what you are doing at the moment,' he said. 'Save the maquisards – save the Maquis.'

I nodded, for this was what I had hoped he would say.

'While you have been doing what you have been doing,' he continued, 'I have been thinking and planning.'

I nodded again, but this time with less enthusiasm.

'I have decided', the Colonel said, 'to get them all out of here once they have been gathered together by you. I will want to regroup at least fifty kilometres from here. We have twenty liaison girls and men, and can move everybody fairly fast. Puech-Samson will take over Marienne's duties.' Without pausing, he went straight on: 'Our plan is –'

'Just a minute, Colonel,' I butted in. 'You know the situation. For the next two to three days I shall do my utmost to save all I possibly can. I don't think at the moment that it's a good idea to alter what's already happening. The Gestapo and *Milice* know who

I am, know what I look like, and are looking out for me. Once I have all our chaps in new safe places I'll hand them over to you, then take a week away to allow my profile to reduce a little. But the main thing is that the less I know about your plans the better, in case I get caught tomorrow or the next day.'

Surprisingly, he agreed, and for another hour we talked about other matters, until I took my leave and headed for Callac.

I knew that the Colonel was bitter. He was a fighter, and one of the very best, but with one arm he was too conspicuous, and no matter how much disguise he might have covered himself with he was still an obvious target.

No one else had come back, so after a hurried meal of what I could find in the kitchen I returned to the road for several hours, catching up men and pointing them to the Trédion woods.

Back again, Babin reported that three more villages had been burned and over twenty men arrested, with four known to have been shot. The general report from the others all indicated an increase in roadblocks and patrols. That night we all, except the members of the Gambert family and 'our' three girls, returned to the fields.

I knew the Germans and *Milice* were on to me, although so far nobody had given my whereabouts away, despite our losing a number of soldiers and Maquis to the enemy. Sleeping in the fields was made more pleasant by the weather, and we thanked God that it was not February – and prayed, also, that it would not be February before the liberation came.

'Bob, are you dreaming?' I opened my eyes. Above me, with her dark silhouette framed by stars, was Geneviève.

'What are you doing here? Why aren't you at home and in bed? If I get caught, that's one thing: this is my job; this is what I'm being paid to do. But with you – well, that's different. You really shouldn't take such unnecessary risks.'

'I came to say that the Gamberts would like you to sleep in the house again – and I'd like that too.'

I thought about it, weighing the risks to them, and decided that it might be less dangerous than having messages relayed through the fields at night.

She saw me wavering. 'The maquisard watching the roads came and threw stones up at my window and asked me to tell you that there have been many vehicles on the road throughout the night. Something is about to happen, and you'll get a better view from the house.'

'Better view maybe,' I said, 'but also a better chance of being caught and dragging all of you down with me.'

'I think you should come back.'

Back in my old bedroom and with no new movement through the village, I slept in snatches until a frantic banging on the other side of the wall by my head brought me quickly to full consciousness with a pounding heart.

But another sound now masked that heavy thumping: laden troop-carrying vehicles trundling through the main street of Callac and heading south.

I dressed quickly and returned the banging, but this time on Geneviève's door. She was still in bed, so, without switching on the light, I crossed to the open window and very slightly drew back a corner of the curtains. My initial thoughts were confirmed.

'It's terrible,' I joked — 'every time I try to sleep something happens. If it's not you it's the blasted Germans, and if it's not the blasted Germans then it's you!'

She ignored me. 'They're moving into the Trédion area. There'll be a search within a couple of hours.'

'I don't think they'll search Callac — at least not yet. They'll be after larger concentrations of men.'

I let the curtain's corner fall back into place, and sat on her bed. 'Do you mind if I stay here a few minutes, to see what else happens?'

'Not at all. Provided you behave. And don't switch on that light to get a better look at me.' She had read my mind. But I still stayed for an hour before slipping away to grab the last of the night in my own bed.

Life swiftly evolved into a routine once more, and one to which I was well accustomed: searching for teams of SAS and Maquis, dodging the Germans, choosing targets for sabotage, arranging supplies of food and cigarettes.

Our military situation gradually improved, helped by the removal of the Cossacks from the area. The *Milice* were down to about a hundred, and there was a marked reduction in the number of enemy heavy vehicles and tanks. They had not been sent to face the advancing Allies, but by and large had been destroyed by our ambushes or had fled to the east, terrified of being boxed into the Brittany peninsula with no chance of eventual escape.

The Colonel and Jim now had everything in order, while stores were being supplied from other Maquis further north.

On 26 July I returned from the Trédion woods to the Gamberts' house with my tired brain full of plans that concerned only Geneviève, but the moment the door was opened I could sense that something was wrong. A new worry had descended on the household. Geneviève quickly told me.

'There's a young man who says he has come all the way from Vannes especially to see you.'

'How the hell did anyone from Vannes know where to find me?' I asked of nobody in particular, and nobody replied.

I sat and listened to their story. At ten o'clock that morning one of the road sentries reported that three cars containing Germans and *Milice* had stopped a few hundred yards from his post. Shortly afterwards a *milicien* in a French parachutist's uniform ran down the street in a replay of an earlier incident, shouting for help and a safe haven from the Germans who were, he cried, on his tail.

He had stopped at no other house until he reached that of the Gamberts, where he tore open the door and continued his screaming.

'Help me! Help me! They're trying to capture me. For God's sake help me!'

Unfortunately for the bravado performance, he was recognized by Geneviève as the man who had so rudely forced my first kiss on her in the woods. 'Oh,' she screamed. 'Just wait a moment.' And with that she ran back into the kitchen.

'I can't wait,' he shouted after her. 'Please hide me from the Germans.'

But there was to be no hiding place as Geneviève ran back

wielding a stiff broom with which she immediately attacked the intruder, raining vicious blows about his ears and shoulders.

'This is what you deserve! And what's more', she screamed convincingly, 'I'll tell the Germans that you're here. You and your lot have caused us more trouble than you're worth.'

Cornered by a reaction that he was not expecting, the hapless traitor had crouched down with his arms shielding his face. Geneviève continued to poke and prod through his defences.

'We want no filthy parachutists here,' she screamed louder, and as the German patrol burst through the door the beating and lunging intensified: there was no mercy.

'Stop it, stop it,' shouted the patrol commander, pushing her aside. 'It's all right. He's on your side. He's not a parachutist. He's a *milicien*.'

'What!' Geneviève shouted back, the broom handle across her front, knuckles white with readiness for her next assault. 'In that case he deserves even more for frightening me and for playing little soldier boys!'

And with that she delivered a final onslaught while the Germans, without success, tried to restrain her. It had, the Gamberts assured me, been a convincing performance which forced the enemy team to leave as quickly as it could.

A little later, when the others had left the room, I looked at her. 'I was going to ask you to marry me!' She didn't look surprised, so I went on, 'But I'm not sure I've enough armour!'

'Stop trying to be funny, Bob,' was her only reply. We had talked vaguely of spending the rest of our lives together, but I had never used the word 'marry', and now I had done so only to make a feeble joke. 'The Germans are up to something, and we must try to stop them.'

'How?' I asked lamely.

'I don't know, but they won't let us get away with this. After all, they came straight to the house – and if that isn't a warning then I don't know what is.'

I had no answers, so I changed the subject. The presence of the man from Vannes was nagging at me. 'I'd better see your visitor. Can you show him in?'

'Are you sure?'

I wasn't at all sure, but I needed to find out how he knew of my whereabouts. 'Yes,' I said with considerable hesitation.

A young man was ushered in, looking shifty and suspicious. I thought him either brave or foolhardy, for if he was a *milicien* he must have known that his chances of survival by himself among us was slim, and if he wasn't he was still taking one hell of a chance. Either way I would give him no leeway.

'Good afternoon, Captain Bob,' he began.

I was expecting that, and showed no sign of recognition. Instead I said curtly, 'I don't know the man. What do you want?'

'Well, sir,' he persisted, 'I was in your first Maquis, and since the withdrawal I've been living in Vannes, where I've met some friends who want to form their own Maquis. They asked me if you could take them on.'

I said nothing.

'They're on friendly terms with the Gestapo, and they tell me they can get anything you might want.'

I remained silent.

'They also asked me to tell you that the German army, the Gestapo and the *Milice* have all been told that there's a 500,000-franc prize for anyone giving information that leads to your capture.'

I didn't like what I was hearing.

'Please will you come to Vannes and meet our small group?'

As an attempt at setting up an ambush it was amateur, and I decided to lead him on a little more to gain some knowledge of his intelligence-gathering methods.

'Why did you think this Captain Bob was here? Who told you?'

'The Gestapo and the *Milice* both know that you have lived here for some time. It's through them that I got the address.'

If he was speaking the truth then it was a terrible piece of intelligence, and if he wasn't then it was a brazen attempt at getting it.

'You must be well in with the Gestapo and *Milice*.'

'Oh yes, we are,' he replied easily. 'We can learn most things that we want through them. It should be very useful to you if you come with me to Vannes.'

I said nothing.

'We'll look after you really well,' he pleaded.

I thought for a moment, then said, 'Today is 26 July. I'm not Captain Bob, but I'll be in Vannes on 2 August.'

He seemed not at all taken aback by this sudden decision. 'In front of the town hall,' he said – 'eleven o'clock?'

'Fine.'

'Good, then you can meet my friends over lunch.'

I smiled and waved him out of the room, then as soon as he had gone I related the conversation to Geneviève, her sisters and Babin. 'The whole thing stinks. I'm dead certain he's not on the level, which makes it odd that he should have taken such a risk. What's certain is that people who shouldn't have known of our whereabouts do now.'

'Anna and Henriette,' I turned to the two sisters, 'you'd better pack your things and push off to your parents tonight. Babin, you go with them.'

I turned to the third sister. 'Geneviève, you and I will stay here until 1 August. I'll sleep in the fields till then.'

Supper that evening was a quiet affair with four of us round the kitchen table, until at ten o'clock we were disturbed by the doctor's anxious knock on the back door.

'On my way back this evening' – he was still breathless – 'I was stopped by a farmer to the south of Trédion. He told me he had seventeen of our parachutists hidden in the woods by his farm. Three of them are wounded. Apparently, earlier this morning they'd received orders from Colonel Bourgoin to move into the area, but while they were doing that they were ambushed by the Germans. They managed to escape, but we're going to have to get them away pretty soon.'

'We'll catch up with them in the morning,' I said, then briefed the doctor on the day's events.

'Do you intend going to Vannes?' he asked.

'No, I don't.'

'Then why did you say you would?'

'I'm just hoping that they'll think I will, and leave us alone till then,' I said. 'It's a risk, but then this is all a risk.'

A night of tossing and turning followed, until the doctor and I were on our bicycles heading for Trédion and the farms to the south. We were just in time, for the farmer was himself leaving for the fields.

'How do you help them?' I asked quickly, for I didn't think we had much time.

'During the day we take them food, otherwise they're left very much on their own.'

'That's kind of you, and I'll reimburse you, but please don't do any cooking for them. Cold meats, bread, butter, eggs and that sort of thing is fine, but if you're caught cooking for seventeen rather than the four of you it won't help.'

'Yes, sir.'

'Go and see them at seven this evening. We'll warn them, so they'll know that visitors at any other time of day are enemy.'

We walked towards where he pointed – the edge of the forest – then, while the doctor did what he could for the wounded, I briefed the two officers on what they should do.

Back at the farm we remounted our bicycles and travelled the first three hundred yards or so in silence. I was not happy with the situation, for the team we had just visited was too vulnerable and would not be able to make any escape while held back by the wounded.

However, my thoughts were interrupted by the doctor, who slowed down to let me catch up. 'Don't look now,' he said out of the side of his mouth, 'but on your right, fifty metres ahead – three Germans. Weapons lying in the grass.'

I looked up without moving my head. 'Keep pedalling,' I whispered. 'Pretend we haven't seen them.'

We passed the embryo roadblock without being bothered, and then after another few hundred yards the reason was clear. We were caught between two armed sections of German soldiers.

'Move to the left-hand side of the road,' the doctor said. 'I'm going to drop my medical bag into the ditch.'

I did as he asked, and slowed a little.

'OK,' he said – 'that's done.'

We were not molested this second time either, but when we

reached Trédion there were six lorries lined up along the main street while men from the army, Gestapo and *Milice* were flooding through the village. Roadblocks had been established at each end and, having been waved through the first, we had to slow down to negotiate the large numbers of enemy milling around. What caught my eye, though, were seven Frenchmen lined up with their faces against a wall. The last roadblock was manned not by Germans but by *miliciens*. I could handle Germans, but the *Milice* might see through me, and I feared them the most.

'Stop! Get off your bicycles,' one shouted, moving into the centre of the road and swinging his automatic pistol from his shoulder. '*Papiers!*'

We did as ordered, and stood astride our bicycles while the papers were subjected to a thorough scrutiny; then, unexpectedly, and with a peremptory wave of the hand, we were allowed to continue.

As soon as we had risen to the saddles another *milicien* blocked our path. 'You two. What are you doing here anyway?'

The doctor spoke sharply. 'We came to Trédion on business. My friend here represents a flour mill in Malestroit – you saw his papers – and my boss, who lives here, supplies the village and the mill with flour. When we saw what was going on we decided to get out until all the fuss has died down.'

'Where does your boss live?'

'You see those seven men against the wall? Well, that's his house. I also look after his three horses.'

For reasons of his own – and they were probably not ulterior at that moment – the *milicien* smiled and said, 'Stop being so scared. Go back and get your work done.'

We had no alternative but to go through with our own charade, and so we reluctantly pushed our bicycles back to the house whose outside wall was lined by the seven men.

'Doc,' I said once out of earshot, 'do you know the owner of this house?'

'Fortunately I do,' he replied with a broad grin.

'Thank God!'

Before entering the outer door to leave our bicycles in the long entrance hall, I managed a glance at the faces of the captured men and was horrified to recognize them all as members of our Maquis. Though conscious of their most likely fate, they seemed full of courage, preferring death to exposing the names and addresses of their leaders and comrades. The sight filled me with a deep anger, and as I racked my brains for some way to help them I realized how impotent I was.

14. Wanted: Dead or Alive

Once through the street door, we left our bicycles in the gloomy passage before I followed the doctor into the front room, unannounced. The owner and a young woman were standing side by side facing us: our presence did nothing for the grim looks on their faces.

'Good morning,' said the doctor first. 'This is Captain Bob, a British officer. We arrived here to find the Germans out in force, and didn't want to get caught in their games, so when a *milicien* started asking questions I had to think of something to say pretty quickly. I told him that I worked for you – in charge of your horses – and that the Captain was a flour representative from Malestroit. I'm afraid I forgot that you deal in butter, but I don't think that the *milicien* noticed. Can you explain what's going on?'

It was a long speech and, I thought, rather presumptuous, but the doctor obviously knew his man, although neither gave much sign of intimate recognition.

'Yes I can,' he said without hesitation. 'But first of all I must present my niece, Mademoiselle Annie Baudouin.'

And with those briefest of introductions our 'host and employer' recounted his version of events. He began, however, by rebuking us for so suddenly putting him and his niece in danger. 'Much as I like you, doctor, and I am sure I will like your friend, it is not good to see you here this morning. However, I can do nothing about that now, so you must feel welcome.'

We mumbled our apologies.

'At eight this morning the village was surrounded by Germans and their bloody spies. The houses were all searched, and while they were doing this house I asked them what was happening. They weren't keen to talk, but I did hear what was being said to the men outside. Seventeen parachutists are known to be in this area, and they are anxious to round them up. If they do not find what they are after, they will start the executions. Nor do I need to tell you what they will do to all of us if they know you are here.'

For the sake of the seventeen parachutists and seven maquisards we had to get out – but on our terms – so I excused myself. At the back of the house there was a small garden with a large shed from whose attic I could see much of our surroundings – and a pretty cheerless sight it was too. A straightforward escape across country would be impossible, and I racked my brain for some other tactic.

'What are you thinking about, Bob?' the doctor asked on my return.

'The same as you, probably,' I replied: 'how to get out of here to warn the parachutists. But if they escape then the seven men outside will be shot.'

'It's seven against seventeen,' he said unhelpfully. One of the two groups would be killed no matter what we did.

The doctor added, 'There's no guarantee that the seven will go free if the others are caught.' He turned to our host: 'Did the Germans give any idea when the men would be killed?'

'Six o'clock.'

'We've got a bit of time. Do they know they are maquisards?'

'No.'

'Doc,' I said, 'I'm going to get out to warn the parachutists, then come back here and see if I can make a diversion and get these men free too. There's not much I can do, but anything is worth a try.'

As he nodded his assent I turned to Miss Baudouin. 'Mademoiselle,' I said, 'do you think you could help me?'

She smiled.

'I've a plan that might just work, but to get away with it I shall need your assistance. In a few minutes I shall open the door and we'll walk out wheeling our bicycles and talking like old friends. Once outside, we'll try to pass through the roadblock on the Callac side. The trick, I think, will be to keep up an animated conversation.'

I turned to her uncle: 'Would you come to the door and give us an enthusiastic send-off – like you would give an old friend? And don't forget that my name is Alfred Havet – at least that's what it says on my papers.'

For a moment or two we practised roughly what would be said, and then with a pounding heart I opened the front door for Annie to wheel her bicycle out past me. Out of the corner of my eye I could see the seven men still standing, but with their hands now on their heads. A few yards in front of us a crowd of *miliciens* were gathered; all turned towards us as we stepped into the street.

From his front door our host played his part superbly. Raising his arm in a farewell salute, he called, '*Au revoir, Monsieur Havet*. My regards to your boss, and don't forget that you're both coming here for lunch tomorrow.'

'I won't forget,' I shouted back. 'And thank you very much. I'll be sending my lorry to collect this month's supply of butter in five days' time.'

'Yes, that's fine. Now you look after my niece – she's young and innocent, so behave yourself!'

'That's a nice opinion you have of me. Don't you trust me?'

'No, my boy,' he laughed. 'I've known you since you were a brat. No girl was safe. Now get on, both of you.'

The *miliciens* heard every word, as they were meant to, and began shouting all manner of obscenities at us – including suggestions that in peacetime would have had Annie's uncle laying into them. But it was what we wanted, and with a final wave over our shoulders we were on our way. Many eyes were on us as we kept up a lively conversation, cycling deliberately and slowly towards Trédion's northern outskirts, where a *milicien* waved us to stop. I offered a silent prayer that no one would recognize me. So far I had been lucky, but that could not last.

'Get off your bikes and let's look at your papers!'

We did as ordered. The scrutiny was thorough and quick, then he searched my pockets and ran a hand over my clothes before turning to Annie. Her papers were in order, but the hand-search of her clothes took a long time, the man smirking and winking over his shoulder at his companions.

Annie had had enough. 'Take your hands off me, you filthy brute,' she half screamed.

'All right, all right, *chérie*. I won't spoil you for your boyfriend. Now get out of here, the pair of you, before I change my mind.'

And we did 'get out', as quickly as we could, by pedalling furiously away.

A few minutes later Annie, in the lead, slowed up, and as I came alongside her she said, 'Alfred, two hundred metres ahead, on the left of the road, there's a track that leads to a farm, and from there you should be able to work your way south again to warn your friends.'

'Thank heavens for that,' I replied. 'It's worth trying.'

I followed her down the track until, turning on to a path that led towards the wood, I quickly changed my mind and continued straight on towards the buildings. Annie followed behind; when she had caught up, I explained what I had seen.

'That path is full of Germans heading this way.'

'I saw them too. One of then is studying us through his field glasses. Keep going as though we don't know they are there.'

By following the track, we eventually made it to Callac. We had failed in our primary aim, but we had at least escaped and were able to move freely while I thought of another way to get the message to our men.

An hour passed, and so did a number of lorries heading away from Trédion. Then, from an upstairs room, a huge fire was visible, gaining in strength and smoke.

'I guess that's that,' I said gloomily. 'They're either all dead or have been made prisoners of war – which is the same thing.'

Depressed and angry, I sat with Geneviève in the Gamberts' kitchen half expecting the doctor to arrive. But I was surprised when, in less than half an hour, his knock did rattle the door.

'Bob, Geneviève, I've got bad news.' I guessed he wouldn't have good news – nobody did.

We found a secluded spot in a nearby field and sat down to listen.

'Ten minutes after you left me,' the doctor began, 'I got fed up with waiting and thought that I too should try my luck. And that luck held, as no one paid me the slightest bit of attention. There was, though, quite a hubbub going on – a good deal of excitement among the Germans and the *Milice*. Something was obviously happening, but I pretended not to notice or care and slowly wheeled the bike along the main street and eventually through the roadblock with no problem.

'I turned down the track to where we could reach our men, and then nearly bumped into a German patrol, but I managed to hide in the bushes. Suddenly there was a great deal of shooting, and a minute or so later a young boy ran past. I called to him, and together we moved into a thicker area of scrub. I asked him to tell me what was going on.'

Apparently the poor child had been shaking from head to toe, but managed to get his story out in small bursts. It seemed that his boss's wife – the farmer's wife – had wanted to cook a meal for all seventeen of the SAS soldiers and, while the farmer had suggested that that was not a wise thing to do, she had insisted. In the middle of her preparing the meal, the Germans and *Milice* had stormed into the kitchen to ask awkward questions before searching the buildings. While some were doing that, others wanted to know how many people were living there. 'Four,' she had said: her husband, herself, their daughter and the young lad. 'Then why are you cooking food for twenty?'

At this the farmer was badly beaten, while the two women were taken outside and lined against the wall. In the confusion, the boy managed to run quickly into cover, where he stayed frozen to the spot and able to hear what happened next. The Germans demanded to know where the soldiers were, and said that if they were told then the family would be left in peace and the men would be taken off as prisoners – and if they didn't then they would all be shot.

The farmer, after more beatings, agreed to give the game away, and led the Germans towards the hiding place – which then housed twenty or so, as the soldiers had been joined by some maquisards. The boy heard the shooting and then silence until the main party returned to the farm, still with the farmer. They had, though, as far as he could see, left some of the troops at the hiding place, presumably to wait for anyone who might come to give a warning.

Once back at the farm, the farmer was shot in the back of the head while his wife and daughter were forced to watch. The boy then ran, and it was during this flight from horror that the doctor had called to him to stop.

Geneviève, who knew the family well, was in tears. 'Where's the boy now?' I asked.

'I don't know.'

Later that day it was confirmed via a number of sources, including the mayor of Malestroit, that fifteen soldiers, two maquisards and the farmer had been shot. Two or three had managed to escape. The farm had been burned to the ground, and the wife and daughter were being cared for by a local family. The only good news was that the seven men lined up for execution had been freed after each had received a severe beating.

'Why does everything go wrong?' I lamented. 'If we don't get liberated soon, I hate to think what will happen next.'

'With Colonel Bourgoin and Jim now running the show,' said the doctor, 'if I were you I'd get the hell out of Callac – do a vanishing trick for a few days.'

Neither Geneviève nor I did a 'vanishing trick'; instead, we worked night and day helping the hidden teams as much as we could, while I also attended conferences with the Colonel and Jim so that by 1 August I had handed over everything – including a working wireless link with England. The doctor had left to join the headquarters two days before.

Over lunch that day I told the Gamberts that Geneviève and I would be gone by the evening, leaving no trace that we had ever been in their house. Her parents had asked if we would like to move in with them, for they had heard that the enemy had traced us both to Callac.

'If you don't move soon,' the warnings were becoming persistent, 'you'll find yourself against a wall as well – and sooner rather than later.'

So we moved out with heavily laden bicycles and headed towards Sérent, then on to join the Malestroit road for about five miles until a narrow path that leads off to the right. A mile or so down this we took another right turn, and at the end of that track stood a small farmhouse that had escaped burning by the Germans. It was close to the original Maquis, and was now the home of the Pondard parents.

'Hello, everyone,' we called as the door came into view beyond a hedge. 'Anything to drink?' It had been a hot ride, but one untroubled by the enemy.

Monsieur Pondard rushed forward. 'Captain!' he exclaimed. 'What do you think of my new farm? Not so big, but it's close to our fields, so we can continue to work them.'

'It's wonderful,' I replied, shaking his hand vigorously before kissing Madame equally warmly. It was heartening to see the resilience of these two people who had been through hell, and it was easy to see from whom Geneviève, Anna and Henriette had inherited their bravery.

'We've only got three bedrooms, but we've made up a bed for you in the attic – which you'll be sharing with Babin.'

'Is he here?'

'He will be. He went out this morning to see some friends, but won't be back till tomorrow evening.'

'Come on, all of you,' Madame Pondard's long-remembered exhortation broke into our conversation – 'supper's ready.'

Dinner with a family, who had lost their farm and much of the year's crops was an oasis of peace and tranquillity, and we all laughed cheerfully as they planned for the future with an unquench-able belief. After supper had been cleared away we strolled, the four of us arm in arm, through the warm evening air with cigarettes and coffee.

'Why are you taking leave?' Monsieur Pondard asked.

'It's not leave in the ordinary sense,' I explained. 'Colonel Bourgoin now has everything under control. My job was to prepare and organize the Maquis before his arrival. Then my job was to advise on training and targets, and to organize the resupply of money, arms, ammunition and explosives. Marienne and I did all of that to begin with, and then again each time we were thwarted by the Boche.'

'I've heard of some of your activities,' Monsieur Pondard said.

'Then you'll know that nearly everybody living in this area knows my face and what I'm doing, and as the *Milice* are getting dangerously curious the Colonel agreed that I should lie low for a day or two. With full-scale operations due to start in about four days, I'll rejoin him then.'

'You certainly look as though you could do with some sleep I must say – both of you,' he added.

I took the hint and climbed the ladder to the attic, where I slept for eleven hours.

The new day did not herald the end of our troubles. Geneviève and I had to return to Callac, to ensure that the supply route for vegetables and cigarettes would stay open during my proposed 'leave'. There was no reply to our knock on the Gamberts' shop door. We tried once more, to be answered by Madame's assistant peering warily round the edge.

'Oh, it's you,' he said. 'I thought it was the *miliciens* again.'

'Again?' I asked. 'Tell me.'

'Come in.'

'Monsieur Gambert was arrested this morning,' he said briefly.

'Go on.'

'Early this morning an SAS sergeant came here in civvies. He was carrying good ID papers, and said he was on his way to see Colonel Bourgoin, or one of the Maquis, but he didn't say why. Monsieur Gambert knew him, as they had been in the same platoon in the Maquis, so he asked him to stay for breakfast. We hadn't started when the house was surrounded and the doors burst open. After a thorough search they left taking Monsieur and Madame Gambert and the sergeant, but leaving the daughter and me. I advised her to go to her grandmother as quickly as she could, while I locked the shop and house. As far as I know they didn't find anything in their searches, so from that point of view it may be all right.'

'They need no excuses to murder,' I added unhelpfully.

'As they were leaving, and after the others had been taken outside, one of them turned and asked me if a captain lived here – or had lived here. I said, "No", but their reply was a strong poke in the ribs. They told me to shut up, and said that they'd be back to catch this Captain Bob as soon as they'd dealt with their prisoners.'

'Did you recognize any of the *miliciens*?'

'I was going to tell you. Remember that young man from Vannes – I think he was from Vannes – who came here a few days ago?' I remembered him well. 'He was sitting in the back of one of the cars.'

'I bet he was.'

I could feel Geneviève getting edgy, while the shop assistant understandably did not want to be seen in my company, so we collected as many cigarettes as we could, pocketed the certificate that gave us permission to redistribute them, and swiftly remounted our bicycles.

On the road to Malestroit, Geneviève slowed and said, 'I'm terribly sorry for the Gamberts. They're such a considerate couple. I dread to think what they're going through right now.'

'They've chanced a lot for us, but provided the SAS sergeant isn't recognized I think they'll be all right. Let's stop for a moment. I need to think now that we're clear of the houses.'

Geneviève needed time to sort her mind out as well, for the enemy seemed to be closing in on me and that meant her too. A convenient gateway led to a field with a hedge tall enough to hide us from the road; behind it we lay down our bicycles and snuggled up to each other, her head on my shoulder.

'Since we came to France,' I started, 'we've made a mess of things. My greatest wish was to see the SAS fighting out in the open as soldiers, and the Maquis helping with sabotage and local knowledge as well as acting as eyes and ears. Up to now I've been lucky – although God knows how, with all this bicycling in public – but in this type of war it's easier, though of course more risky if caught, to fight in civilian clothes, acting like a civilian on the surface – no weapons, good false papers: you know.'

Her head nodded against my shoulder. Not knowing what I was leading up to, she said quietly, 'I'm beginning to understand.'

'Only when the time comes can we get into uniform and start the battle. In my case it's not so complicated – I had a different training from the SAS. They learned to be soldiers, whereas I was taught to be a civilian first and a soldier second!'

I knew this would puzzle her, for we had never talked about my role: she just saw me as a British soldier acting as some form of go-between for the SAS, the Maquis and the people in England who organized the air drops.

'You're a strange person, Bob,' she said, 'and I realize I know nothing about you.' I let her go on. 'You behave like a man who knows Brittany inside out. You understand the people, you talk with them, you act like them, and frequently you visit places without anyone directing you. You speak French better than most of the people around here, yet still understand them when they talk in their own patois.'

Surprised perhaps by her own summing-up, she rolled on to her stomach, propped her head on a hand, and looked closely at me with a friendly but distant expression spreading across her face. There was, though, a touch of fear about it – fear, probably, for the answers to the questions she knew she now had to ask.

'What exactly are you? No – *who* are you? Are you British or are you French? Why are you always escaping when others are being caught? Why are the Boche and the *Milice* looking for you but somehow never seem to find you – although they know where you are?' The look of fear intensified, leaving nothing friendly in her eyes.

'Oh, I'm British all right,' I assured her slowly, not wishing to appear too keen to allay her suspicions in case that only aggravated them. 'I lived in France for most of my life before the war started – in Le Havre as a matter of fact. My mother was Welsh and my father French, but I had – still have – a British passport. Then when the war started she moved away from the front to a little town called Guer – about twenty kilometres from here.'

'Yes, I know it.'

'Well, I managed to get a job working in the railway station. Once it's liberated, there's a German there I want to meet. Actually, my mother is still there – or at least I hope she is, as I haven't for obvious reasons been able to contact her.[1] My father died some time ago.'

'Who is this man?'

'Stop asking questions,' I said, smiling, and to put her at ease I kissed her forehead. 'All will be revealed if you'll just listen.'

'Sorry!'

'It took me a great deal of hard work and patience to get employed by the French railways. I was under age for the war, and had lost my passport when a ship I was in was sunk.'

'You never mentioned that.'

'Long story – tonight, perhaps, over a Calvados.'

When I had finished telling her of my time shunting engines and copying manifests, she was still studying my face. 'Is that the end?'

'Not quite. I went to work with Jim – except that he wasn't known as Jim then . . .'

'So that's how you know him!'

'Yes. And when the people in England heard that there was this British boy who spoke the local language better than his own, and who knew the countryside, they arranged for me to be lifted out by boat early in 1944 so that I could be trained properly as an agent, but one with a British rank and uniform. So you see I'm not either really. But that was after I'd helped Emile – Jim – run a pipeline of escaping pilots and other agents.'

'Is that all?'

'I want to get to Guer, so that I can be the first to give Bahnhof Guer the Younger some of his medicine back.'

'Thank you for telling me. Now I understand . . .' she paused for a long time, 'and I love you even more for it.'

'You don't mind that I'm British?'

'Of course not. But I know that you're not as safe among the enemy as I was beginning to think you might be. Now, don't you think it's time we called on the mayor?'

We rejoined the road and pedalled on.

'Good afternoon, both of you,' the mayor greeted us. 'What can I do to help?'

'First of all,' I said, 'do you know what the Germans have done with the Gamberts and one of the SAS sergeants?'

The mayor was taken aback. For once, bad news had not reached him first.

'What! The Gamberts? The Gamberts of Callac?'

'Yes. This morning.'

He nodded, and turned away muttering to himself, 'I'll have to try and find out what's happening to them and see if I can help.' He swung back to us. 'As for the parachutists who escaped, they're in prison in Vannes and will be treated as prisoners of war. I get very little news nowadays, but I'll see what I can do.'

'Thank you,' I said. 'Have you anything else for us?'

'You remember that tough-looking girl who attached herself to your organization? Well, I'm glad to say she's making herself a thorough nuisance.'

'Tell me more.' I was sorry that she had been lost to the enemy, but maybe she could do as much harm in prison as outside captivity.

'The first thing she did was to refuse to be searched, so they beat her up. In the fight, she bit on to a German's finger so hard and wouldn't let go that they had to hit her until she was unconscious. Even then they found it difficult to get her mouth open. After that they left her in peace for a day, but when they offered her food she flung it back at them and now just sits there singing patriotic French songs. They may regret having captured her.'

Sadly, I doubted it.

'You know there's a million francs being offered for your capture?'

'I do now,' I said with a laugh. 'It's gone up. Does it say "dead or alive"?'

'You shouldn't joke about it, Captain,' the mayor rebuked me. 'A million is nothing to them, and they hold you responsible for almost everything that's happened to them since the landings in Normandy. It's still possible that they'll find a man – or woman – who'll sell their soul – and yours – to the devil for much less.'

'Thank you,' I said – 'I'm grateful for your warning. I'll be on my guard.'

We shook hands, and Geneviève and I collected our bicycles. A mile or so out of the town we stopped and leaned against a field gate.

'The mayor was not too optimistic. Rather morbid in fact. I wonder if he's applied for the million francs himself.'

'Don't be silly, Bob.'

'Only joking!'

'It's not a joking matter. One of these days they'll find somebody who can use it, and my guess is that it'll not be a member of the Gestapo but a bloody *Milice*. If I were you I'd stick to the attic for a few days and we'll do the running around for you.'

'No. I won't have you out on the roads from now on without either myself or Babin. And it's best to send Anna with him. I'd never forgive myself if anything were to happen to you now.'

'You really care?'

'Better than that. I love you.'

We kissed before wobbling back on our bicycles.

Babin was waiting for us at the Pondards' house.

'From here', he began, once settled as lookout by the attic window, 'I went straight home, where I was greeted well – that's what absence does even for my family. But they'd been visited by *miliciens* on a number of occasions – once disguised as tourists from Paris trying to buy butter and eggs from the farm. They said that they'd become very friendly with me in Paris, and wondered what I was doing now. Luckily my family were up to that sort of thing, and the bastards went away empty-handed.'

'Good,' I nodded.

'I then pushed on to Jim and the Colonel, who seem to have things well under control. Already two successful operations have been carried out, and there are more planned for daylight now they have their confidence back.'

I nodded again.

'But the best news is that the Allies have at last broken through in the Avranches area, and are heading towards Rennes. With luck it'll be only a matter of days before they reach us here. In the meantime the Germans seem to be gradually withdrawing from the Brittany peninsula. The Cossacks have already pushed off altogether, and I for one won't be sad to see the back of them. Half the *Milice* are reported to be out of the area – and I'm not sad to see them go either – and at least one section of Gestapo has left for Paris.

'A number of trains loaded with men and matériel have recently left from Vannes and Guer for Paris – but I doubt that they'll reach their destination, as we knew well in advance of their departure. And finally, Bob, the German High Command are concentrating their troops mainly in the larger towns, for safety. They're abandoning mobile patrols, roadblocks, searches and so on. We should be a bit safer on the roads.'

'I still won't trust them.'

'Quite. Now what do you want me to say to the Colonel?'

'Ask him to bring me up to date. Tell him I'll join him the

moment he needs me.' And with that settled Babin left – he would, we estimated, be back by dawn.

Monsieur Pondard now took me aside in a conspiratorial manner to tell me of a farmer friend of his, living a mile away, who was keen to meet me.

Always suspicious of 'blind' meetings, I quizzed him further.

'He used to supply the Maquis,' he told me. 'I've known him for a number of years, and have no doubts about him. His name is Monsieur Lumière – you may have met him.'

Although his name was familiar, I could not see the point in a meeting just for the hell of it, and said so.

'He wants to start helping again. And . . .' Monsieur Pondard paused, 'I think he has some Americans hiding in one of his woods.'

'That's more like it! Does Geneviève know the way?'

'I'm sure she does, and you can reach his farm without crossing any roads.'

'Do you know anything useful about this man?' I asked Geneviève after a few hundred yards.

'Hardly anything. He's a friend of father's, and supplied Jim with food before the battle at the farm.'

I changed the subject, for another thought was filtering its way into my brain. 'Are you sure we go nowhere near any roads?'

'Certain. Why? That's the third time you've asked.'

'It's just that this field – these fields – seem ideal for parachute drops. Not men, but definitely supplies. I thought I knew this area as well as anyone, but obviously not, and while La Baleine was operational I hadn't really looked at anywhere else in detail. Stupid of me! We should always have emergency alternatives.'

We walked on in silence, until after an hour a collection of darkened buildings loomed out of the night. As we turned a corner, in front of us the owner was framed in a doorway by a light shining dimly through a flimsy curtain.

'Geneviève?' he said softly.

'*Oui.*'

Monsieur Lumière ushered us both inside, hugged each of us in turn, then offered cider with the excuse 'These evenings are very warm, are they not?'

Once we were settled, he leaned forward across the kitchen table. 'Two days ago, Captain, I was working in one of the fields when I stumbled across – literally – three men hiding in the long grass where the wood begins. They were wearing uniforms, and had what seemed to be a large wireless set. I'd never seen one before, but I guessed that that is what it was.'

I smiled as he continued, 'They were not at all worried by being discovered, and introduced themselves as American soldiers. I asked them if there was anything they wanted, but they said, "No" – unless I had any food and water I could spare. During the past few days I have been supplying that, and all they have asked is that I keep their secret.'

'I can't imagine that they're doing much good just sitting in their hide. They'll have no information to pass back – if that's what they're here to do.'

'That's what I thought, so I took a risk and said that there was an English officer in the area and that I could fetch him if they wanted. I also told them what had been happening in this part of France since the invasion, and they seemed most interested in that and asked all sorts of questions, but as I could not answer them I agreed to fetch you.'

'They could still be *miliciens*,' I suggested cautiously.

'Precisely. And if that is the case the sooner we know the better, before they can do any damage.'

'Did they speak French?'

'Yes and no! Sort of broken French, with a strange accent.'

Monsieur Lumière had probably never heard a real American speaking his native tongue. 'Not convincing – anyone can fake that,' I said. 'Anything else about them? Were they smoking Gauloises, for instance – or smelling of garlic?'

'No! But they did have some small books which they closed when they saw me, and once I heard a di-di-di sound coming from their wireless. They were nervous – which probably the *Milice* would not have been – and one man had a strange contraption tied on his head that was linked to the wireless. Every time it made that di-di noise he would write something down. He seemed to be pretty busy.'

I held back my laughter at the description of a wireless operator, for fear of hurting the farmer's feelings, and looked towards Geneviève, but she was already smiling broadly.

'I'll come tomorrow morning at seven o'clock, with a colleague.' I was pretty certain the risk was minimal. 'In the meantime, tell your new friends that I'll wish to speak to their leader. We'll follow you to the field, but remain under cover while I watch how they react to you this next time. Then I'll decide.'

Geneviève and I slipped, arm in arm, back into the night and walked quickly until we could just make out her parents' house, with no chinks of light visible from behind the curtains. Inside, though, we imagined the warmth and smell of hot coffee and cognac. Although enticing, it was not enticing enough. I glanced at my watch – midnight, or very nearly – then at Geneviève.

'Did you have the same idea?' I asked, and she laughed.

'It's about time we talked of things other than the war.'

'Yes, but we haven't had that many chances recently.'

'There are so many things I want to talk about, but not tonight – they must wait until the day before you leave.'

I pulled Geneviève to the ground and snuggled alongside her, our backs resting in the hedge.

'Bob, what feeling do you get when you jump from an aircraft?'

It wasn't the question I was expecting, and I thought for a moment. 'It's awkward to explain. All I know is that it's not dangerous provided your parachute opens!'

'But the first time . . .'

'The first time there were twelve of us, and we were all terrified – and the look on the face of the man opposite made things even worse!'

'What happens if your parachute doesn't open?'

'Then you go straight round to the person who packed it and give them a piece of your mind.'

'Don't be silly!' she retorted.

We stayed for an hour, enjoying a rare moment of peace, certain we would not be discovered by anyone, let alone the enemy. Eventually and none too eagerly we left our warm patch of grass, and with a final kiss goodnight I climbed to my attic bed and slept, dreaming only of Geneviève.

At four o'clock I was woken by Babin's heavy tread on the ladder.

'Any news?'

'Plenty.'

I pulled myself up and sat on the edge of the bed, filled my pipe, and offered Babin the tobacco pouch. He recounted his night-time excursion.

'I arrived there at eleven, and told Jim and the Colonel what you wanted. The Colonel suggested that some of the girls at his farm could act as a link between us, and is happy for that to start immediately.'

'At last!'

'Yes. Well, they've carried out a number of successful operations, and in a day or so will be widening their area of interest. The main problem is that there are now so many small Maquis in the Brittany area that coordinating them is a bit of a nightmare. They've been dispatching daily sitreps to London, but so far have received no reply. Obviously London think he's been overrun.

'Captain Leblond is trying to make his way to the Normandy area, from where he hopes to get a lift back to England. If he makes it he'll call in at your HQ and tell them what's happening. In the meantime the Colonel is hoping to occupy Malestroit with two thousand maquisards in a couple of days. He wants you to find out the enemy strength in the town and, if you can, where their defensive positions are.

'The Allies have broken through and are heading for Rennes and then on to this area. To make that easier for them, the Colonel wants you to advise him on the right time to launch a series of large attacks against the Germans in the smaller towns and villages. He'll use the girls to keep you informed and for you to pass back the information he needs.

'The Germans are beginning to move back, but we must continue to harry them and inflict as many casualties as possible, with the dual aim of preventing them reinforcing Normandy in strength and destroying their overall will to fight – and from all accounts there's plenty of that still left in them. They know that it's a long way to Berlin and they have plenty of time. Anyway, all seems to be going well, and the new plans are working.'

Babin then leaned back across the bed and blew out a cloud of smoke while I explained about the three men we assumed were Americans.

There was no time for more sleep, so we washed and were soon banging on the door of Monsieur Lumière's kitchen, from where we followed him to the woods.

The new arrivals were so keen to please that before we had had time to put our delaying tactics into effect they were walking across the open field with their arms outstretched. I patted the pistol in my trouser pocket for reassurance that I had not forgotten it – I did not usually carry one, for fear of being searched, but had thought this occasion warranted the extra precaution. If they had been armed *Milice* they would have held the upper hand, for we were not expecting such trust. For their part they had much to learn, as we too could have been *Milice*.

'Just keep on walking,' I said out of the side of my mouth to Babin. 'They look pretty genuine to me.'

Half a minute later both parties had come to a halt in the middle of the field and were staring at each other across about five yards of grass.

'My name is Bob,' I began – 'British Special Forces. This is Monsieur Babin, civilian intelligence officer to the Free French forces in this area, and this gentleman' – I touched Monsieur Lumière on the shoulder – 'you already know.'

At that one of the men took a step forward: 'And I am Captain Cyr, American OSS.[2] With me are Lieutenant Jackson and my wireless operator.'

Any doubts I might have had disappeared the moment Captain Cyr opened his mouth, for no Frenchman could have imitated that accent! Nevertheless, I questioned them on a few points about their stay in England: where they had trained, the names of their officers and so on. Although I was satisfied, they were not sure that I should be, and so we were led back to their hide in order to witness a wireless schedule with London. All was as genuine as I had thought it would be.

'We'll get all your kit back to the farm, and then see how we can help each other,' I offered. And with that we hoisted their packs and equipment and were soon drinking coffee from huge bowls around the kitchen table.

I gave the newcomers a rough idea of recent events and the present situation as we saw it, telling them of Colonel Bourgoin's plans – including his problems with the wireless link.

Captain Cyr followed my briefing with a short account of his own operation. They had dropped ten days earlier with a remit to keep the Allies in Normandy up to date with events in our area. I thought that without making contact that would have been difficult, but kept my mouth shut until the Captain had finished. Apparently they had tried to reach us, but could find no one willing to talk – which hardly surprised us. They had been remarkably lucky that none of their contacts had been *Milice*.

'We must have been mistaken for the enemy, which is why, I guess, nobody would speak.'

'You guessed right,' I replied, 'and were bloody lucky.'

'In thanks for finding us, why don't you give me a sitrep and I'll get it passed through to your headquarters, and then perhaps your Colonel will be back in the communicating business.'

For five or so minutes I sat in a corner of the room scribbling out a résumé of our position and intentions, which was sent once the operator had reset his aerials.

'Bob,' the American said, 'tell your Colonel that another French colonel dropped with us.' This was news to me, and I wondered who he was. I expected that it would also be news to Bourgoin.

'Tell me,' I demanded.

'When we arrived at the airfield we were met by this elderly colonel who appeared to find the business of fixing his parachute very complicated, and his kit seemed to bother him. We gave him a hand, but it was not until we'd taken off that he explained that at fifty-five years old he had been suddenly called by his office that morning and told to report immediately. He was asked if he had ever parachuted, and when he said "No" to the general he added that at his age he had no intention of starting. The general looked at him and said, "Well, you jolly well are – and tonight. I want you to take overall command of the Maquis in Brittany."'

We laughed, but there was more to come.

'In the aircraft he asked us about parachuting and how to land, and we did our best to assure him it was safe. For some reason he was due to jump first, and once the hatch was opened he lay on the deck and literally blew kisses at the French countryside as it rushed past below. Just before the moment came he combed his hair and checked his tie, but left us to check his parachute.'

The story had been told to us in broken French with extravagant and wild gesticulations which had brought tears of laughter to all our eyes.

'Do you know where this wonderful man is now?' I asked.

'No. My guess is that he took things quietly for a day or so – probably to get over the excitement of parachuting and being back in France, while getting the low-down on the position here. I expect he'll pop up somewhere when he's got himself organized: he appeared pretty confident of his capabilities.'

That might have been so, but I wasn't sure that Colonel Bourgoin would share the American's enthusiasm for this unexpected interloper.

With the business side of things settled – the wireless operator confirmed that he had managed to pass on our message – Monsieur Lumière agreed to take the American team under his wing and see to their security and personal needs, and with that settled Babin and I took our departure.

Yet more strangers were waiting in the wings, for no sooner had I dispatched Anna to tell Colonel Bourgoin of our American contacts than Monsieur Pondard walked in with the news that the Colonel had himself sent a girl with a message, and that she was waiting outside.

'I've not told her you're here or that I know you, just in case she's a plant.'

'If she'd come a bit earlier we could have saved Anna the trouble. Never mind, I'll take the risk – provided she's alone.'

She was alone, and she was genuine.

'As the Allies are now advancing faster than we expected, Colonel Bourgoin began a series of full-scale attacks early this morning and in a day or two hopes to be occupying Malestroit. Every Maquis in Brittany has already been in some sort of action today, including the capture of two small towns. The Germans are being tied up all over the place and are unable to regroup.'

'Thank you,' I said. 'Anna has only just left for the Colonel, so I've no return message except to say that I'm delighted with the news and any help I can give he only has to say.'

Our efforts at keeping the Maquis together – despite the earlier lengthy and understandable absence of its leader – had at last borne fruit.

15. The Last Kiss

Between 3 and 10 August 1944 the days passed quickly, for they were full of excitement and a great deal of work.

Our Maquis was carrying out full-scale attacks, by day and night, under the direct and forceful command of Colonel Bourgoin. Trains were blown up, roads were mined, and convoys were ambushed. Every route that the Germans tried to take was fraught with danger for them, as it became more and more difficult to leave the comparative security of the towns and villages that they had been occupying. Supported by larger and larger air drops, the Maquis were in the ascendancy – and raring to avenge the years of cruel torture and subversion.

The enemy were reaping their reward for the crimes they had committed, while several well-known *miliciens* and Gestapo agents had already joined their brutish ancestors – but not their victims – and there were others who realized that unless they left the area they would soon follow the same path. The most satisfying sights were those when members of the 'master race' came face to face with our motley bands of guerrillas, who possessed few uniforms but wielded a range of assorted and effective weapons.

Our jeeps were also doing a splendid job with their well-armed crews of four – including a sprinkling of SAS men – as they patrolled the roads we had not mined, often forcing their way through the enemy with bursts of machine-gun fire. The Germans began to show signs of panic – the more so as the possibility of an Allied victory became a certainty.

They knew that they had to fight on, but increasing pockets of men – to begin with in their ones and twos – began creeping into our areas in the dark to surrender, utmost relief etched deep into their young faces.

German camps were raided, ammunition dumps were blown up, and transport was damaged beyond quick repair. All across the peninsula the story was the same, while interrogation of prisoners indicated a swift-growing realization that the crimes they had committed would be avenged with interest. By surrendering, some hoped that they would be spared, but not all those hopes were upheld. Prisoners were treated as prisoners, and with regard for the normal conventions – but some, inevitably and perhaps understandably, did not get that far.

Now well trained and plentifully armed, our Maquis fought like lions under the one-armed Colonel. With pride and exhilaration – but little pity – they fought also with professionalism and dedication. Men and women who had suffered long years of imprisonment were quickly being replaced in their cells by the very men who had incarcerated them in the first place.

By 6 August much of the surrounding country had been liberated ahead of the Allied advance, but Malestroit remained a lone German stronghold, with an estimated three thousand soldiers still 'in residence'. The German commandant's plan, as relayed to me via the mayor, was to wait for the approaching American troops and then, after a token battle, surrender. What he was not prepared to do was to lay down his arms to the Maquis. He had been led a merry dance by us and, I supposed, his pride would not allow him to surrender to what he had always regarded as a rabble and little more than an irritating thorn in his side.

All the town's roads were mined, as was the bridge that crosses the river Oust in the centre. The Germans sat back and waited. Other road routes linked western France with Paris and Berlin, but the road that ran through Malestroit also led to – or from – the major German garrison just north of Guer and, whether for reinforcements heading west – increasingly unlikely – or for an escape route via Coëtquidan and the railway link with Paris, the town was regarded as a 'fort' of importance to the German rearguard action.

By now the Allies had reached and occupied Rennes, some fifty miles to the north-east, and, with that position consolidated, advance columns had begun heading our way. We, however, were determined that it should be the Maquis who routed the hated Germans, for we saw this as the culmination of our own struggle. We knew personally the tribulations with which this particular

Boche group had visited us and our civilian supporters and guardians in the farms, on the roads, through the woods and by the landing zones, and it was we who wanted to – needed to – extract the final toll, claim the ultimate prize.

What we did not know was the likely reaction of the garrison: would it run or would it turn and fight and, either way, what would be the fate of the civilians in the town?

These last days, although freer of the earlier heart-stopping harassment of roadblocks and dawn cordons and searches, were nevertheless tense and busy. Captain Leblond was on his way to the Normandy beaches, the American team based on Monsieur Lumière's farm had re-established Colonel Bourgoin's credentials and wireless links, while Babin and I ran the Maquis's intelligence network from the Pondards' new farm.

In Malestroit, out of bounds to us now, Monsieur Legrand remained our prime contact: his daily sitreps were added to ours before being forwarded, via Geneviève, to the American team, who would in turn pass them to London and direct to Allied headquarters in Normandy.

Then, early on 8 August, the deputy mayor came to the farm asking to see me. He was worried.

'Captain,' he blurted out, his voice full of anxiety, 'you have to find some way of helping me.' He paused. 'In fact you must help all the civilians in Malestroit.'

This seemed a tall order under the circumstances, but I nodded and asked, 'Anything gone wrong?'

'Plenty,' he replied. 'The German commandant called the mayor in at six this morning, and what he had to say made frightening listening.'

I could guess what was coming, but it was worse.

'He said that he – the commandant – knew that there were two thousand maquisards on the outskirts of the town preparing to attack, and he did not intend to put up with that threat. As long as he was still in control of the town, he would not under any circumstances surrender to irregular troops. He said they would murder his men' – with good reason I thought – 'or, at best, ill-treat them. He went on to say, "I will only surrender my officers and men to a regular army that is a representative of your Allies. If those maquisards attack the town my troops will blow up every building and kill every civilian. If the maquisards leave us in peace I will withdraw in my own time, but until then nobody – military or civilian – is allowed to leave." He gave me a pass on the understanding that I told you what he had said and that if I don't return he will shoot my entire family. He then added with a smirk, "And you have quite a large family I understand." '

For several minutes I considered this unwelcome problem. During the previous few days events had been running too smoothly for our luck to have held. We didn't want any withdrawal, as that was precisely what we were there to prevent. We wanted a surrender or a battle, and we wanted it to be to, or with, the Maquis!

'As you know, my job in this area was to organize the Maquis and then, when it was ready, to hand it over to the French. That has now happened, and therefore I no longer have the power to stop or order an attack. But I think there may be a way in which we can sort this problem out.'

I turned to Anna, 'Go to Colonel Bourgoin. Ask him to wait until four this afternoon before launching his attack. Explain what the deputy mayor has just said and what I am now about to say to Geneviève.'

I turned to Geneviève. 'Go to the American team and get them to send an emergency message to London immediately. Explain to them what you've just heard, and ask them to pass the following message: "Send air support over Malestroit – aircraft to fly in as low as possible, circling over town for twenty minutes from two, repeat two p.m. No shooting." That's all. They'll know how to put it into message form.'

Once the girls were on their separate missions, I turned back to the deputy mayor. 'Go back to the town and tell the German commandant the following: he has got until three this afternoon to withdraw in peace; if he does not do so the Maquis will attack in force with air support. He will remember the last time we had air support, and realize that his days of giving orders are over. The aircraft will not be used to damage the town, but their machine guns might be used to damage him.'

The deputy mayor looked a little calmer, but still had some reservations. 'Do you know why the Germans refuse to withdraw now?'

'I do,' I answered. 'They've committed so many crimes in this area that they're scared stiff that we'll give them back their own medicine. They think that the Americans won't know about these crimes and will simply take them as prisoners of war. But what they don't know or are failing to realize is that the Yanks will treat a war crime every bit as seriously as we will and that they'll stand trial as necessary. They think we'll kill them before a trial. But the Yanks will do so afterwards, so what's the difference?'

The deputy mayor was not yet convinced. 'But what if they refuse to withdraw?'

'They will,' I said with unwarranted confidence. 'But you'd better get back before the Commandant thinks you've stayed with me too long.'

We shook hands, and he pedalled furiously away on his bicycle.

I was far from happy, and sat nursing a mug of coffee until, gently to begin with, a distant rumble began to drift through the open farmhouse windows. It was unmistakable, and with a last gulp I leaped up to my window. American tanks were approaching from the north-east along the Rennes–Vannes road. Minute by minute the rumble increased, until by ten that morning the air was filled with that wonderful, distant noise.

Anna returned to say that the maquisards had never intended attacking Malestroit that day, but were waiting until early the next morning, when they hoped for close support from the approaching American tanks.

The next visitor was the deputy mayor, carrying yet more news from the German commandant. The officer had apparently listened very carefully to my message, and then left the room to think 'deeply' on its effect on his standing among his men. He returned a few minutes later to state that he would blow the two bridges only to delay the advancing armour. He would not destroy the town – but, he had added, if a battle should start through no fault of his own he would not be held responsible for the civilians. And with that warning in his ears the deputy mayor had jumped on his bicycle to tell me.

There seemed now to be no end of callers, for next a liaison girl puffed in from Colonel Bourgoin to say that the Colonel had established a new headquarters at Rochefort-en-Terre, a small village eight miles south of Malestroit. He wanted me to visit as soon as possible, and certainly sooner than a bicycle ride would allow – but he had not sent a jeep. With the roads, by and large, now clear of the enemy, Monsieur Pondard suggested I called on a friend of his, the garage owner in the local hamlet. 'I think he has a car that he's kept in running order.'

After a little pushing and grunting we managed to coax the engine into some form of life, and with a top speed of twenty miles per hour and followed by a cloud of blue-black smoke Geneviève and I headed towards Rochefort-en-Terre, where we were met by a crowd of armed maquisards, SAS soldiers and two jeeps. There was a village-fair atmosphere and youthful excitement among the maquisards, which made finding the Colonel a protracted business, but eventually I tracked my quarry and Jim to a small café, where they were enjoying an early meal and more than one bottle of red wine.

'Good morning,' I said, swinging two empty chairs round from a nearby table.

'Hello, Bob, Geneviève,' they greeted us together, as though we had been gone only a few minutes. 'This area will be liberated by tonight,' the Colonel continued. 'Then, as soon as Malestroit is in our hands, I'm going to push on as fast as we can towards Vannes.' He looked across the table and poured two fresh glasses of wine. Pushing them towards us he asked me, 'And what are you going to do now?'

I thought that that was up to him, and was the reason why he had called me so quickly to join them. Clearly he had everything under control and no longer needed the services of a liaison officer. 'My orders are to report back to England as soon as the area is liberated,' I explained. 'So I guess that in four or five days I will be in my Colonel's London office getting myself briefed for another job.'

Beside me I felt Geneviève tense. I reached for her hand under the table.

'Bob,' the Colonel explained, 'I shall be staying here for another ten days or so. I'll establish my HQ at Vannes, and once that's secure I'll signal London to find out what happens next. Come and see me before you leave the country.'

'Of course, Colonel,' I replied, although I suspected that once London had their claws into me there would be little opportunity. We shook hands, and I shepherded Geneviève back into the car. Suddenly it all seemed to be over.

Once alone, she took my hand from the wheel and slowly raised it to her lips. As I felt the tears run across my fingers, concentrating on the road ahead became difficult.

Back at the farm the rumbling of tanks was closer – so close that we could now hear the clanking and squeaking of their tracks, while occasionally the crack of a rifle shot and a short rattle of light-machine-gun fire added a little drama. Although elated at the apparent lack of heavy opposition to this relentless advance, I was still concerned about the aircraft. There was no doubt that, with or without the Americans, the Maquis would attack Malestroit. Then, for the second time in my life, the longed-for drone of heavy fighters caused an involuntary and deep sigh of relief. Quite suddenly two squadrons were over us, turning in towards the town, where I could imagine pairs breaking off one after the other to dive to roof level before pulling up steeply, as instructed, their engines screaming.

Exactly as I had ordered, not a bullet was fired. Then, as suddenly as they had arrived and after a final continuous stream of individual aircraft, they headed north-east, leaving us with the silence of a summer's day. Even the tanks had stopped their rumbling during the twenty-minute air display.

It was all over. Or at least I hoped it was, and with no firing coming from the direction of the beleaguered town the signs were good. Nevertheless, I had to wait for an hour before the deputy mayor, flushed with victory and Calvados, arrived again – this time in a car.

Once I had persuaded him to speak slowly, he explained that the trick had worked to perfection and that, as the Germans withdrew in good order and without fuss to the north-east, the Maquis had entered Malestroit's south-west outskirts. Now, as he spoke, the town was in our hands and, he gushed, it had all been thanks to me. I tried to explain that all I had done was to pass on orders, but he seemed adamant that I should share with him the remnants of a bottle he fetched from the boot of his car.

'The people would like me to bring you to them, so that they can thank you in person.'

I thought for a moment. This was not my victory: this was the Maquis's victory, and it was they who deserved the plaudits – they and the fighter pilots.

'*Pah!*' he exclaimed. 'You made it possible. You must come with me now.' And with that he swung open the passenger door. But, just as I was stepping inside, two jeeps careered round a bend in the farm track. I waved them to stop.

'Where are you going?' I asked the leading driver.

'Malestroit, sir,' he replied.

'Good,' I said. 'Can you give me a lift?'

He nodded, and the deputy mayor waved his agreement. 'Better that you arrive in military style,' he said. 'But I suppose it doesn't really matter how you get there, provided you do get there!'

Our little convoy snaked its way down the lane towards the main road, and within ten minutes we had slowed to a crawl as the streets were swamped with girls, women, old men and maquisards. The SAS were helping to decorate every building and flagpole with the *tricolore*, the Stars and Stripes and the Union flag. Quite where they had come from no one seemed to know, but with contact now made with the approaching Americans it was possibly from them. We were forced to drive at a snail's pace through cheering crowds to the town hall.

There were also tears of sadness for many who could now mourn in public the loss of husbands, brothers, sons and fathers, as well as a significant number of young daughters, mothers and sisters. I remembered too my friend Marienne, and reflected how much we owed to his professionalism and courage: it had in effect been his Maquis, and it was to him that any praise should be directed.

The mayor pressed my hands warmly and pointed to a Citroën car that already had a small British flag fluttering from a makeshift flagstaff on the bonnet. 'That's for you,' he said, handing me the keys.

The party lasted well into that night until – exhausted with relief – men, women and children drifted off to their beds. For them, the inhabitants of Malestroit plus the outlying farms, villages and hamlets, the ghastly nightmare was over.

But for the Maquis and the SAS it was not yet finished, for it was vital that the fleeing enemy should not – in even the smallest group – join up with their colleagues closer to the coast. And there were still scores outstanding which could be settled only in honest combat.

Across the fields and through the woods the enemy was chased and harried relentlessly and mercilessly. Groups were divided and split by those who knew the lie of the fields and forests better than any fleeing soldier. Captured Germans were taken in a steady stream to the cells of the now 'ex-German' camp at Coëtquidan, where they were incarcerated with ill-disguised glee in the very rooms that had, until two days earlier, held innocent French men and women.

The day after Malestroit's freedom had been restored we drove to see Colonel Bourgoin and Jim, and talked to them for an hour or more until, with nothing sensible or constructive left to say, we bid them a fond and emotional farewell. For their part they had numerous other towns and villages to liberate, in order that the advancing allies could have as clear and as quick a run as possible towards the Atlantic ports.

That afternoon Geneviève and I drove to all the villages that had regained their freedom, to thank everyone who had helped during those difficult and dangerous days when the Maquis had been split across the country. Everywhere we went we were fêted, while I tried, with little success, to explain that nothing would have been possible without their willing and courageous cooperation. They could not have escaped so easily as we had been able to do – and many had not: the dread of a pre-dawn battering at the door by storm troopers must have been hell to live with. The next day we made our way to Coëtquidan – an establishment I had never visited, despite it featuring prominently during my time as Guer railway station's office boy. It was full of sullen prisoners of war, and I delighted in their discomfort.

It took the American infantry another two days to reach Malestroit, by which time the effects of too much Calvados and rejoicing had begun to take their toll on the inhabitants – so much so that I felt it necessary to find an officer and explain why their reception had been warm but hardly ecstatic.

I introduced myself to the leading tank commander from the US Army's 4th Armored Division.

'What in hell's name is going on here?' were his first words once we had exchanged names. 'We came in expecting a town occupied by Jerry, but instead it's full of French airborne types, armed civilians and you, Captain. Is the town free? Were you dropped in?'

'We've been here about two months, and liberated the place two days ago,' I said, then briefly recounted the 'story so far' while watching his expression turn from astonishment to disbelief.

'Hey,' he replied, leaning against his tank and pulling out a Camel cigarette from a soft pack of twenty, 'are you kidding? I'm going to wake up in a minute to find it's all a dream.'

'It's no dream,' I said. 'This area has suffered badly over the last four years, and what I'm telling you is true.'

'Well, that's great. But my men need to find a Jerry or two. They're afraid that they'll miss out if all they come across are places like this.'

'There are still plenty of opportunities for good sport to the west,' I said, and his eyes lit up as I promised him guides who also knew where the mines were. Maps were produced as we sat chatting about his advance down from Avranches and the earlier landings. They had had a bad time of it in places, but were now raring to go – and especially so now that the odds of success had turned in their favour. 'One or two scores need to be settled,' he said.

The rest of that day passed in a haze – and mix – of celebration and mourning until, dazed and tired, Geneviève made her way back to her parents' temporary home, leaving me to continue looking up old friends and listening to their stories. It wasn't until well after midnight that I crept back to my attic.

There was, however, still a war to be fought – a fact emphasized by a messenger at dawn the next morning.

'The Colonel has asked me to tell you', he gushed as I wiped the hangover and sleep from my eyes, 'that the American tanks have passed through Rochefort-en-Terre but have now been halted twenty-two kilometres further on at a mined bridge over the river Vilaine. The enemy are defending it vigorously. It's the main approach route from the north to Saint-Nazaire.'

I guessed where he meant, and knew that if the bridge was blown the Allies would be forced into at least a fifty-mile detour – there and back via Redon, which I didn't think was yet in our hands. I decided to take a look myself.

'Tell the Colonel I want two jeeps and a handful of men. I don't care if they're SAS or Maquis, but they must know the area where these tanks are held up.'

'Yes, sir.'

'And I want them now!'

He drove off, leaving a cloud of dust rising behind him: now it didn't matter, but before liberation it would have been a dangerous sight.

Within half an hour we were on our way, and it was wonderful being on the open road, free to drive as we pleased with no fear of ambush or roadblock. We were openly armed – another freedom – and heading with, we hoped, impunity to carry on our work.

After an enjoyable twenty minutes' drive, with me map-reading in the front right-hand seat, a bend in the road brought us abruptly to a halt behind the rear tank of a long column. I had hoped that they might have been closer to the bridge.

I jumped out, checked my pistol, and walked down the line of Shermans. It was odd that there were no supporting infantry, without which – according to my limited training – it is unusual to manoeuvre tanks in close country. I felt decidedly naked.

Walking quickly on I found the leader's mount, and there, sitting on the turret, was my new friend from Malestroit.

'What's the problem?' I asked rather lamely.

'We're stuck, Captain,' was the equally inadequate reply.

'I can see that!'

'Three kilometres ahead they're still holding the blasted bridge. The locals say that it's mined . . .'

'It is,' I interrupted – I'd hoped that American infantry might have been able to outwit the enemy before the tanks reached it.

'. . . and that the enemy are waiting for us to get on to the damned thing before they push the plunger.'

'Wouldn't you?'

'They also say that there are four thousand Jerries in the surrounding fields and woods. The trouble is I've got the tanks but no infantry – just my crews.'

'I thought tanks weren't supposed to manoeuvre alone.'

'That's right . . .' He said no more, then, 'It's no good just shooting into the hedges. I need a recce party ahead to work out the best way to advance.'

'Just give me a moment,' I said, reaching the ground again. 'I may have a solution.'

At the rear of the column I waved up the second jeep, so that I could explain the position and suggest a way out of it. My few SAS and Maquis men were keen to get to grips with the enemy in what they regarded as a 'proper' battle, while we were all keen to get the Americans on their way. We drove up to the column leader.

'With our two jeeps and a handful of men,' I stood on my seat and shouted up to the turret, 'we're going down to the bridge to find out what the hell's going on. Follow us with a couple of tanks, and if we get into trouble give us support with your main armament. OK?'

'OK, buddy,' he shouted back above the noise of his idling engine.

Settling back into the seat I nodded for the driver to move on, which we did for nearly a mile and a half with all weapons, including a newly acquired heavy-calibre machine gun, cocked and ready. Progress was slow, for each time we were suspicious or the country closed in on us a few men patrolled ahead on foot to clear the hedges and bushes while the two tanks kept a respectable two hundred yards behind. There was no opposition, and I began to wonder if the 'fuss' was part of an American ploy to get some form of ground support that had obviously not been supplied by their infantry.

According to my rough map we had now reached the last bend

in the road before the bridge, so the driver reduced his speed to a crawl and I beckoned all but the machine-gun operators to dismount. With our pistols and rifles, we crept round the corner, crouching low.

Immediately ahead was a German gun crew in a foxhole by the side of the road. Though probably as surprised as we were, they instantly opened fire. A shell whistled close overhead, and machine-gun rounds kicked up the dust to our left. The shell landed close by the leading jeep some yards behind us, covering it and the remaining occupants in dust and stones. From the safety of a ditch we watched a second shell being loaded and fired while my soldiers crawled into fire positions. This round missed, but it was joined by more accurate machine-gun fire that forced us to keep our heads well down.

'Let's get out of here,' an SAS soldier muttered. 'It's a bit unhealthy.'

'I agree,' I replied. 'But I want to see if the tanks can help.'

I crawled back along the ditch to the bend, in time to see the leading two tanks being joined by the others: all were firing at targets I could not see. For several minutes this minor skirmish raged over our heads, while all we could do was to lie as flat as possible and wait for a result. The SAS soldier was quite right, it was a thoroughly unhealthy situation – with the whole battle lasting for over two hours. At one stage the tanks managed an advance of a few yards, but I still feared that my last minutes would end in an inglorious death from our own side. But eventually a lull allowed us to scramble back to our jeeps and make a hasty and less than dignified retreat to comparative safety behind the tanks. The lull ended with a burst of machine-gun fire aimed at our departing backs.

No matter what they did, the Americans could not get past that final bend in the road, and although they harried the German infantry with both their heavy guns and secondary armaments they were unable to prevent a mass exodus of the enemy back across the bridge. That meant only one thing, and it happened almost as soon as the last man had reached the far side: an enormous explosion and shock blast almost had us off our feet. The bridge had been blown.

While the Americans could now retaliate by approaching closer than before, they made little impact on the individual soldiers on the other side of the wide river.

I went forward again and, with only spasmodic rifle fire to trouble me, was able to get a closer look at the bridge and the damage it had suffered. There was no doubt that until a pontoon bridge could be brought forward the detour was now the only way by which Allied forces could continue their advance. With our two jeeps leading, we headed first north and then east until I could point the tanks in the direction of Redon and the next bridge upstream.

This, I thought, was now out of my area, and so, after handshakes all round and promises to contact each other after the war, my men made their way back to Malestroit engulfed in a feeling of failure. If – but it was only an 'if' – we had been able to reach the bridge before the tanks we might have managed some way of diverting attention. But the blowing of bridges was a well-practised art for the fleeing Germans, and it was probably going to happen no matter what we did or did not do.

Back at the *hôtel de ville* I was confronted by the 4th Battalion's intelligence officer and the news that the headquarters had moved on. He could not tell me where, but instead relayed some story that his jeep – evidently his pride and joy, which he had kept roadworthy despite 'all the odds' – had been commandeered to be turned into a light aircraft! I listened with patience until it was time to ask about Geneviève. She was waiting for me at her parents' house.

It was now clear that, with the Maquis under full command of a formal military unit and chasing errant Germans through mined areas, I no longer had a role to play either with the considerably expanded Maquis de Saint-Marcel or with the 4th Battalion of the French SAS, so I recovered the keys to the Citroën and drove steadily back to the Pondards and their daughter. Time passed too quickly for Geneviève and myself. I had managed to get a message through to London with my final sitrep, and received the welcome military news that I was to report on 14 August to the nearest Allied headquarters, which by then was stationed in

Rennes. This news was less welcome from a personal point of view.

Using the Citroën, I drove again all over the liberated sectors of Brittany across which we had been fighting, escaping, evading and watching, continuing to thank everyone I could find for their help and courage. My list of people to thank seemed to grow rather than diminish! I even made a special trip to Guer to see what news there might be of Bahnhof Guer the Younger. I had no intention of thanking him for anything: indeed, I did not expect to find him other than in a prisoner-of-war cell. After some cursory detective work I learned that he had left the area two months earlier and was most likely on the Russian front. I thought maliciously that he would certainly have lost some weight, and if caught by the Russians would be made to light many fires. I was not sorry.

Although it was the most important of all our farewell visits, I had been subconsciously delaying the final visit to Plumelec and its cemetery, but now that cheerless moment could be put off no longer. With tears in our eyes, Geneviève and I laid fresh wild flowers on the graves of Marienne and the other maquisards and SAS soldiers who had meant so much to us and to that small corner of France.

Then, having said all my goodbyes, I reported as instructed to the Allied HQ in Rennes on 14 August. The mayor of Malestroit had also given me a driver for occasions such as this, and so with Geneviève beside me I travelled the fifty or so miles in the back seat of the Citroën. Most of the journey was passed in silence, knowing that this could be the beginning of the end of our relationship and that what might – or might not – happen after the war was way beyond a bridge that had yet to be faced, let alone crossed. The war in our area had been won, but there were other areas yet to be liberated and as a serving officer in the King's army I had no choice but to obey whatever orders would be given to me in Rennes. We both silently prayed that any subsequent duty would again be in Brittany, but we also knew that that was unlikely.

The agony of that drive to Rennes was lengthened by the volume of military traffic heading in the opposite direction and, in a number of places, by the state of the road where long stretches had been fought for. Guns, tanks, troops and supplies all slowed our progress, until after many enquiries we managed to locate the building that now housed the Allied headquarters.

I tracked down the senior British representative and introduced myself, then explained the nature of the operations we had conducted over the previous two months and the present position as I saw it.

'All right, Captain,' he said. 'I saw your Colonel before I left England, and he also told me what you'd been up to – and pretty exciting it sounds too!'

'It had its dull moments,' I added cheerfully.

'My orders are to get you back to England by the fastest possible means.'

'I can't be that important!' I protested.

'Your CO says that he has another operation waiting for you. You've obviously done a good job here, and he needs you elsewhere in France.'

'We weren't that good at it . . .'

'My next convoy north across the Channel is not for three days, so', he looked at a desk calendar, 'be here on the 17th. At six in the morning, please.'

I sighed with relief, and resolved that I would not now say goodbye to Geneviève in the less than romantic and rather public confines of a British army camp. 'Thank you, sir.'

Supper that night was quiet, although there was laughter when we recalled the happier moments of the previous weeks. And then, as the Calvados flowed, it became less jolly as we remembered the burned farms and murdered friends.

With the washing-up finished, and far from sober, we decided to call on other friends in the area, ending up – as we had heard that they were back – in Monsieur and Madame Gambert's Callac house. The even better news was that their daughter had returned: the sight of this reunited family was wonderful for our morale.

Unexpectedly – and at two in the morning – Madame Gambert announced in a serious voice that our old rooms were ready and made up for us should we wish to spend what was left of the night in Callac.

'We do indeed,' Geneviève said before I could open my mouth.

'*Très bon!*' Madame replied, and swept the rest of her family off to their own rooms.

Suddenly alone, Geneviève and I looked at each other. There were tears in both our eyes, but she managed a smile and said, 'Let's go down to the river for the last time.'

I replied quickly, 'Maybe it won't be for the last time.'

'Maybe.'

Hand in hand, we made our way without difficulty and lay back on the grass, each trying to sound more cheerful than we felt. I took her in my arms, and we stayed together until the dawn of 15 August.

The next day, the two of us returned to the site of the original Maquis de Saint-Marcel, where we picked our sad way among the ruins and fields where our military and personal adventures had had their beginnings.

Back once again with Geneviève's family, we were joined by Anna and Henriette for a last meal together. I had left instructions for my driver to be at the farm at two the next morning, and in preparation for that Geneviève helped me pack a small bag of my few remaining possessions. When everyone had gone to bed we walked hand in hand through the fields, smoking cigarette after cigarette and talking only of events since 6 June – and if not of them then we didn't talk at all, for neither of us could summon the courage to guess the future. It was so much easier to hide behind a façade of silence.

'I'll see you off,' Geneviève said with a brave attempt at a smile.

Neither of us slept as we sat holding hands until the Citroën rumbled up to the door.

We kissed, hesitantly.

'God bless you,' she said, and turned away.

The journey to Rennes was miserable.[1]

16. Another Moon – Another Task

'Ah, Captain Hue. In time I see. Thank you.'

'Morning, sir,' I replied to the senior British Army representative.

'Yes, of course, good morning,' he said. 'The convoy I'd planned for you to join has been cancelled. Couldn't contact you I'm afraid. Never mind – I'm sure I can fix something.'

The thought of Geneviève looking so lost in the pre-dawn light just those few hours ago flooded back as I realized that the parting had been premature. But I could not return.

'That's all right, sir.' I put a braver face on it than he knew. 'If it's fine with you, I'll push on to Twenty-first Army HQ. I've got a private car, a driver and plenty of fuel.'

The further we drove from Rennes the worse conditions became. Most bridges had been blown and replaced by army-built constructions with one-way-traffic controls, but longer hold-ups were caused by the mass of discarded German equipment. If nothing else, however, the delays at least took my mind away from the men and women – and the one special woman – of the Maquis de Saint-Marcel.

At army headquarters I finally parted with my Citroën and its patient driver and was once more in the hands of the military machine – a machine of which I had never, in practice, been part. An intelligence officer debriefed me at great length, although he already seemed to know more than I did, and once that ordeal was completed I was free to wander off to the Movements Branch, where a lift was organized for the coast and the prospect of a waiting tank-landing ship for the penultimate leg of my journey home.

I was, however, deeply conscious of the state of what up till then I had proudly called a uniform. In the midst of the staff, I now realized that fighting clothes were not de rigueur and that mine were simply unacceptable. After inspecting my allocated tent, I therefore went in search of the stores depot, only to find a notice saying that 'due to the impending move' it was now closed until relocated.

A shout from behind stopped me, and, turning, I saw the officer who had escorted me during my trip to London from the sealed camp where I had begun my journey for France just ten long weeks before.

'Come and have a drink. The Pay Corps is still reeling from our last lunch together.'

'It must have been pounds.'

'Not as much as they feared it might have been!'

'I'll bear that in mind next time.'

The next morning I boarded the tank-landing ship some three or four hundred yards off the beach. The anchor was weighed on the dot of eleven, and as the coast of France faded into memories my mind returned, as it so often still does, to those friends and colleagues who had helped that country to regain its freedom.

'Welcome back, André,' Colonel Buckmaster began. 'In two weeks — maybe less, depending on the next moon — you'll be in the Nièvre area of France training maquisards — part of the Gondolier circuit under Captain Sawyer. Your new name will be "Hendrik", so you'd better practise living with it. Now, why don't you push off on a week's leave?'

Epilogue

André was parachuted back into France on the night of 30/
31 August 1944. The SOE report states, 'Captain Hunter-Hue,
who had previous experience on Brittany, undertook the training
of approximately 250 men in the use of arms, ambushes, camouflage
etc. He himself blew up three bridges and after the liberation of
Luzy was instrumental in neutralising and removing a large number
of mines left behind by the Germans.'

With the war in Europe over, André was parachuted into Burma
with SOE's Force 136, and when the war in the Far East ended he
served with the 9th Parachute Battalion at Haifa in the Canal Zone.
Subsequently, like so many of his kind, he was recruited into 'the
firm' – MI6 or, more correctly, the Secret Intelligence Service –
with whom, as a lieutenant-colonel, he was employed as the military
attaché in the British Embassy in Phnom Penh. It was in Cambodia
that he met his future wife, Maureen, herself a member of 'the
firm'. On their return to the UK André became a founder member
of the Special Forces Club in London, while Maureen continues
to look after 'the firm's' elderly from those days.

Appendix 1
André Hue's SOE Record of Service

The following are extracts from the surviving SOE Record of Service on André Hue and are reproduced here – most unusually – with permission of the SOE adviser to the Foreign and Commonwealth Office. A number of details are not contained in his diaries, while others cannot be corroborated – in either 'direction': tragically, André has not been able to see – and thus comment on – these reports. Due to the nature of the reporting/recording system of the time there is some duplication, although I have tried to eradicate that which is out of context.

Folio 1

To F/Recs   From D/CE 5
2rd [*sic*] March 1944

Hunter-Hue A. A. Hubart A.

As you know the above named was released from the R[oyal] V[ictoria] P[atriotic] S[chool] yesterday having successfully established a claim to British nationality. He was not accordingly interrogated while at the RVPS but in accordance with the usual drill in such cases, MI5 will require to see him at Devonshire House in due course. They have asked that I should make an appointment for him to report to Devonshire House for this purpose at 10.30 a.m. on Friday, 10th March and I should be grateful if you will make the necessary arrangements and confirm that it has been done. I will then advise you the exact address and to whom Hubart should report when he gets there.

I would also remind you that when he arrived at Dartmouth he was fitted out with a battle-dress by the MI6 representative and

D/FD has undertaken that it should be returned to MI6 as soon as possible. Would you be good enough, therefore to keep in touch with D/FD.

Signed . . . [illegible but believed to be Major Haylor]

[PS] Have told Hubart the address below and arranged transport to pick him up at 10.15 a.m. Friday: Major Jones, Room 514, Flat 50, Devonshire House, Mayfair Place.

Folio 2

F.RECS/FR/273   3rd March, 1944
To: F, FB, FP, FM, FG   From F/RECS

Lieut. Alfred Hubart (Alfred Hunter-Hue)

This man was released from R[V]PS owing to his dual nationality on Wednesday, having satisfactorily substantiated his claim to be regarded in the future as a British subject. He is available for interview at Malvern Court in the usual way.

He worked for a certain time for Oscar, whom he knew as Captaine François, in a rather minor role. He has assisted at one reception with his friend Réné (now Lieut. Bachelier) and was instructed by the latter in the use of small arms. He has however no experience whatsoever of sabotage work. He is very anxious to get back into the field as soon as possible. He is blown in Brittany but knows Le Havre very well and has many friends there including workmen, Merchant Navy men, shopkeepers, garage owners and various other people who might be useful to us. He also knows the district round Le Havre very well. He knows Marseilles fairly well, but has no contacts there and would prefer to work in the north.

He has been a writer in the Merchant Navy.

Folio 3

SAB [Students' Assessment Board] report 31.3.44

Grading   C
Intelligence 5
Morse   Average
Mechanical   Good
Instructional Average

Remarks: A very active, energetic, enthusiastic man with a reasonably stable personality, although inclined to excitement at times. He is self-confident, practical, hard-working and conscientious. Capable of planning on a simple level. He has a high sense of duty and is genuinely keen to return to the field where he has already gained valuable experience. He has the right temperament for W/T [wireless telegraphy] work and is also recommended, if required as an instructor in weapons and demolitions.

Folio 4

STS 24 [Special Training School, Inverie, Inverness, paramilitary training] – 12.4.44

[1st report] Seems to be very suitable for this work – he is keen, punctual, sociable and well-disciplined. Although he appreciates and enjoys the training he is very anxious to get back to the 'field' and for this reason wonders whether it would be possible for him to go into action soon after STS 51 [parachute training at Ringway, Manchester].

STS 24–25.4.44

[2nd report] This student works well. He is very anxious to please, always endeavouring to be at the top of the class. It is interesting to note that although he is not really disliked by his comrades they do not care for him particularly . . . although I am tempted to think that the fact he is so anxious to please at all costs is the main reason for his unpopularity. Despite the faults he might have, it is largely compensated for by his extreme keenness to do this work and I consider him a very suitable man altogether.

[Private note] Lt Ashley to Major Philipson-Stow STS 24–25.4.44

This student has progressed steadily throughout the course. Due to his keenness and perseverance he has done better in most subjects than the three other members of the party . . . I consider this man very suitable for this work – he is keen, sound, courageous and reliable.

Most suited for: Small Organizer but preferably Assistant Organizer (on account of his age which he himself considers a handicap when dealing with older men than himself). He has expressed the desire of doing some instructing in the field . . . a course STS 17[1] would benefit him considerably.

STS 24A–6.5.44

Ins. remarks: A student who, in spite of his youth and lack of education has done excellent work. He is slow at grasping things but having learnt them he remembers them. Is very thorough in his work and would probably make a good second in command and with more experience a leader.

Comms: Report

A very pleasant student with just the right temperament for the job For one of his age he has had a fairly wide experience of life . . . Should do well in the field.

Folio 5

STS 51 [Parachute training]

This student performed well on the ground training. He tried hard and completed the course satisfactorily. Four descents.

Folio 6

[Undated]

Hubart

Of British nationality, born in 1923 at Swansea. His father was of French origin and died in 1938 and his mother is an Englishwoman. He was educated in Swansea and at Le Havre and entered the French merchant navy as an interpreter and writer in 1938, serving on various large ships. He was torpedoed [*sic*] on the 'Champlain' and with most of the crew was taken to Bordeaux, where he joined another ship and went to Casablanca, returning to Marseilles in November 1940.

He subsequently joined his mother in Morbihan and occupied himself in giving private lessons in English and French. He was recruited for resistance activities in 1943 by a man called Touzet and at some time met Rene Bichelot (Bachelier) and he assisted a reception which was given away to the Germans.

Subsequently Hubart and Bichelot met 'Oscar' for whom they did a certain amount of work. After Bichelot's departure for England Hubart went into hiding near Ploernel and came to this country direct by sea.

He knows Brittany extremely well but the extent to which he is blown there would seem to need investigation. His mother was arrested in September 1942 while he was on the run.

He has done a full course at Group A and has jumped and I am proposing to send him to STS 42 [Thame Park, Oxford] for a fortnight's revision on Wednesday next. He has proved to be an extremely keen student although not a very popular one, possibly due to his extreme anxiety to please. His mixture of French and Welsh blood makes him inclined to be excitable but I think he would be reliable within his limitations.

Folio 7

Extracts from André Hue's own official summary of his SOE service

SECTION I – PERSONAL PARTICULARS

Schools　　　College of Swansea and French school
Degrees taken　English *Diplome*, French *Certificat* and French
　　　　　　　Diplome cours supérieur

SECTION II – QUALIFICATIONS

Civilian occupation: Second *écrivain* at Compagnie Générale Trans-atlantique, French Navy, from 3.9.39 to 3.11.40. Sunk in action on SS *Champlain* 17th of June 1940. From 3.9.39 convoys of weapons from America to England and France

Professional, technical or other qualifications: Navy and Army since 14 years old (*écrivain* – interpreter)

Language qualifications: French, English: bilingual. German: knowledge

Special knowledge and experience: Trains: one year attached to station

Sporting achievements: Shooting: good. Diving: fair. Swimming: good. Mountaineering: good. Boxing: fair.

Hobbies and other interests: Voyage [travelling?]

SECTION III – MILITARY HISTORY

Date of commission: 2.2.44
Honours, rewards: DSO, authority L/G d/d 21.6.45
[*Further details:*] Sunk on SS *Mexico* 20 of June 1940 on mine.[2]

SECTION IV — ACCOUNT OF SERVICE WITH SOE

Special remarks: In September 1943 with Captain François reception committee at Guer; from September to January 1944 recuperation [*sic*] of British pilots shot down in France; sea operations;[3] [illegible] of December failed and attacked by German coastguard; lived in coast area for one month.

SOE courses of instruction: 1.3.44 School 22 [*sic*] Inverie; School 41 [*sic*] at Hislip, Ringway: 5 weeks of training SOE. Paramilit. Agent. W-T. Driving. Course on Jeeps. Jumping course and committee of reception. Weapons. Demolition. Sabotage. Sea operations . . . PT. Foreign weapons.

Chronological record of Service with SOE:[4] 26.5.44. F Section. Sent to Major Bourgoin 4th HET [*sic*] of SAS. For planning 25 operations of sabotage in Brittany. Jump on D-Day with 12 SAS. Dropped in German camp in civvies. Arrested by Germans on landing. Fight all night to get out of camp. Next day contact with Maquis of St-Marcel. Sent several [men] to find rest of party; all came to camp except four. For 10 days reception of ten-to twenty planes by night . . . Attacked by one German division . . . Killed 1,200 Germans, wounded 900. Evacuation of camp . . . After all the camp was mined with plastic . . . Put 120 SAS in farms; put the wounded in doctor's hands. For 30 days intelligence work on all German movement in south Brittany. Arrested twice; got out. Back to England.

15.9.44. F Section. Sent to the field to St-Honoré-les-Bains as instructor. Mined roads, bridges, instructor of 1,500 [illegible].

[Date illegible] Back in England 30 October 1944. At ME 25 Ceylon 15.12.44. Training. On operations the 29.1.45. Out the 6 April 45. Attacked on D-Z by Japs – BTA. 27 days without rations. Put report in the 6 April 45 for inefficient leadership of our commanding officers.

Folio 8

Undated [1945]: Recommended for the Military Cross

The summary reads, 'By his tireless energy, personal courage and leadership, Capt. Hue set a magnificent example to the FFI troops with whom he worked.'

7.4.45: Recommended for the Distinguished Service Order

The summary reads, 'An excellent man who in a short time did an immense amount of work and achieved most important results.'

Note by E. S.-T.: Although André Hue was awarded the DSO and not the MC, the following letter was written by Colonel Buckmaster on 27 June 1945:

> My dear Hunter Hue,
> I am delighted to tell you that you have been awarded the MC for your gallant actions in Brittany last summer. The announcement is contained in the London Gazette of the 21st June. All of us here send you our most sincere congratulations on this very richly deserved award.

Folio 9

Extract from an Undated Miscellaneous Report

INTRODUCTION

[Hubart] is an 'F' agent who was given a special mission by Lt Col. Buckmaster and Major Bourne-Paterson, namely that of acting as guide, in Brittany, to a body of SAS men and to assist in arranging landing grounds and accommodation for further parachutists . . .

MISSION

[Hubart] set about the task of carrying out his mission [on arrival at Saint-Marcel], and within 48 hours had organised farms and houses, three landing grounds for men and material, and one landing ground for gliders. Marienne then arrived with 5 men, having lost four of his men, one killed and three taken prisoner, in engagements with enemy troops. [Hubart's] mission was then, in reality, accomplished and Marienne took over.

FURTHER ACTIVITIES

[Hubart] remained with Marienne and attended several receptions of men and material. He also acted as assistant to Marienne in organising the 'effectifs', and took part in various brushes with the enemy.

Marienne was, unfortunately, caught by the enemy after some time, his whereabouts having been given away inadvertently by a member of the camp, and was shot by them. [Hubart] then took over the military operations, regrouped both parachutists and partisans, and had more brushes with the enemy, both miliciens and troops.

Other activities were: – [Hubart] set up, in conjunction with a certain Pieche Sanson [*sic*] and the FFI, a 'bureau de renseignements' for the whole of the Morbihan which enabled them to secure information on the enemy's moves; he supplied dossiers on several miliciens which enabled the patriots to liquidate them; on D-Day for the Morbihan he mounted LMGs [light machine guns] on cars and directed and guided American convoys, also carrying out reconnaissance patrols which brought him into contact with the Germans.[5]

Appendix 2
Operational Orders for the 4th French Battalion (SAS)

Extracts from Instructions for Operations of 4th French Parachute Battalion (SAS) in Brittany, dated 22 June 1944 (following the Battle of Saint-Marcel on 18 June)

1. The base in the Dingson area will be reconstituted as soon as possible in some convenient area.
2. The new base will be kept as dispersed as possible . . . the local Maquis should not be concentrated in the base area . . . but should come [only] in small numbers to collect arms and ammunition.
3. Your main task of interrupting communications between Western Brittany and the remainder of France can now be considered as completed.
4. Your main task now is to organise and equip the Maquis for important operations which may take place at a later date . . .
5. You will endeavour to have small groups of Maquis spread throughout Brittany so that they can be concentrated in the most important areas when the moment for action shall arrive.
6. You will in particular make arrangements for Maquis to be established or if necessary move into areas within striking distance of the more important ports i.e. St Malo, Morlaix, Brest, Lorient and Vannes.
7. You will endeavour to make contact with workers in these ports . . . to ensure that when the time comes German attempts to destory the port installations shall be interfered with as much as possible . . .
10. Meanwhile you will carry out such minor acts of sabotage as will embarrass the Germans and prevent their free movement throughout the area . . .

12. In the event of any major German withdrawal from Brittany you will ensure that the earliest possible information of such movement is sent to England.

Comment by E. S.-T.
Earlier tasks included:

1. The severance of communications between Brittany and the rest of France in order to prevent reinforcements located in the province coming to the assistance of enemy troops engaged in the beach-head area.
2. The recruiting, arming and organising of resistance elements in Brittany . . .

Enemy troops in Brittany before D-Day were believed to include at least the following:

- one division at Rennes (possibly the 17th SS Panzer Group)
- 721st Infantry Division at Dinan
- 5th Parachute Division (elements) west of Rennes
- 25th Infantry Division at Vannes
- 265th Infantry Division at Lorient
- 3rd Parachute Division in the Carhaix area
- 353rd Division at Morlaix
- 343rd Infantry Division north-west of Brest
- 266th Infantry Division in the Saint-Brieuc–Guingamp area.

Appendix 3
André Hue's Citations

André Hue's DSO citation reads:

THE DISTINGUISHED SERVICE ORDER.
Captain (temporary) André Hunter Alfred HUE (322545)
General List

This officer was parachuted into France in June 1944 with a party of SAS troops whom he was to guide in operations with the FFI in Brittany.

He was dropped some distance from the reception committee,[1] and in trying to join up with the rest of the party, ran into a group of Russian enemy troops. He kept his head, and pretending to be a German,[2] passed through this and another group, and ultimately made his rendezvous.

Hue set to work to split it into smaller units to arrange for the supply of arms by parachute, and to instruct in the use of weapons. On the 15th June[3] the camp was attacked by 800 heavily armed Germans. After a long battle the Maquis withdrew. Hue distinguished himself in the fighting, and in organising the successful dispersal of the FFI troops.

When the Commander of the SAS force was killed, Hue took over command and worked untiringly. Five times he was arrested by the Germans. Each time he was put up against a wall, threatened with sub-machine guns and beaten up. Each time he kept his head and got away.

When the American armoured forces arrived in his area, Hue guided armoured reconnaissance columns and took part in numerous engagements with the enemy.

Hue volunteered for a further mission and was again parachuted into France on the 30th August, 1944, as instructor to a circuit in the Nievre. With this mission Hue blew up three

bridges, and undertook the removal or neutralising of the mines
left behind by the enemy.

And his citation for acceptance into *L'Ordre de la Légion d'honneur
– au Grade de Chevalier* reads:[4]

DECRET
AU GRADE DE CHEVALIER
Capitaine Hue Hubart A. Hunter General List 322545

Officier Britannique qui a pris une part active en 1943 a
l'organisation de la Resistance en Bretagne. Rentre en Angleterre a ete parachute le 6 Juin 1944 avec un groupe de parachutistes français auquel il a par la suite servi de guide. Tombe loin
du Comite de reception, n'a pu rejoindre son equipe qu'en
traversant les lignes ennemies. A contribue au succes des operations de parachutage et a instruit les groupes qu'il a armes.
S'est distingue par sa bravoure au combat de St-Marcel. Arrete
plusieurs fois, menace de tortures, est toujours parvenue a
s'echapper. Au moment de l'avance allie, a servi de guide aux
avants-gardes. Retourne en Angleterre en Aout 1944 a ete
parachute une seconde fois dans La Nievre, le 30 Aout. A detruit
trois ponts empruntes par la retraite allemande. S'est ensuite
consacre au deminage de la region.
Ces citations comportent l'attribution de la Croix de Guerre
avec Palme.
Paris le 16 Janvier 1946.
Signe: Ch. De Gaulle.

Appendix 4
Le Musée de la Résistance Bretonne, Saint-Marcel

The Museum of the Breton Resistance lies towards the south-eastern corner of the battlefield covered in Chapter 8 and just outside Saint-Marcel itself. Nearby, at the monument to the resistance movement (erected in the grounds of La Nouette farm) a service of commemoration and remembrance is held annually. A section of the museum, which enjoys over a million visitors a year, is devoted to André Hue and for that and numerous other connected reasons is well worth a visit. Below is a translation of the museum's pamphlet.

Rendezvous with History

Saint-Marcel, situated in the Landes de Lanvaux, was home to the largest Breton Maquis, where, on 18 June 1944, a historic battle was fought – a crucial part of both France and Brittany's history.

Before the Allies even landed in Normandy, Free French parachutists had landed in Brittany and joined the 2,500 Bretons who had started to congregate at Saint-Marcel.

The Resistance in Brittany, one of the first regions in France to be recognized for its heroics and its sacrifices, deserves recognition, explanation, commemoration and to be preserved for ever.

Built on the battlefields themselves, in a wooded area of six hectares, the Museum of the Breton Resistance in Saint-Marcel preserves the memory of this army of the shadows who refused to surrender to Nazi occupation.

This museum of history, unique in Brittany, enables you to discover a permanent exhibition of 1500 sq. m. showing the life and commitment of the Bretons during the Second World War. Since 1994, this has also been the location where the Free French parachutists have decided to keep their national exhibition.

With the aim of playing an educational role, the museum has benefited from a dynamic style giving it an original look in both its presentation and its understanding.

Some of the items exhibited are unique in France – the collection spread of six rooms is also complemented by audio-visual presentations and model layouts.

Notes

Prologue

1. A form of French security force which degenerated from its original high ideals of restoring French military honour into a semi-gangster organization composed of local men from the villages who were, in the words of George Millar, DSO, MC (SOE), in his book *Maquis* (London: Heinemann, 1945), 'the scum of the jails, brutalized of the most brutal, cream of the offal'. *Miliciens* were particularly dangerous as they knew the local areas better than the Germans or even the neutral gendarmes, both of whom could be bluffed by the Resistance – not so these local thugs. They could also detect a false French accent, which the Germans could not do.

2. See M. R. D. Foot's *SOE in France: An Account of the Work of the British Special Operations Executive in France, 1940–1944* (London: HMSO, 1966), C. E. Lucas Phillips's *Cockleshell Heroes* (London: Heinemann, 1956), Madeleine Duke's *No Passport: The Story of Jan Felix* (London: Evans, 1957), Ewen Southby-Tailyour's *Blondie: A Biography of Lieutenant-Colonel H. G. Hasler, DSO, OBE, Croix de Guerre, Royal Marines* (London: Leo Cooper, 1998), M. R. D. Foot and J. M. Langley's *M19: Escape and Evasion 1939–1945* (London: Bodley Head, 1979) and Barry Wynne's *No Drums . . . No Trumpets: The Story of Mary Lindell* (London: Arthur Baker, 1961). By and large this exodus took place before SOE was formed, and many Frenchmen were lost as agents. Thus SOE was, partially, forced to use those Englishmen who either had one French parent or had spent so much of their life in France that they spoke without any trace of an English accent – a rare achievement even for the most educated. Such was André Hue; hence his early recruitment, repatriation and training.

3. 'Maquis' generally refers to an area or a team (also known as a *réseau*) of the French Resistance movement, with the individual members called 'maquisards'. The word 'Maquis' comes from the thick brushwood or

thicket traditionally used as a refuge by fugitives on the island of
Corsica and referred to in Corsican Italian as *macchia*.

Introduction

1. M. R. D. Foot, *SOE in France*.
2. Military Intelligence, Research File No. 10, PRO.
3. *Report to the Combined Chiefs of Staff on Operations in Europe of the Allied Expeditionary Force* (London: HMSO, 1946).
4. Ibid.
5. See C. E. Lucas Phillips's *Cockleshell Heroes* and Ewen Southby-Tailyour's *Blondie*.
6. M. R. D. Foot, *SOE in France*.
7. Note to H. N. Sporborg of the SOE, PRO.
8. Max Hastings, *Overlord: D-Day and the Battle for Normandy* (London: Michael Joseph, 1984).

Acknowledgements

1. In 1944 the future Professor Michael Foot (then a captain in the Royal Artillery) was flown into France to work with the SAS in Brittany. He was captured, wounded during an escape, and exchanged. He was awarded the French *Croix de Guerre* and, much later, the Dutch Order of Orange Nassau. He has a CBE for services to SOE history. His many books on SOE operations are considered to constitute the definitive history of that organization.

1: Shipwrecks and Marshalling Yards

1. Winston Churchill, *The Second World War*, Vol. 2: *Their Finest Hour* (London: Cassell, 1949).
2. Caroline Hue was later captured by the Gestapo, interned in a concentration camp, and very badly beaten. She returned to Wales after her release, and died on 19 May 1962.

3. Now the *office de tourisme*; the marshalling yard is a wide, open recreation space which includes a children's play area. The route of the former single-track railway line is a popular country walk. Otherwise the appearance of the station and the town square remains unchanged from before the war.

4. Although various names were used to describe the enemy, the most popular was '*doryphores*' – after a particularly unpleasant little insect that eats potatoes. '*Mort aux Doryphores*' was painted on the front bumper of the heavily armed Maquis jeeps.

5. Vallée had already won the Military Cross with the SOE in Tunisia, where his most audacious operations included passing by hand, twice, papers to a British submarine off the coast and receiving wireless equipment and explosives in exchange; sabotaging the engines of a convoy of lorries at Tunis railway station before they were delivered to the Italians in Tripolitania; damaging with incendiary grenades the petrol tanks of another convoy of lorries; attacking the Italian ships *Sirius* and *Achille* by swimming out to them with 'special charges' (both sank); and placing more charges on the tanker *Beauce* just before her departure from Tunis. He was discovered and arrested, but was released after seventeen months in prison. His award of the MC was approved by the French on 18 October 1943. Vallée's Parson circuit in Brittany was to be penetrated by the Gestapo in December 1943, forcing him to seek a safe house in Paris. He was picked up by the Gestapo on 4 February 1944 on his way (with his second in command, Lieutenant Henri Gaillot) to a Lysander landing strip. They were last seen in the prison at 3 Place des Etats Unis before being deported to Germany and execution, probably in the Gross Rosen concentration camp. Gaillot had been an equally remarkable man, and before joining SOE had been awarded the *Médaille Militaire*, the *Ordre de Léopold*, and the *Croix de Guerre*.

6. Especially that run by Monsieur Francis Fourché (himself a member of the Resistance) in the main square: called the Café de la Place, it is largely unchanged, although now a crêpérie as well as a bar.

7. Monsieur Pondard began a diary of events at this time which was later taken over by his daughter Anna and kept up until liberation. The opening lines read, 'In around February 1941, Emile Guimard accompanied by Raymond Provins [?] came to see me at La Nouette. Emile

Guimard asked to speak to me privately – we both went outside and he asked me if I was for or against the English. When I replied that I was [for the English], he suggested making a parachute dropping zone with which I was in complete agreement. He asked me to locate an area which would become a depot which was well hidden. He asked me particularly to maintain the greatest secrecy regarding our conversation. It was agreed that he would return some time later with a parachutist specialist to select the area which would best meet their needs. Fifteen days later, Emile returned to La Nouette with a friend whom I did not know but whom I guessed to be the specialist to whom he referred. The three of us went out into the farm and I took them to an area which I thought might best meet their needs.'

8. Sadly, André's saviour from the railway yard was not so attentive to his own safety, for he did not heed Touzet's advice and was arrested on 10 December 1943. Touzet himself moved to Paris under a different name, but, like Durandière, was never seen again. André has always assumed the worst.

9. See Ewen Southby-Tailyour's *Blondie*.

10. The wing commander did get home – but not in time to placate his wife. For many years André and he exchanged Christmas cards.

11. On this occasion – code-named Operation Easement II – one of the two incoming agents was a young François Mitterrand. See Sir Brooks Richards's *Secret Flotillas: The Clandestine Sea Lines to France and French North Africa 1940–1944* (London: HMSO, 1996).

12. This was the much-used MGB 502 under the command of the hugely experienced Lieutenant Peter Williams, DSC, RNVR, of the 15th Flotilla. She was later mined – three days after VE Day – with only two survivors. MGB 502 was armed with a two-pounder gun forward, twin 0.5 inch guns, two twin .303s, twin 20 mm mountings, and another six-pounder aft. She displaced 109 tons, and had a trials speed of 28 knots.

2: Headhunted

1. M. R. D. Foot quoting from Thomas Carlyle in *SOE in France*.
2. Teams of three, one each from France, the UK and the USA, trained to liaise with and organize the Maquis.
3. André learned later that the dispatcher had 'forgotten' these and hurriedly pushed them out through the floor hatch some seconds after the other containers. Plenty of notes were available from soldiers – back from Dunkirk – who had raided bombed-out banks, and from black-market dealings in such capitals as Lisbon: neither source being creditable, neither was claimed at the time. SOE was expressly forbidden to forge European currencies – a ruling that was obeyed.
4. The parachutes of the dropped supplies were coloured to make identification of the containers' contents easy: for instance arms and ammunition dropped beneath red parachutes. Other commodities such as food, clothing and money all had their own colours: green, blue, black and so on.

3: Maquis

1. The first French victim of the battle to liberate France on this day was Corporal Emile Bouëtard.
2. Before turning in, Marienne sent the first of his formal sitreps, which read, in part, 'For Commandant Bourgoin . . . Confirm 10 lightly armed companies out of 25 – Urgent send all available officers, men and equipment . . . in particular Bren guns – Very impressed by organization and immense capabilities . . . can assist Samwest from here . . . Confirm DZ [dropping zone] – may also suit gliders . . . 50 three ton lorries, 50 family cars available. Have large supplies of food and animals, except flour. Urgent send petrol, medical equipment and uniforms with identity.'

4: 'My Grandmother will Smoke a Pipe with You Tonight'

1. In the end two infirmaries were established: one in the garage of La Nouette's owner, Madame Salles, who lived in a nearby house, and the other in the loft above the Pondards' kitchen.
2. 'For Commandant Bourgoin . . . Situation superbly re-established despite difficult arrivals . . . 3,500 men in regular training await your arrival. Dropping Zone will be defended by 500 men on night of your arrival . . .'

6: Enter the Colonel

1. From André's diaries it has not been possible to establish where this occurred. However, it is probable that it took place either on the branch line between Guer and Messac or, more likely because of the direction, on the north–south line that runs through Malestroit.
2. The logistic support was impressive: an abattoir had been established, as had a meat store, a field kitchen, bread-making ovens next to the older pigsties, a cobbler's workshop, and tailoring facilities where FFI armbands were sewn on to shirt sleeves and alterations were undertaken by the Pondard sisters. There was a motor-transport repair 'garage', while generators provided lighting and power for the wireless sets.

7: Trouble with the Neighbours

1. In her journal Anna Pondard wrote that she and her sisters were at some stages helped by up to eight 'bakers', producing bread for twelve hours a day to feed the men spread across the whole of La Nouette's grounds. The cellar distributed up to six barrels of cider a day and one barrel of wine. There was insufficient water at the farm, which meant a continual stream of vehicles to supply the required fifteen or twenty barrels a day. All day local farmers would arrive – in broad daylight – with livestock, vegetables and cider, while three maquisards were on

a permanent rota for the collection of wine, cider and general groceries from merchants in Malestroit.

2. Included in the drop was a Second Lieutenant Jasienski – an intelligence officer – who was to liaise with any disaffected Russian troops. Jasienski was working for M. R. D. Foot at the time.

3. A total of 581 containers were scattered over four square miles.

8: A Grand Battle

1. Anna had been dispatched earlier – on 10 June – to give Commandant Caro his orders in person: thus his battalion was well established and knew its tactical area of operations intimately.

2. In practice the battalions were named after their commanding officers – thus the Garrec Battalion (No. 2, of 750 men) was detailed to the south and east; the Gouvello Battalion (No. 9 – despite, according to André's notes, there being only eight) was to guard the north-east; and the Caro Battalion (No. 8, of 1,200 men) was to guard the north and west. The SAS were not only responsible for their own sector to the east, but augmented the Garrec Battalion to the south. Two days earlier the 3rd Company FFI had taken up defensive positions to the east and south of the chateau at Les Hardys-Béhélec and covering the Saint-Marcel road. The 2nd Company was positioned in a sunken lane to the north of the 3rd Company. Units from the Rochefort-en-Terre Battalion and FFI groups from La Gacilly, Peillac, Saint Martin-sur-Oust and Les Feugerets and a section from the FFI company in Guer contributed a further 200-plus men. The other battalions and many of the SAS were about their business away from the Maquis de Saint-Marcel.

3. Contemporary reports suggest that at that stage Marienne himself, with his well-armed jeep, had accounted for over forty enemy dead.

4. The Germans, believing that the Maquis HQ was in the vicinity of Sainte-Geneviève, to the north of Saint-Marcel, had unwittingly taken on the strongest of the SAS positions, where one Bren gun had been placed every ten yards.

5. The message was received at the SAS Brigade's operations desk (of which M. R. D. Foot was 'momentarily' in charge) in clear, at about

1310 hours. The apparent time difference is possibly due to the various time zones being kept: GMT, double British Summer Time and French Summer Time.

6. The Maquis counter-attacked and won ground at Sainte-Geneviève, but failed to do so at Le Bois Joli. Les Hardys-Béhélec came under intense pressure, as did the land to the east of L'Abbaye.

9: Suspicions

1. Contemporary reports state that there were no further drops into Brittany that month because of this renewed spell of bad weather.
2. The bravery of these farmers was to haunt André for the rest of his life and is why, when the terrible saga was over, he spent much time trying to get not only compensation but also medals for them. He was successful with some, while with others he was less so.
3. The house and shop were unchanged to April 2003, when they were owned by an Englishman, who knew nothing of their history. The 'emporium' – to the right of, and attached to, the main building – is being converted for domestic use.

10: The First Kiss

1. One ruse adopted by many was to carry a photograph of Marshal Pétain with their papers as a tangible sign of 'loyalty'.

11: Regrouping

1. Not, now, to be confused with a newer, higher water tower a few hundred yards to the north-west. German fortifications still exist at the base of the original tower, plus a monument to all those killed in the area at that time. This original still stands sentinel over the place near by where Marienne, André and their men landed on D-Day.
2. The start of the track to Kérihuel farm is now difficult to find: the formal route to the farm leads off to the right along the paved road.

Although the buildings remain much as they might have been, there is no longer a café.

12: *Hay Barns and Dawn Cordons*

1. A large bay tree now obstructs this view.
2. A wedding dress made from parachute silk is on display at Le Musée de la Résistance Bretonne at Saint-Marcel.

13: *Tragedy*

1. The 4th Battalion's report for the week of 27 June states: 'Finisterre – 10,000 men awaiting arms; only 1,000 so far organized. Côtes-du-Nord – nothing yet organized. Ille-et-Vilaine – more dangerous – tighter enemy control. Loire-Inférieure [now Loire-Atlantique] – also tricky, from both enemy and political viewpoints. Morbihan . . . 2,500 organized and armed.' Grog, in particular, could boast of five battalions, of which three were already armed. Posters across Brittany warned all captured paratroopers and their helpers that they would be shot as *francs-tireurs*.
2. Kérihuel is the site of one of the most poignant memorials to those military and civilians murdered by the Germans and *Milice* on that day: a tall cross marks the place where the executions took place. Marienne himself is now buried by the war memorial in Plumelec, which lies against – and outside – the cemetery wall. Colonel Bourgoin, who died in 1970, is buried, by request, with his former colleagues and lies immediately on the inside of the wall, opposite Marienne.

14: *Wanted: Dead or Alive*

1. André did not yet know that his mother had been imprisoned by the Germans for burning his papers.
2. Office of Strategic Services.

15: *The Last Kiss*

1. In due course Geneviève was to marry Alexis Babin.

Appendix 1

1. Held at Brickendonbury Manor, Hertfordshire. The course included industrial sabotage, counter-scorching, and the manufacture of home-made explosive devices.
2. This is not mentioned in André's diaries.
3. It is assumed that this refers to escorting pilots to the beaches from where they were lifted out by MGBs.
4. There are minor discrepancies between this SOE Account of Service, André's diaries and other official reports such as 4th Battalion's war diary. After many comparisons, it has been concluded that this account is the least accurate.
5. Not covered in André's diaries.

Appendix 3

1. Not strictly accurate, as there was to be no planned reception party – see Chapter 2.
2. In fact he pretended to be a member of the treacherous *Milice*.
3. Interestingly, other records give the date as 18 June.
4. No accents were typed in the original.

Bibliography

Books

There are numerous books on the SOE and associated subjects, but only those publications that have been of help in corroborating André Hue's narrative are listed here.

Foot, M. R. D. *SOE in France: An Account of the Work of the British Special Operations Executive in France, 1940–1944* (London: HMSO, 1966)
——, *The Special Operations Executive 1940–1946* (London: Pimlico, 1999)
Gaujac, Paul, *Special Forces in the Invasion of France*, trans. Janice Lert (Paris: Histoire & Collections, 1999)
Hampshire, A. Cecil, *The Secret Navies* (London: William Kimber, 1978)
Jefferson, David, *Coastal Forces at War* (London: Patrick Stephens, 1996)
Leroux, Roger, *Le Morbihan en Guerre 1939–1945* (Mayenne: Joseph Foch, 1983)
Mackenzie, William, *The Secret History of the SOE: 1940–1945* (London: St Ermin's Press, 2000)
Public Record Office, *SOE Syllabus* (London: PRO, 2001)
Richards, Brooks, *Secret Flotillas: The Clandestine Sea Lines to France and French North Africa 1940–1944* (London: HMSO, 1996)
Stafford, David, *Secret Agent: The True Story of the Special Operations Executive* (London: BBC, 2000)

Archive Material

PRO Archives:

WO 218/114	SAS Brigade Operation Instructions
WO 218/193	Operational reports
WO 277/2	SAS Reports
HS 2/323	Government correspondence

HS6/572

HS6/586

Air/27/956 and Air 20/8012   Sup
                               Over

Archive material in Le Musée de la Résistanc
Saint-Marcel.